Montgomery County Tennessee

County Court Minutes

1808-1810

By:
Work Projects Administration

Copyright 1940
By: Works Projects Administration

New Material Copyright: 2018
By: Southern Historical Press, Inc.

All rights reserved. No part of this publication may be reproduced, stored in a retrieval system, transmitted in any form, posted on to the web in any form or by any means without the prior written permission of the publisher.

Please direct all correspondence and orders to:
www.southernhistoricalpress.com
or
SOUTHERN HISTORICAL PRESS, Inc.
PO BOX 1267
375 West Broad Street
Greenville, SC   29601
southernhistoricalpress@gmail.com

ISBN #0-89308-677-0

Printed in the United States of America

MONTGOMERY COUNTY

COUNTY COURT MINUTES VOL. 2
1808-1810

(p-1) State of Tennessee, Montgomery County -- Monday March 28th 1808.
The Worshipful Court of Montgomery County have met according to adjournment from Saturday March 26th 1808.
Present:

        John Blair)
        Samuel Gattis) Esquires
        James Hambleton) Justices
        Thomas Smith)
        Sterling Neblett)

TARPLEY MADDUX)
   Vs   ) Debt
JAMES ADAMS)

    The Defendant in this case was solemnly called and came not but made default, therefore it is considered by the Court that the Plaintiff recover against the Defendant the Debt in the Declaration mentioned amounting to one hundred and sixty Dollars with interest thereon from 13th day of September 1807 as also his costs about his suit in this behalf expended.

JAMES M. REYNOLDS)
   &   )
JOHN R. MCFARLAND) Debt
   Vs   )
ROBERT WELLS)

    This day came the Plaintiff by his attorney. The Defendant was solemnly called and came not but made Default therefore it is considered by the Court that the Plaintiff Recover against the Defendant the sum of one hundred and twelve Dollars and fifty cents, the debt in this Declaration mentioned with Interest thereon from the 6th day of March 1808, as also their costs about their suit in this behalf Expended and the Defendant in Mercy &c.

Deed of Conveyance Morgan Brown to Wm. Clements was proven in Open Court by the Oath of William Stallings and William R. Clements subscribing witnesses thereto and ordered to registeration for one Lot in the Town of Palmyra No. 69.

THOMAS BATTSON Assee)
   Vs   )
JAMES BOWERS)

    The Defendant in this case being solemnly called and came not, but made Default, therefore it is considered by the Court that the Plaintiff recover against the Defendant the sum of one hundred and twenty Dollars the

Debt in the Declaration mentioned with Interest thereon from the first day of January 1808 & also his costs about his suit in this behalf Expended & the Defendant in Mercy in Mercy.

```
STATE            )
  Vs             ) Presentment
STEPHEN THOMAS   )
```

1 Richard Pardue
2 Wright Bonds
3 John Marshall
4 William Corlew
5 Isaac Morgan
6 Isaac Gattis

7 Samuel Creswell
8 Stephen Handley
9 John Trotter
10 Barny Duff
11 Benjamin Hawkins
12 Joshua Weakley

Who being duly elected tried & sworn upon their Oaths do say that they find the Defendant not Guilty as declared in the Presentment.
therefore it is considered by the Court that the Plaintiff take nothing by his Bill but that the Defendant may Depart without Day.

```
(p-2)    STATE          )
           Vs           ) Presentment
     JOSEPH PENRICE     )
```

To wit

1 Richard Pardue
2 John Marshall
3 William Corlew
4 Isaac Morgan
5 Samuel Creswell
6 Stephen Handlen

7 John Trotter
8 Barny Duff
9 Benjamin Hawkins
10 Joshua Weekley
11 Stephen Thomas
12 John Thomas

Who being Elected tried & sworn the truth to speake upon Presentment upon their Oaths do say that the Defendant is not Guilty as Declared in the Presentment, therefore it is considered by the Court that the Plaintiff Take Nothing by his bill but that the Defendant may Depart without Day-

Ordered that John Thomas be appointed overseer of the road from Vaughn's Mill to Deason's Creek in the place of Stephen Thomas & that Samuel Vance Esquire gives the list of hands to work thereon

```
ALEXR. FAITH    )
     Vs         ) Case
                )
WILLIAM ALLEN   )
```

Dixon Loggins proves 6 days as a witness 2 ferriages-

(p-3) STATE) Presentment
       Vs   )
   REUBEN GRAYSON)

   Jury to wit

1 Richard Purdue
2 John Marshall
3 William Corlew
4 Isaac Morgan
5 Samuel Creswell
6 Stephen Hendley

7 John Trotter
8 Barny Duff
9 Benjamin Hawkins
10 Joshua Weakley
11 Stephen Thomas
12 John Thomas

who being Elected tried & sworn the truth to speak upon the Bill of Presentment & upon their Oaths do say that the Defendant is Guilty as charged in the Presentment-
therefore it is considered by the Court that the Defendant be fined & that he pay the sum of one Cent as also his Costs about his suit in this behalf Expended & the defendant in Mercy & C-
Motion of Defendants attorney for a New trial Granted to Defendant-
Court adjourned for one Hour-

Court met according to adjournment present-
The Worshipful.

        Sterling Neblett)
        Samuel Vance   )
        John H. Poston)
        Thomas Smith   )
        Samuel Gattis   ) Esquires
        James Hambleton)
        John Blair   )
        Hugh McClure   )

John Thomas shewing sufficient reasons to the Court is Exonerated from attending as a Juror this Term-

(p-4) STATE) Indictment
       Vs   )
   SAMUEL CRAFT)

              John Ohira the prosecutor in this case who was bound in Recognizance to appear to give testimony in behalf of the State was solemnly called & came not but made Default agreeable to his recognizance-
Therefore it is considered by the Court that the State recover against John Ohira the Prosecutor agreeable to his Recognizance as also his Costs about his suit in this behalf Expended -

STATE   )
Vs   ) Indictment
WILLIAM HUBBARD)
     Jury to wit

1 Richard Purdue	7 John Trotter
2 John Marshall	8 Barney Duff
3 William Corlew	9 Benjamin Hawkins
4 Isaac Morgan	10 Joshua Weakley
5 Samuel Creswell	11 Stephen Thomas
6 Stephen Hendlen	12 John Thomas

Who being Elected tried & sworn the truth to speak upon the Issue Joined do upon their Oaths say that the Defendant is Guilty as is Declared in the Bill of Indictment in Manner & found & the Court fines the Defendant one Cent therefore it is considered by the Court that the State recover against the Defendant the fine of one Cent as also the Costs about this Suit in this behalf Expended & the Defendant in Mercy &

STATE)
Vs) Indictment
SAMUEL CRAFT)

On motion of Defendant by his attorney ordered by the Court that the defendant be realesed from his recognizance in this case & that he be at Liberty to Depart without Day—

(p-5) STATE)
Vs) Presentment
JOHN MINOTT)

Jury to wit

1 Richard Purdue	7 John Trotter
2 John Marshall	8 Barney Duff
3 William Corlew	9 Benjamin Hawkins
4 Isaac Morgan	10 Joshua Weakley
5 Samuel Creswell	11 Stephen Thomas
6 Stephen Hendlen	12 John Thomas

Who being Elected tried & sworn the truth to speak on the Presentment do upon their Oaths say that they find the Defendant the Defendant is Guilty as declared in the Presentment in Manner & form & the Court fined the Defendant two Dollars therefore it is considered by the Court that the State recover against the Defendant John Minott the aforesaid sum of two Dollars the fine afflicted by the Court as also his costs about his suit in this behalf Expended & the Defendant in Mercy & C

STATE)
Vs) Indictment
SAMUEL VANCE)

Same justices on the bench except Samuel Vance

The Defendant in this case comes into Court & submitted & the Court fined the Defendant Samuel Vance one cent, therefore it is considered by the Court that State recover against the Defendant the fine of one Cent as also the Costs about his suit in this behalf Expended & the Defendant in Mercy & C.

Stephen Hendly a witness proves three Days & two ferriages in this suit.
Darden Brown a witness proves 4 days attendance & two ferriages—

(p-6)   STATE
               Vs   ) Indictment
       WILLIAM LYONS)

Nathan King a witness in behalf of the State was solemnly called out upon his Subpoena but made a default & came not, therefore it is considered by the Court a Judgment by Default Ni Ci be entered against him & that Sci fa Issue against the said Nathan King

STATE
   Vs   ) Indictment
WILLIAM LYONS)

Error   William Lyons the Defendant in this case was solemnly called & came not but made Default therefore it is considered by the Court that Sci fa Issue—

STATE
   Vs   ) Indictment
WILLIAM LYONS)

Error   Samuel Vance who was Security for the Delivery of the body of the said Defendant to this term

for sufficient reasons shewed to the Court by John Thomas was Exonerated from attending as a Juror the Balance of this Term—

for sufficient reasons shewed to the Court by Joshua Weakley he was Exonerated from attending as a Juror the Balance of this Term.

(p-7)   STATE
               Vs   ) Indictment
       WILLIAM LYONS)

William Lyons who stands bound by Recognizance in the sum of one hundred Dollars for his personal appearance at this Term to answer such charges as should be exhibited against him was solemnly called to answer upon an Indictment exhibited against him for an Assault & Battery & came not but made default, therefore it is considered by the Court that his Recognizance be forfeited & that a Sci fa Issue accordingly

Samuel Vance who respectively stands bound by Recognizance in the penalty of fifty Dollars for the personal appearance of William Lyons at the present Term of this Court to answer such as should be exhibited against him was solemnly called to bring into Court the said William Lyons to answer the State upon an Indictment exhibited against him for an Assault & Battery & failed to do so, but made Default, therefore it is considered by the Court that his Recognizance be forfeited & that Sci fa Issue accordingly.

Court adjourned untill tomorrow at 9 O'clock.

Court met according to adjournment
     Present

John Blair
Hugh McClure
Samuel Vance
Samuel Gattis

(p-8) STATE OF TENNESSEE) March Term 1808
MONTGOMERY COUNTY)

Samuel McCulloch & Alexander McCulloch & Benjamin McCulloch, apply to the Court now here in session for an Order that their Clerk Issue a Warrent directed to Duncan Stewart, Willie Blount & James Baxter to be named Commissioners they or any two of them, to attend said Benj. McCulloch, Samuel McCulloch & Alexander McCulloch on the 25th day of May next at a red Oak & Hickory tree the begining corner of a six hundred & forty acre Tract of land claimed by said Benjamin McCulloch, Samuel McCulloch & Alexander McCulloch Heirs of Benjamin McCulloch Deceased to whom said tract of land was granted by the State of North Carolina by patent Number 1968 and bearing Date the 20th May 1793 for the purpose of taking the Deposition & doing whatever else they may deem proper for assertaining said begining corner & Boundaries of said tract of land & for perpetuating the evidence thereof in pursuance of an Act of the General Assembly passed 23rd October 1799 entitled an Act to assertain the boundaries of land & for perpetuating testimony & that the Clerk of this Court be directed to Issue Subpoenas for William Crutcher & Nicholas Conrod witnesses to be examined before said Commissioners at the day & place aforesaid & your applicants as in Duty &.
                                                Signed
                                                Benjamin McCulloch
                                                Samuel McCulloch
                                                Alexander McCulloch

Whereupon it is ordered by the Court that the Clerk Issue a Commission & Subpoenas agreeable to the petition of the applicants Benjamin McCulloch, Samuel McCulloch & Alexander McCulloch.

(p-9) GUTHRIDGE LYONS)
          Vs   ) Certio &
      MONTGOMERY BELL) Super's

                On motion of the Defend't by his Attorney and Reasons filed. The Court is of oppinion that the Origl attachment be Quashed- Therefore it is considered by the Court that the Defend't recover his costs of Suit in that behalf Expended of the plant'f-
                Same Justices on the Bench.

SELAH PUKETT Asses of)
Pukett & Long   )
      Vs   ) Appeal
LEWIS PUKETT &   )
MOSES KNIGHTON   )

                Jury viz

1 John Marshall   7 Peter Oneal

2 Isaac Morgan	8 James Loggans
3 Samuel Croswell	9 Stephen Cocke
4 Benjamin Hawkins	10 William Loggans
5 William Curlew	11 Reuben Loggans
6 John R. McFarlan	12 Timothy Drake

Being Elected tried and sworn the truth to speak upon the matter & Controversy upon their Oaths do say that Defendants hath not paid the debt as declared by the plaintiffs & do find for him by Reason of the detention thereof Eight Dollars & Sixty Six Cents – Therefore it is ordered & Adjudged by the Court that (p-10) the plaintiffs recover against the Defendants the said sum of Eight Dollars & Sixty Six Cents as found by the Jury in their Verdict – And also their Costs of Suit in that behalf expended –
John Blair, Thomas & James Hambleton, Esquires.

JAMES RUSSELL)
    Vs   ) Case – William B. Ross who
JOHN JONES)

was called out upon his subpoena last term came here into Court gave his reason on Oath for not attending which the Court Deemed sufficient & ordered that he be released from the forfeiture of the Sci fa & have leave to depart without day–
John Blair, Thomas Smith & James Hambleton Esquires on the bench.

JOSEPH PHILLIPS)
    Vs   ) Debt
ISAAC MORGAN)

Jury viz.

1 John Marshell	7 Peter Oneal
2 John Trotter	8 James Loggans
3 Samuel Criswell	9 Stephen Cocke
4 Benjamin Hawkins	10 William Loggans
5 William Curlew	11 Reuben Loggans
6 John R. McFarling	12 Timothy Drake

Being duly Elected tried & sworn the truth to speak upon their Oaths do say that the defendant had not paid the Debt in the plaintiffs Declaration mentioned (p-11) and do assess his Damages by Reason of the detention thereof &c by Consent of boath parties John Marshall withdrew & the rest of the Jury is discharged from rendering their Verdict & the cause is continued untill next Court, it is allso agreed that the pleadings in this cause be amended–
John Blair, Thomas Smith, James Hambleton, Samuel Vance.

HUGH MCCOLLUM)
    Vs   ) Certiorari
ROBERT GRAYSON)

The plantiff in this case suffered a Non Suit, therefore it is considered by the Court that the Defendant recover against the Plaintiff his Costs about his suit in this behalf Expended & the Plaintiff in Mercy & C

39. - Deed of Conveyance James Ford To Reynolds & McFarland was proven in Open Court by the Oath of Thomas Martin & John Baker junr. Subscribing witnesses thereto for one Lot in Port Royal No. 23.
Same Justices on the Bench.

JAMES MCCARRELL)
Vs) Certiorari
JAMES LOCKERT)

The plantiff in this case was solemnly called & failed to appear & prosse, his suit, therefore it is Considered by the Court that he be Nonsuited-
Therefore it is considered by the Court that the Defendant recover, against the Plaintiff his cost about his suit in this behalf Expended & the Plaintiff in Mercy & C.

(Entered before) Deed of Conveyance Morgan Brown to William Clements was proven in Open Court by the Oath of William Stallings & W. R. B. Clements subscribing Witnesses thereto & ordered to Registeration for one Lott in Palmyra No. 69.

(p-12) Same Justices on the bench.

GEORGE WILLIAMS)
Vs) Appeal
MOSES STEEL)

The plantiff being called failed to appear and prosecute his suit therefore it was Ordered by the Court that he be nonsuited and that the Defendant recover his Costs of suit in that behalf Expended & the Plaintiff in Mercy & C.
Same Justices on the Bench.

JAMES BLACKWELL)
Vs) Debt
WILLIAM LOGGANS)

Jury viz.

1 John Marshall   7 Peter Oneal
2 John Trotter   8 James Trice
3 Samuel Creswell   9 Timothy Drake
4 Benjamin Hawkins   10 Isaac Morgan
5 William Corlew   11 John Baker Junr.
6 John R. McFarling   12 Jesse Martin

Duly Elected tried and sworn the truth to speak upon the Issue Joined do say upon there Oaths that the Defendant owe to the Plaintiff the sum of Fifty four Dollars the debt in the Decleration mentioned and assess his Damages by Reason of the Detention thereof to Three Dollars Twenty Two & a half Cents-
Therefore it is Ordered adjudged & Decreed that the plantiff Recover against the Defen't His Judgment as by the Jury in their Verdict set fourth and also his Costs of suit in that behalf expended-
Dixon Leggins a witness proves 2 days attendance & C.

(p-13) JAMES BLACKWELL)
       Vs   ) Debt
       WILLIAM LOGGANS)

Joshua Gardner a witness in this case was solemnly called out on Subpa'a. & failed to appear therefore it is ordered by the Court Sifa Issue to next Term-
John Blair, James Hambleton, & Samuel Vance Esquires on the bench-

FREDERICK GOSS)
      Vs   ) Appeal
HANER HAMBLETON)

Jury viz

1 John Marshall   7 Peter Oneal
2 John Trotter   8 James Trice
3 Samuel Creswell   9 Isaac Morgan
4 Benjamin Hawkins   10 Jesse Martin
5 William Corlew   11 Thomas Brantley
6 John R. McFarling   12 Timothy Drake

Duly Elected tried & sworn the truth to speak on matters & Controversy do upon their Oaths say that the Defendant hath not paid the Debt as declared by the plantiff & do find for him by Reason of the detention thereof to the sum of Ten Dollars & Fifty Cents- Therefore it is ordered & Adjudged by the Court that the plantiff Recover against the Defen't his Damages as assessed by the Jury and also this Costs of suit in that behalf expended-
John Campbell a witness in this suit proves 4 day attendance.

(p-14) Court adjourned untill tomorrow at Nine O'clock.

Court met according to adjournment Present - The Worshipful Hugh McClure, Thomas Smith & Samuel Vance on the Bench.

JAMES STEWART &   )
ALSEMUS KENDRICK &)
WILLIAM KENDRICK   ) Original Attach't.
      Vs   )
THOMAS HAWKINS   )

The Defendant in this case being Solemnly Called failed to appear and defend his suit, therefore it is Ordered by the Court that final Judgment be Entered up against him as also their Costs about their Suit in this behalf Expended -
        Same Justices on the bench.

DANIEL JONES)
     Vs   ) Sci fa
ISAAC MARTIN)

The Defendant being solemnly called failed to appear & Defend his suit, Therefore it is ordered by the Court that Judgment final be Entered up against him according to Sci fa & also his Costs about his Suit in this behalf Expended -
        Same Justices on the bench-

STATE)
Vs) Jurors
DELINQUENTS)

Jacob Brient, John Edmondston, John Nevill, Peter Hubbard, Robert Wells, John Waggoner, Richard Perdue, Edward Leech, William R. Bell, all being duly summoned to attend this Term & serve as Jurors to answer when Solemnly called, Therefore it is ordered by the Court that Judgement-

(p-15) Hugh McClure, Thomas Smith, Samuel Vance Esq.

DIXON LOGGANS)
Vs) Case
WILLIAM LOGGANS Senr.)
Jury Viz

1 John Marshall
2 William Corlew
3 Benjamin Hawkins
4 Isaac Morgan
5 Samuel Creswell
6 John Trotter
7 Hugh McClure
8 Jesse Martin
9 Joseph Oneal
10 Stephen Cocke
11 Sterling Ingram
12 John Rudolph

Being duly elected tried and sworn the truth to speake upon the Issue Joined, do upon their Oaths say that they do assess the plantiffs Damages to Thirty Dollars & Seventy five Cents. Therefore it is adjudged & Deemed by the Court that the Plantiff Recover of the Defendant his Damages as assessed by the Jury in their Verdict, And also his Costs of suit in that behalf Expended & the Defendant in Mercy & C

Samuel Vance Esqr, a Witness proves 5 days & 2 ferriages.
William Loggins a Witness proves 6 days & 4 ferriages.
Reuben Loggins a Witness proves 8 days & 4 ferriages.
William Loggins New Comer a Witness proves 6 days & 4 ferriages.
Jesse Martin a Witness proves 6 days & 4 ferriages.

Court adjourned for one hour-

Court met according to adjournment - Present, Hugh McClure, Thomas Smith, Samuel Vance.

Esquires on the Bench & Joseph Woolfolk Esq.

(p-16) SAMUEL THORNTON)
Vs) Debt
AMOS ROCHELL)

The Defendant was solemnly called and failed to come and defend his suit. Whereupon the Court Ordered that Judgment Final be entered up for the sum of Eighty Eight Dollars Sixty Nine & one half cents with Interest from the first day of January 1808, and that the plantiff Recover against the Defendant his Costs of Suit also in that behalf Expended -

Same Justices on the Bench.

THOMAS FIGURES Assee)
RICHARD HOLLAND)
    Vs) Covenant
MINOAH TAYLOR)

    The Defendant was called & failed to appear, Therefore Judgment by Default & Writ of Enq'y was awarded to next Term—
    Same Majestrates

JOSHUA WEAKLEY)
    Vs) Cov't.
ISAAC MARTIN)

    The Defendant was Solemnly called & failed to appear whereupon Judgment by Default & Writ of Enq'y awarded to next Term—

(p-17) Hugh McClure, Joseph Woolfolk, Thomas Smith Esqrs.

ROBERT RAY)
    Vs) Certiorari
DANIEL ANDERSON)

    The plantiff being called & came not the Court is of oppinion that a Non Suit be entered, and that the Deft. Recover his Costs against the plantiff in that behalf expended—

41 Deed of Conveyance King & Peston To Richard Weatherford for part of a Lot in Clarksville No. 57 was acknowledged in Open Court by John H. Peston.

JAMES RUSSELL)
    Vs) Case - Motion for a New trial at last Term over ruled by
JOHN JONES) the Court, Therefore it is considered by the Court that the
    Plaintiff recover against the Defendant his Damages so assessed by the Jury in form aforesaid as also his costs about his Suit in this behalf Expended & the Defendant in Mercy &c.

(p-18) Thomas Clinton, James Stewart, Hugh F. Bell, James Ford, William R. Bell, Isaac Peterson & Reuben Pollard)
    Vs)
    JOHN SAUNDERS)

    The Plaintiffs by their Attorney bring here in Court a Certified Copy of a Judgment Recovered in the Superior Court of Law for Mero District, at their May Term Eighteen Hundred & form by John Sevier Governor of the State of Tennessee against the said Defendant John Saunders as principle. And the said plantiffs as his Securities for the sum of Three Hundred & Fifty Six Dollars & Eighty Four & Three Forths Cents together with his Costs in that behalf expended and it appearing to the Satisfaction of this Court that the aforesaid Judgment has been Discharged Satisfied & payed by Thomas Clinton, James Stewart, Hugh F. Bell, James Ford, William R. Bell,

Isaac Peterson & Reuben Pollard the above named Plantiffs as Securities of Saunders the above named Defendant, And on Motion it is thereupon Considered by the Court that the said pltffs. recover against the said Defendant the aforesaid sum of Three Hundred & fifty six Dollars Eighty four & three forth Cents together with their Costs in this behalf expended-

(p-19) Joseph Woolfolk, Benjamin Weakley & Thomas Smith, Esquires on the Bench.

JOHN COCKE)
   Vs   ) Case
BENNET SEARCY)

         Jury Viz

1 John Marshall   7 Moses Parker
2 John Trotter   8 Joseph Oneal
3 William Curlew   9 Timothy Drake
4 Benjamin Hawkins   10 Robert Temple
5 Isaac Morgan   11 Charles Murry
6 Samuel Creswell   12 Henry McBride

Being duly Elected tried and sworn the truth to speake upon the Issue Joined do upon their Oaths say that the Defendant did assume upon himself in manner & form as the plantiffs have declared against him and they do assess the Damages to the plantif by Reason thereof to Eighty four Dollars Forty five Cents besides his Costs. Therefore it is considered by the Court that the plantiff Recover against the Defend't the Damages aforesaid by the Jurors in their Verdict in form aforesaid and also his Costs in that behalf Expended & the Defendant in Mercy-

Court adjourned untill tomorrow at 9 O'clock-

Court met according to adjournment. Present-

                 Joseph Woolfolk)
                 Thomas Smith   ) Esquires
                 Hugh McClure   )

(p-20) STEPHEN CANTRELL Junr)
     & GEORGE M. DEADRICK)
            Vs   ) Covenant
     JOHN BAKER Junr   )

     In this case Demurer over Ruled & a Writ of Enquiry awarded to next Term-

JOHN COCKE)
   Vs   ) Case
BENNETT SEARCY)

     The Defendant in this case prays an appeal which the Court Granted.

he having given Bond & Security & Reasons filed for the Appeal-
Henry Small & Benjamin Hawkins bound in the sum of Five Hundred Dollars
as Security-

JAMES JACKSON &
WASHINGTON JACKSON
  Vs   } Debt
HAMLIN HICKS
                          Jury to Wit

1 John Trotter   7 Colmore Duvall
2 John Marshall   8 William Kerr
3 William Corlew   9 Barny Duff
4 Isaac Morgan   10 James Brantly
5 Benjamin Hawkins   11 Richard Perdue
6 Samuel Creswell   12 Robert Temples

Who being elected tried and sworn the truth to speak upon the Issue Joined
upon their Oaths do say that the Defendant hath not paid the Debt in the
Declaration Mentioned of three hundred & twenty four Dollars & fifty three
Cents and do assess the Plaintiffs Damages by the reason of the Detention
thereof to Eight Dollars & Eleven & one fourth cents (p-21) therefore it
is considered by the Court that the Plaintiff Recover the Debt in the Declaration mentioned & the Damages so assessed the Jury in their verdict in form
aforesaid assessed as also his Costs about his suit in this behalf Expended
& the Defendant in Mercy & C-

CHARLES ANDERSON)
    Vs   } Case
ISAAC MORGAN   )

Reasons in arrest of Judgment filed continued untill next Term for argument
Same Justices on the Bench

JAMES M. REYNOLDS &
JOHN R. MCFARLING
    Vs   } Debt
DIXON LOGGANS
                     Jury Viz

1 John Trotter   7 Colmore Duvall
2 John Marshall   8 Barny Duff
3 William Curlew   9 William Carr
4 Isaac Morgan   10 James Brantly
5 Benjamin Hawkins   11 Richard Perdew
6 Samuel Creswell   12 Robert Temples

Duly Elected tried and sworn the truth to speak upon the Issue Joined do
upon their Oaths say that they find that the Defendant hath not paid the
Debt in the Decleration mentioned of Fifty four Dollars Twenty six Cents &
do assess his Damages by Reason of the Detention thereof to Ninety five
cents- (p-22) Therefore it is considered by the Court that the plaintiffs
Recover against the Defendant their Debt & Damages as assessed by the Jury
in their verdict, and also his Costs about his suit in that behalf expended

and the Defendant in Mercy-
Same Justices on the Bench

JAMES M. REYNOLDS
& JOHN R. MCFARLING) Case
Vs)
JAMES BUNTING)
Jury Viz.

1 John Trotter   7 Colmore Duvall
2 John Marshall   8 William Karr
3 William Curlew   9 Barney Duff
4 Isaac Morgan   10 Daniel Epps
5 Benjamin Hawkins   11 Richard Perdue
6 Samuel Creswell   12 Robert Temples

Who being duly Elected tried & Sworn the truth to speake the Issue Joined do upon their Oaths say that the Defendant hath not paid the Debt in the Declaration mentioned and do assess his Damages by Reason of the detention thereof to Two Hundred & sixty one Dollars Thirty seven & a half Cents- Therefore it is considered by the Court that the Plaintiffs recover against the Defendant the Damages so assessed by the Jury in form aforesaid as also their Costs about their Suit in this behalf Expended & the Defendant in Mercy & C. The Defendant prayed an appeal & gave Bond with John Steel & Samuel Smith his securities bound in the sum of Five Hundred & Twenty Two Dollars seventy five Cents-

(p-23) Thomas Smith, Joseph Woolfolk, John H. Poston Esquirers on the Bench-

H. MCCLURE & JAMES ELDER)
Vs) Debt
GEORGE TROTTER)

The Defendant being called failed to appear & Defend his suit whereupon it was ordered by the Court that Judgment by Default for Seventy one Dollars & Seventy seven Cents with Interest from the first of January 1807 & also that the plaintiffs Recover their Costs of Suit in this behalf expended & the Defendant in Mercy &

JAMES RUSSELL)
Vs) Case Motion for a new trial at last Term over ruled.
JOHN JONES)

The Defendant in this case prays an appeal which is granted & entered into bond with Montgomery Bell & Lemuel Peters his securities in the sum of Six hundred & forty three Dollars & fifty two Cents & filed reasons for an appeal-

WILLIAM TAIT Assee)
of THOS. DAVIS)
Vs) Covenant
JAMES C. BROWN)

Demurrer over ruled and a Writ of Enquirery awarded to next Term-

ADAM DUNCAN & ALEXANDER JACKSON)
                Vs   ) Case
HUGH MCCOLLUM   )

      Demurrer over ruled & a Writ of Enquiery awarded to next Term-

(p-24) Same Justices on the Bench.

JOHN D. GARRETT Assee)
DANIEL A. DUNHAM Assee)
ROBERT WEAKLEY   )
         Vs   ) Debt
BENJAMIN WEAKLEY   )

      Demurrer over ruled & Judgment final for one Hundred Ninety Eight Dollars & fifty Cents with Interest thereon from the first day of April Seventeen Hundred & Ninety Nine - and also his Costs of suit in that behalf Expended-

      Ordered by the Court that Henry Small present Ranger Demand & Receive of James Moore the former Ranger, all the Books & other Documents belonging to the County as touching the Office of Ranger-

                                              J. Woolfolk
                                              John H. Poston
                                              Thos. Smith

(p-25) The Worshipful Court of Montgomery County have met according to Adjournment Monday June 20th 1808.
       Present -
                    Samuel Gattis   )
                    James Hambleton) Esquires
                    Sterling Niblett) Justices

Grand Jury (Viz) 1 Robert Nelson - foreman

2 William Jordan   8 Lewis Thompson
3 Robert McLaughlen   9 Alexander Brown
4 Jacob Rudolph   10 Robert Nowlen
5 William Grayson   11 Alexander McCrabb
6 Joseph Dickson   12 Martin Goss
7 James McCarrell   13 Samuel Mitchell
                                      14 John Rudolph
                                      15 Abraham Hall

Being Elected and sworn to enquire for the body of the County Retired to make their presentments-
The Grand Jury served four days & was discharged.

David Enloe a Constable was Sworn to attend the Grand Jury during this Term & served four days.

(p-26) 1 Deed of Conveyance

15 a

Guthridge Lyons to Burrell M. Williamson for a Town Lott in Palmyra proven by the Oaths of John H. Hyde & Samuel C. Hawkins & Ordered to Registration-

On Sufficient Reasons shown to the Court, Dempsy Hunter is excused from Serving as a Juror this present Term-

Thomas Williams is excused from Serving as a Juror this Term he being an overseer of a public Road-

John McKey is also cleared as being an Overseer of a public Road-

2 Deed of Conveyance Samuel Harvey to Benjamin Adams proven by the Oaths of James Fentress & Adam Harman Junr, for one Hundred Acres of land and Ordered to Registeration-

3 Deed of Conveyance David Outlaw to Wright Outlaw for 100 acres of land and Ordered to Registeration-

3 Deed of Conveyance David Outlaw to Wright Outlaw for 100 acres of land proven by the Oaths of James Moore and Robert Vance Subscribing Witnesses thereto & ordered to Registeration-

4 Deed of Conveyance John Bailess to Abraham Whitehead for 215 Acres acknowledged in Open Court & Ordered to Registeration-

(p-27) Thomas Smith & Sterling Neblett Esquires who was appointed by the Court to settle with Edward Leech Admr. of the Estate of David Bell Decd. Returns to this Term accordingly their Report of Settlement-

5 Deed of Conveyance John Cooke Sheriff of Montgomery to Thomas K. McElrath for one Town Lott in Palmyra No. 152-
Acknowledged in Open Court & Ordered to be Registered-

6 Deed of Conveyance John Cooke Sheriff of Montgomery County to Frances Tomkins for 282 Acres of Land acknowledged in Open Court & Ordered to be Registered-

7 John Cooke Sheriff of Montgomery acknowledges a Deed for one Town Lott in Palmyra No. 130 to Frances Tomkins and Ordered to be Registered-

Ordered by the Court that John Chisham be and is hereby appointed Overseer of that part of the Road in this County in place of Stephen Mallery & that he have all the hands which said Mallery & that he have all the hands which said Mallery was entitled to work under him-

Ordered that Joseph Ray be & is hereby appointed Overseer of that part of the Road in this County that James King was & that he have all the hands liable to work on said Road that Said King had-

(p-28) JOSEPH GRAY Assee of)
       WILLIAM B. WILLIAMS)
           Vs   ) Debt
       PETER HUBBARD   )

                    The Defendant Peter Hubbard at this day comes in proper person & confesses Judgment according to Specialty with Interest &

the plantiff stays Execution Three Months-
Therefore it is considered by the Court that the plantiff Recover his Debt in the Declaration mentioned with Interest & also his Costs of Suit in that behalf expended-

8 Deed of Conveyance Sarah Stewart wife of Andrew Stewart to Robert Biggar for 290 Acres Land being the same Tract of Land once conveyed by his husband Andrew Stewart, and acknowledged by her before William McDaniel & Benjamin Weakley two of the Justices for Montgomery County on her private Examination seperate from her Husband to be her free Act & Deed and ordered to be Registered- The State Tax on this Land has been paid before-

9 Agreeable to an Order made at October Term 1807 and Continued at January Term 1808 & at March Term 1808.
Revised on Motion of Alexander Tait formerly Alexander Joyce, appointing Commissioners to make partition and sett of to the Said Alexander Taite his part of Joseph Taite's tract of Three Thousand eight hundred & forty Acres of land as an Heir- Made their Return this Term-

10 Deed of Conveyance for 500 Acres of Land Heydon Wells to Charles Jones acknowledged in Court and Ordered to Registeration-

(p-29) James Fentress, Sterling Neblett & Abner Harris Esquires on the Bench-

On Motion Ordered that it is the Opinion of this Court that the whole of the proceedings on a Motion for Viewing and Laying off a Road from Clarksville to Smith's ferry and from thence to Intersect Humphries Road has been entirely

On Motion it is ordered that the Return made to this term by the Jurors appointed at last Term to view and lay of a Road from Clarksville to Smith's ferry from thence to Intersect Humphrey Road be quashed-

11 Deed of Conveyance, Duncan Stewart to William McDaniel for Eighty four & a half acres of Land acknowledged in Open Court & Ordered to be recorded-

12 Deed of Conveyance Joel Pace to James Mallery for 125 Acres of Land proven by the Oaths of Zenas Fox, Pray Whipple witnesses thereto & ordered to be Recorded-

On petition ordered that Vincent Cooper be excused for non attendance as a Juror last Term-

William McDaniel Esq. Returns a list of Taxable property for Capt. Bates Company for the present year.

(p-30) James Fentress, Sterling Neblett & Abner Harris - Esquires on the Bench.

THOMAS K. MCELRATH)
Vs)
BENJAMIN DOWNS)

On motion of the Plantiff's Atterney and it appearing by the Return of Darden Brown Constable that a Writ of Fiere facias Issued by James Moore Esq. Justice of the Peace for this County in favour of said Plantiff Vs said Defendant for the sum of Six Dollars sixty two & a half Cents & Costs of Suit has been levied by said Constable on Eighty Acres of land in this County the property of said Defendant. It is ordered & Considered by the Court that a Writ of Vendetioni Exponas Issue to expose said tract of land to sale to satisfy said Judgment & Costs of suit in that behalf expended-

ISAAC MORGAN)
Vs) Case
CHARLES ANDERSON)

The Plaintiff in proper person dismisses this Suit the first day of Court – therefore it is considered by the Court that the Defendant recover against the Plaintiff his Costs about his Suit in this behalf Expended-

13 Deed of Conveyance George Payne to Alexander McCrabb for 320 Acres of Land proven by the Oaths of Britain Bayless & William Bayless Witnesses thereto & Ordered to be registered-

(p-31) On Motion Ordered that John Cocke Sheriff have a Credit for five hundred & forty Acres Given in the name of Alexander Outlaw for the year 1807 the same having been Returned for Taxation in the Name of John Steele for the same year-

On Petition ordered that D. R. Slater be excused from serving as a Juror this Term-

GREEN HILL)
Vs)
LEMUEL PETERS &)
JOHN STEELE)

On Motion of the said Green Hill & it appearing to the satisfaction of the Court that the Lemuel Peters & John Steele were bound in a bond dated the 28th day of April 1808 to John Cocke Sheriff of Montgomery County as the Securities of Benjamin Weakley for said Weakleys keeping the Prison bounds of Montgomery County to which said Prison bounds he the said Weakley was committed on a Writ of Capias Adsatisfau An dum sued out of this Court at their January term 1808 at the suit of the said Green Hill Vs the said Benjamin Weakley and that said Benjamin Weakley has Broken the aforesaid Prison bounds contrary to the condition of said Bond – It also appearing to the satisfaction of the Court that the said Lemuel Peters & John Steele have received legal notice of this Motion and that the said Bond has been legally assigned

18

to the said Green Hill according to the Act of Assembly- Therefore it is
(p-32) considered by the Court that the Court that the said Green Hill
Recover Vs the said Lemuel Peters & John Steele the sum of Three Hundred
& Sixty eight Dollars, Eighty Eight & a half Cents, the ballance due on
the said Writ of Capeas Ad Satisfau Andum (which said Writ was founded on
a Judgment of this Court in favour of said Green Hill as Assignee of Benjamin Seawell Vs the said Weakley) and also for the sum of one Dollar the
ballance unpaid of the amount of costs due on the Judgment & Execution
aforesaid & his Costs by him about his Motion herein this behalf expended-

James Fentress Esquire Returns the list of Taxable property for Capt. Har-
mans Compy. for the present year-
Ordered that Joseph Woolfolk & Joseph Robinson Esquires be appointed to
settle with Alexander Brown Administrator of Nathan Ray decd. & make report to next Court-

Ordered that Nathan McGraw & William McDaniel Esquires be appointed to
settle with the Administratrix of the Estate of James Watt Deceased & make
report to next Court as the law requires-

Court adjourned untill tomorrow at 9 O'clock.

Court met according to adjournment 25th June-
    Present

        Willie Blount   )
        James Fentress &)
        Sterling Nibblett)
        Abner Harris   )

James Baxter Esq. took the necessary Oaths on the bench & had his Seat-

(p-33) Samuel Gattis Esq. Returns a list of Taxable property for Captain
Enloe's Company for the year 1808-

GLEN KING & POSTON)
    Vs   } Debt
JAMES BOYD & EDWARD CHEATHAM)

The plaintiff by his Attorney being Made in Court a Certified Copy of a
Judgment Recovered before Henry Small Esq. on the 9th of October 1807
against James Boyd the

JAMES BOYD   )
  Vs   } Debt
EDWARD CHEATHAM)

On the Motion of said Boyd and it appearing to the satisfaction of the Court
that the said Boyd has paid the sum of Twenty six Dollars Ninety seven & a
half Cents on Account of a Judgment obtained before Henry Small Esq. in
favour of Glen King & Poston on which the same was founded, the said James
Boyd was Security for said Defendant, Therefore it is considered by the Court
that the said James Boyd Recover & the said Edward Cheatham Def't. recover the
sum of Twenty six Dollars Ninety seven & a half Cents for his Debt aforesaid-

Tother with his Costs about his Suit in this behalf expended-

14 Deed William Ross Senr. & Thomas Watson to John Shelby for 110 Acres of land proven by the Oaths of William E. Williams & James Lockert subscribing Witnesses thereto & Ordered to be Recorded-

(p-34) JAMES DICKERSON }
              Vs   } Case
        JESSE JAMES   }

Dismissed by letter or Note from Plaintiff- Therefore it is considered by the Court that the Defendant Recover of the Plantiff his Costs about his Suit in this behalf expended-

The Jury that was appointed to clear out a Road from near the State line at James Watkins Blacksmiths Shop to intersect the Clarksville Road, Reports as follows-

Begining at a point on the State line near the shop at a Black Jack in the Barrens Running by Robert Searcy's leaving said Searcy's plantation to the left then crossing the Brushy fork between Clanton's & Shelby's (Bogard Pjantation) Then a direct course to John Frenche's leaving said Frenche's house to the Right hand and thence to the Great Road keading to Clarksville a small distance from Fletcher's Fork-
Given from under our hand this 10th day of June 1808-
John French is appointed overseer from West Fork Road to the Brushy Fork of the Piney Fork & Robert Searcy from thence to the State line-
James Lockert Esquire to name the hands-

15 Deed Thomas Sellers to Henry Ford 115 Acres of land proven by William Ford & John Hignight witnesses thereto & Ordered to be Recorded-

(p-35) On Motion ordered that Joseph Woolfolk Esq. & Drewry Ford have letters of Administration on the Estate of James Ford Dec'd, they qualified & gave Bond with Robert Searcy, Henry H. Bryand, Joseph Roberson & James Huling their Securities, bound in the sum of Twenty Thousand Dollars for their faithful performances-

Ordered that the Administrators of James Ford Decd. Sell all the Perishable property of the said Dec'd. Giving nine months credit on bond & Security-

The Administrators of the Estate of James Ford Decd. renders into Court an Inventory of said Estate.

Ordered by the Court that the Clerk advertise at the Court House Doors that the Court will on the first Tuesday of the next term do the County business & that on the Second Monday of said Term they will take up the States Docket-

Ordered that Robert Tygert be appointed Overseer of the Road from Palmyra to Coonrad's Creek instead of David Standley and the same hands continue to work on the road as heretofore-

John McCauley Esq. Returns a list of Taxable property for Captain Porter's Company for the present year-

Ordered that William Corbin be appointed Overseer of the Road from Benjamin Organs to Charnel Corbins instead of Alexander Faith & the same hands to work under Corbin who worked under Faith-

(p-36) Present the Worshipfull, Robert Prince, Willie Blount, James Hambleton, James Fentress, John Blair, John McCauley, James Moore, Abner Harris, Nathan McGraw, Hugh McClure, John H. Poston, John Sterling, James Baxter, James Lockert, Joseph Woolfolk, Joseph Robinson, Thos. Smith, Samuel Gatis.

The Court then proceeded to the Choice of a Sheriff for the County of Montgomery persuent to the Acts of the General Assembly of this State - and upon Counting the tickets it appeared that John Cocke Esq. was duly Elected Sheriff for Montgomery County-

The said John Cocke Entered into bond with Josiah G. Duke, Edward Niblett & George Humphries, Stephen Cocke Securities bound in the sum of Five Thousand Dollars for his faithful performance as Sheriff-Also gave the same Securities bound in a bond of Eight Thousand Dollars for the faithfull collecting & Accounting for public Monies-

Same Justices except John Blair, Hugh McClure, John H. Poston & Joseph Woolfolk & Abner Harris-

The Court then proceeded to the Choice of a Coroner for Montgomery County, when it appeared on Counting tickets that Abner Harris was duly Elected Coroner for the County aforesaid, Gave bond with Josiah G. Duke, Stephen Cocke & John Cocke his Securities bound in the sum of One Thousand Dollars for his faithfull performance as Coroner for Montgomery County.

(p-37) 16 Deed John G. Fletcher to William Mitchell for 320 Acres of Land proven by Samuel Fillingim & Josiah Horn Witnesses thereto & Ordered to be Registered-

17 Deed John Cocke Sheriff to Stephen Cocke for 500 Acres of land proven by William Allen & Edward Neblett Witnesses thereto & ordered to be Registered-

Jury to Decr. Superior Court 1808 James Moore, Samuel Vance, Thomas Smith, Willie Blount, Robert Prince, Joseph Woolfolk, James Lockert, James Boyd, John Bayliss, James Baxter, James Hambleton, Abner Harris-

Venire to September Term 1808- Reuben Bullard, Brittain Bayliss, David Brigham, Samuel Creswell, Burrell M. Williamson, David Pritchard, Isam Trotter, Joseph Whitehead, Richard Whitehead, Benjamin Adams, Andrew Irwin, Samuel Thornton, Blodget Bird, David Dupree, William Ross, Senr. Glidwell Killebro, Joseph French, David McFadden, William Williams, William McGowen, Ralph Williams, John Teasley, Robert Beggars, Isaac Weakley, William Hightower, Jacob Leech, Moses Oldham, William Montgomery, Peter Oneal, Thomas Brantly, John Harris, Alexander Carnes, James McGowen, James Trice, Thos. Dodd, Joseph Price, David Pasmore, William Whitehead, Guthridge Lyons-

Court adjourned for one Hour —

Court met according to adjournment —
Present —

      Willie Blount }
      John Blair & } Esqrs. Justices
      John McCauley }

(p-38) JESSE MARTIN }
     Vs   } Original Attachment
   GEORGE WILLIAMS}

John Rutledge being duly summoned & sworn as a Garneshee, says that he had at the time of being Summoned Thirty Dollars in Cost besides some pewter & & a Desk, four plates & Two Basons a Trunk & .

Therefore it is considered by the Court that the Said Jessee Martin the Plaintiff Recover of the said John Rutledge the sum of Thirty Dollars —

On sufficient Reasons shown to this Court Edward Leech is excused for his Non attendance as a Juror at last term —

Ordered that Benjamin Organ be appointed overseer of the road from George Humphrey's ferry to William Curlews & that the hands of Mrs. Cooke's, Abraham Cooke hands, Stephen Cooks Hands, Edward Neblets hands, Mrs. Sandersons hands, Joseph Price hands, Andrew Ingrams hands, James Downey, Sam'l. Roberts hands, John Coffee hands, Thomas Smiths hands, William Goods hands, Benjn. Organ's hands, Ambros Martin's hands, Andrew Tribble hands, Spelsbee Tribble hands —

Nathan McGraw Esquire returns the list of Taxable property for Capt. Weakley's Company for the present year —

Joseph Robinson Esquire returns the list of Taxable property for Capt. Bryant's Compy, for the present year.

(p-39) JOHN BAKER, Junr }
    ROWLAND PETERSON } Debt

The Defendant in this case comes here in proper person & Confesses a Judgment According to Specialty with Interest & the plantiff stays Execution Six Months.
Therefore it is ordered by the Court that the plantiff Recover of the Defendant his Damages as is Confessed with his Interest as Damages Together with his Costs about his suit Expended —

Willie Blount, Joseph Robertson, John E. Poston, Hugh McClure, Nathan McGraw, Abner Harris, James Fentress, John Blair, John McCawley, Sterling Neblett, James Lockert, James Baxter & Robert Prince, Esquires on the bench —

On Petition of Hardy Murfree by his Attorney in fact Thomas Smith Esqr. Ordered that he have a Ferry across Cumberland River at his own landing

Just below the first Island above Clarksville, which is granted by the Court, And ordered that Robert Whitledge, Stephen Cooke, Alexander Faith, Samuel Roberts, John Coffee, William Corlew, Benjamin Organ, David Burney, William Corben, Joseph Price, Robert Wells, David Pritchard, be appointed a Jury to lay off a View a Road leading from Clarksville Town To Thomas Smith's Ferry as Agent for Hardy Murfree and from thence to Intersect Humphries Road the nearest and best way with as little damage as the nature of the case will admitt off.

(p-40) WRIGHT BONDS)
    Vs   ) Appeal
JOHN W. LOWTHER)
         Jury (Viz)

1 Henry Funk   7 David Outlaw
2 William Corbin   8 James Pearee
3 William Stroud   9 Stephen Cocks
4 Isham Mathews   10 Isaac Morgan
5 Stephen O'Gwin   11 Abraham Cocke
6 Wright Outlaw   12 George Humphries

Who being duly Elected tried and Sworn the truth to Speake upon the matter of Controversy upon their Oaths do say that they find that the Defendant ows to the plantiff as is set forth against him & assesses his Damage to Forty six Dollars & Seveny four Cents, therefore it is considered by the Court that the plantiff Recover of the Defendant his Damages as assessed by the Jury in their Verdict and also his Costs of suit about his suit in that behalf expended- Motion by Defendant for appeal, appeal Granted & gave Bond with Marmaduke Oneal & Joel R. Oldham, his Securities bound in the sum of Ninety three Dollars & Forty eight Cents & filed his reasons for an appeal.

Leonard Hays a witness in the above suit proves Two days attendance and two Ferriages-

Henry Williams a witness in said Suit proves also Two Days attendance & Two Ferriages-

Wm. Ross, Senr. a witness proves five days attendance six ferriages-

(p-41) Ordered that a road be viewed & marked from Mosley's ferry on Cumberland River the nearest & best may so as to Intersect with the road leading from Weakley's ferry to Cole Richard Napiers forge on Barton's Creek & that William Hightower, Martin Goss, Simeon Miers, James Trotter, Hollow Morris, Fredrick Goss be appointed a Jury to View the same-

Ordered that William Hightower be appointed overseer of the same, & that Samuel Smith be Esquire name the hands to work thereon-

On motion, Ordered that Adam Harmon be allowed the sum of Fifteen Dollars for his Services as an Officer in Executing a States Warrant against Eli Smith & that he be paid the same by the County Treasurer-

June 21st Court Adjourned untill Tomorrow 9 O'clock

22nd the Court met according to Adjournment

Present- the Worshipful James Fentress, James Moore & John Blair Esqrs. on the bench.

JOHN BELL)
  Vs)
REUBEN GRAYSON) Trespass
& JAMES TRIBBLE)

On motion ordered that De po Fa Issue to take the Deposition of Daniel McKinney & John Waggoner in favour of the plantiffs Twenty days notice to be given the Defendant-
(p 42)
Abraham Whitehead, John Mosely & James Mallery who was duly summoned by the Sheriff to serve this day as Jurors being solemnly called & failed to answer or appear, it is Ordered by the Court that Sifa Issue accordingly. Ordered that the above order be Recorded

James Fentress, John Blair & John McCaulley Esquires on the bench.

JAMES MOORE
  Vs
REBECCA DOWNS ALMINISTRATRIX)
ISAAC SATERFIELD ADMR. OF) Original
WM. DOWNS DECD.) Attachment

(Jury Viz)

1 William Corbin   7 Isham Mathews
2 David Outlaw   8 Stephen Cooke
3 Stephen O'Gwin   9 Peter Oneal
4 Wright Outlaw   10 Robert Searcy
5 Henry Funk   11 Benjamin Wells
6 William Stroud   12 Robert Whitledge

Being duly Elected tried & sworn the truth to speak upon the Issue Joined do upon their Oaths say that they find that the Defendant owes to the plantiff the sum of Eighty Two Dollars & nineteen Cents as is Declared in the Declaration- Therefore it is considered by the Court that the Plaintiff Recover of the Defendants the Debt in the Declaration mentioned agreeable to the Verdict of the Jury in form aforesaid. As also his Costs about his suit in this behalf Expended- Burrell Bayliss a witness proves Eight Days & five Ferriages-

(p-43) John Blair, Thomas Smith, Sterling Niblett, Samuel Smith & John McCaully Esquires on the bench-

PETER BRAWNER)
  Vs) Appeal
ISRAEL ROBERTSON)

Jury (Viz)

1 Lewis Pukett   6 Josiah G. Duke

23 a

2	Abraham Whitehead	8	William Allen
3	James Mallery	9	Thomas Whitledge
4	Isaac Saterfield	10	John B. Tompkins
5	William Baker	11	Charles Anderson
6	Josiah G. Duke	12	Owen Perdue

Who being duly Elected tried and sworn the truth to speak upon the matter of Controversy do upon their Oaths say that they find that the Defendant ows to the Plaintiff the sum of Twenty Dollars. Therefore it is considered by the Court that the Plaintiff recover against the Defendant the sum of Twenty Dollars the Verdict of the Jury in form aforesaid as also his Costs about his suit in this behalf Expended & the Defendant in Mercy & ".

John Yoes a witness proves three days attendance & 32 miles traveling. Ordered that the plaintiff pay this witness his Costs-

(p-44) James Fentress Esquire gives in his resignation as a Justice of the Peace-

John Blair Esq. Renders to Court a list of Taxable property for Captain McCrabbs Company for the present year.

NATHANIEL DICKINSON)
        Vs   )
JOSEPH PENRICE   )

Hugh F. Bell proves two Days as a witness in this suit-
Wright Outlaw, David Outlaw, John Stewart, Charles Stewart being duly & Solemnly called failed to answer as Jurors. Therefore it is ordered by the Court that the Clerk Issue Sofa to next Term-

The fine Receded as to Wright Outlaw & David Outlaw, Charles Stewart & John Stewart all excused.

18 Deed of Conveyance George Payzer to James Baxter, James Jackson & Washington Jackson for Town Lotts No. 6 & 10 in the addition to Clarksville proven by the Oaths of William Smith & J. B. Reynolds witness thereto & Ordered to be Registered-

THOMAS DODD   )
     Vs   ) Case
ROBERT SEARCY)

The Plaintiff in this case Dismissed this suit & the Defendant assumes all Costs, therefore it is considered by the Court that the Plaintiff recover against the Defendant his costs about his suit in this behalf Expended & the Defendant in Mercy & ".

(p-45) John Blair, John Sterling, Thomas Smith, Sterling Neblett, John McCaully, Samuel Smith, Abner Harris, Justices on the Bench-

STEPHEN CANTRELL Junr. &
GEO. M. DEADERICK
Vs
JOHN BAKER Junr.

Jury (Viz)

1	Henry Funk	7	Andrew Batie
2	Stephen Cocke	8	William Killebrew
3	James Puree	9	Nedham Whitfield
4	Stephen O Gwin	10	Benjamin Wells
5	William Strocier	11	Peter Oneal
6	Isham Mathews	12	William Corbin

Being duly elected tried & sworn to enquire of Damages on their Oaths do say that the plaintiff has sustained Damages by Reason of the Defendants non performance of his Covenant in the declaration mentioned to the sum of Five hundred & Eighty Dollars-
Therefore it is considered by the Court that the Plaintiff Recover of the Defend. the sum found as Damages by the Jury assessed in their Verdict and also their Costs about their suit in that behalf expended-

19 Deed John Cocke Sheriff of Montgomery to Richard Whitehead for three Hundred & Twenty Acres of Land- Acknowledged in Open Court and Ordered to Registeration-

(p-46) John Blair, John Sterling, Samuel Gattis, Sterling Neblett, Thomas Smith Esquire-

ISAAC MORGAN
Vs   } Case
CHARLES ANDERSON

1	Stephen Cocke	7	Isam Mathewes
2	James Pearce	8	William Killebro
3	William Corbin	9	Abraham Whitehead
4	David Outlaw	10	Abraham Cocke
5	Henry Funk	11	Stephen O'Gwin
6	William Stroud	12	Isaac Saterfield

Who being elected tried & sworn the truth to speak upon the issues joined upon their Oaths do say that the Defendant is Guilty as is charged in the Declaration & assess the Plantiffs Damages to Twenty five Dollars. There it is considered by the Court that the plantiff do Recover his Damages as assessed by the Jury in their Verdict and his Costs about his suit in this behalf expended-

Motion for new trial by the Defendant, which being duly argued on both sides it is the Opinion of the Court that no New Trial be Granted-

John Johnson a witness in the above suit proves Nine days & seventy miles Travelling & Two Ferriages.

(p-47) STATE)
     Vs) Indictment
REUBEN LOGGANS)

John Sinsel the prosecutor acknowledges himself bound in the sum of one hundred & fifty Dollars to be levied off his goods & Chattels Lands & Tenements but to be void of condition that the said John Sinsel does come here into Court at Friday next Court & there to give Evidence in favour of the State against Reubin Logans & not to depart the Court without leave-

                                   John Sensil

STATE)
  Vs) Indictment
WILLIAM LOGGANS)

John Sinsel the prosecutor comes here into Court & acknowledges himself bound in the sum of One hundred & fifty Dollars to be levied off his goods & Chattels Lands & Tenements but to be void on condition that he personally appear on Friday next at the Court House in Clarksville & there to give testimony in the suit the State against William Loggans & depart the Court without leave

                                   John Sensil-

(p-48) STATE)
     Vs) Indictment
William Loggans)

Martin Loggans comes here into Court & acknowledges himself bound in the sum of One Hundred & fifty dollars to be levied of his goods & Chattels lands & Tenements but to be void on condition that he personally appears at our present term on Friday of next the 24th June at Court to be holden at the Courthouse in Clarksville then & there to give Testimony in behalf of the State Vs. William Loggans & not depart the Court without leave-

                                       his
                                Martin / Loggans
                                   mark

Alexander Faith comes here into Court and acknowledges himself bound in the sum of One Hundred & fifty dollars to be levied of his goods & Chattels lands & Tenements but to be void on Conditions that he personally appear on Friday next of this present Term than & there to give Testimony in favour of the State in Two Suits against William Loggans & one against Reuben Loggans & not to depart the Court without leave-

                                   Alexander Faith

On Motion Ordered that the Treasurer of Montgomery County pay to Robert Prince Esq. the sum of Fourteen Dollars for a Book furnished by said Prince for Records of Registers Office.

James Moore Esquire Returns the list of Taxable property for Capt. Vaxce's Company for the present year-

(p-49) Sterling Neblett, John McCaully & Abner Harris, Esquires on the bench.

LEWIS PICKETT)
    Vs   ) Case
CELA PICKETT)

                Jury (Viz)

1. Wright Outlaw
2. Allen Anderson
3. William Baker
4. Peter Oneal
5. James Mallery
6. John Henderson
7. Benjamin Wells
8. Isaac Morgan
9. William Loggans
10. Josiah G. Duke
11. Robert Whitledge
12. Charles Anderson

Who being duly elected tried & sworn the truth to speak do upon their Oaths say that the Defendant is Guilty as the Plaintiff hath so Declared & do assess the Plaintiff's Damages to twelve dollars by reason of the Detention thereof-

Motion for a new trial by Defendants Attorney-

Motion withdrawn by consent of the parties-
Therefore it is considered by the Court that the Plaintiff recover against the Defendant the damages so assessed by the Jury in form aforesaid as also his Costs about his suit in this behalf Expended & the Defendant in Mercy &.

George Gibson a witness proves 9 days attendance in this Suit & four Ferriages-

Power of Attorney Cela Pickett to Frances Long proven in Court by the Oaths of Colmore Duvall, Henry Minor, & James Williams witnesses thereto & ordered to be Registered-

(p-50) The last Will & Testament of William White Deceased was proven in Open Court by the Oaths of John Henderson & John Dims subscribing witnesses thereto & ordered to be Recorded-

20 Deed of Conveyance Robert Nelson to John Henderson for Six & one Fourth Acres Land acknowledged in Open Court & ordered to be Registered.

Same Justices on the bench.

JOSEPH PHILLIPS) The plea of release
    Vs   ) Debt & replevation thereto withdrawn
ISAAC MORGAN)

                Jury (Viz)

1. James Persee
2. William Corlew
3. William Stroud
4. Lewis Pickett
5. Henry Funk
6. David Outlaw
7. Isom Mathews
8. Abraham Whitehead
9. Abraham Cocke
10. Stephen O'Gwin
11. Isaac Satterfield
12. William Allen

Who being duly Elected tried & sworn the truth to speak upon the Issue

Joined do upon their Oaths say that the Defendant hath not paid Three Hundred & Eighty Four Dollars & fifty Cents of the Debt in the Declaration mentioned & that hath paid the remaining part of said Debt and they do assess the plaintiffs Damages by Reason of the detention of the Sd. Debt to Eighteen Dollars & forty five cents. Therefore it is considered by the Court that the plaintiff Recover his Debt & Damages as assessed by the Jury and also his Costs about his suit in this behalf expended & the Defendant in Mercy & C.

(p-51) Court adjourned untill tomorrow at 9 O'clock-

Court met according to adjournment

Present - The Worshipful

James Moore
Sterling Neblett
John McCauly
Abner Harris) Esquires
Thomas Smith) Justices
James Hambleton

AARON FLETCHER Assee)
  Vs) Debt
STERLING INGRAM)

Jury (To wit)

1 Henry Funk
2 William Stroud
3 William Corben
4 Wright Outlaw
5 Stephen O'Gwin
6 David Outlaw
7 Isham Mathews
8 Martin Loggans
9 William Baker
10 Josiah G. Duke
11 William Allen
12 James Loggins

Who being duly Elected tried & sworn the truth to speak upon the Issues Joined do upon their Oath say that they find said Issues for the plaintiff & that the Defendant has not paid the sum of Three Hundred & Three Dollars & forty ninee cents of the debt in the Declaration mentioned & that the said Defendant hath paid Thirty Dollars of the said Debt & do assess the plaintiffs Damages by Reason of the detention thereof to Ten Dollars & Eleven Cents-
Therefore it is considered by the Court that the plaintiff do Recover of the Defendant the balance of his debt & his Damages as assessed by the Jury in their Verdict, and also his Costs about his suit in this behalf expended-
Motion by Defendant for appeal Granted filed reason for an appeal, the Defendant gave Bond with William Gordan & Richard Lee his Securities bound in the sum of Six hundred & twenty seven Dollars & seventy Cents-

(p-52) Same Justices on the bench only James Moore Esq. & John McCaully Esqr. & James Hambleton Esq. on the bench-

JOHN GARDENER)
  Vs) Asst. & Battery
JOHN BAKER Junr.)

Jury (Viz)

1. Henry Funk
2. William Stroud
3. William Corbin
4. Isam Mathews
5. David Outlaw
6. Stephen O'Gwin
7. William Brown
8. William Killebrew
9. John Stewart
10. Peter O'Neal
11. William Gordan
12. Thomas Whitledge

Who being duly Elected tried & sworn the truth to speak upon the Issue Joined do upon their Oaths say that they find the Issue for the Plaintiff & do assess the plaintiffs Damages to Forty Two Dollars, Therefore it is considered by the Court that the plaintiff recover against the Defendant the Damages as assessed by the Jury in their Verdict together with his Costs about his suit in this behalf expended-

Isaac Dorch a witness in the above suit proves four days attendance & Sixty Eight miles Travelling.

Thomas Martin a witness proves five days attendance

Elias Laurence a witness proves Two days attendance & Thirty six miles Traveling.

Zachariah Grant a witness proves Two days attendance-

Pray Whipple a witness proves Two days attendance & Fourty six miles Travelling -

(p-53) GARDNER)
   Vs)
   BAKER)

James Gardner a witness proves three days attendance & forty miles travelling-

James Grant a witness proves four days attendance-

Whitmill Fort a witness proves three days attendance.

James Hambleton, Sterling Neblett, Abner Harris & John McCauley Esquires on the bench-

(p-54) ALEXANDER FAITH)
   Vs) Case
   WILLIAM ALLEN)
      Jury (Viz)

1. James Pierce
2. Josiah G. Duke
3. James Bray
4. Wright Outlaw
5. Wilson Gibson
6. Reuben Grayson
7. Robert Temple
8. James Lister
9. William D. Wilson
10. Moses Oldham
11. Moses Parker
12. Needham Whitfield

Who being Elected tried & sworn the truth to speake upon the Issue joined upon the Oaths do say that they find the Defendant Guilty as the Plaintiff

hath so declared & assesses his Damages to five Dollars-
Motion for a new trial by Defendants Attorney- Therefore it is considered by the Court that the Plaintiff recover against the Defendant the Verdict of the Jury in form aforesaid as also his Costs about his suit in this behalf Expended & the Defendant in Mercy & C.

ALEXANDER FAITH)
    Vs   ) Case
WILLIAM ALLEN)

Allen Anderson a witness proves four Days Attendance-

George Humphries a witness proves Six days attendance-

Dixon Loggins a witness proves four days attendance & two ferriages.

John Coffee a witness proves six days attendance four ferriages-

Peter Holt a witness proves six days attendance four ferriages

Benjamin H. Watkins a witness proves one day & two ferriages

Abraham Cocke a witness proves six days attendance & four ferriages

Court adjourned untill tomorrow at 9 O'clock.

Court met according to adjournment June 24th 1808-
    Present
                Hugh McClure   )
                John McCauly   ) Esquires
                Sterling Niblett) Justices

On motion ordered that Wright Outlaw be exonerated from serving as a Juror for the rest of this Term.

THE STATE)
    Vs   ) Indictment
WILLIAM LYONS)

The Defendant comes into Court & submits himself.
The Court orders him to be fined Twenty five Cents, Therefore it is Considered by the Court that the said Defendant pay this Costs of this suit in this behalf expendant-

(p-55)   STATE   )
           Vs   ) Sifa
      WILLIAM LYOND)
      & SAMUEL VANCE)

The Defendants in this case being solemnly called out upon their Recognizance at last term & forfeited- On motion & good reasons shown here to the Court, they are of oppinion that the forfetture be set aside, and it is the oppinion of the Court also that the said Defendants pay the Costs of their suits in this behalf expended-

STATE
Vs   ) Aleas Sifa
JAMES TRIBBLE)

The Defendant in this case was at our January term 1807 and second Monday thereof Called out upon his Recognizance and failed to appear whereupon he forfeited agreably to the Acts of Assembly. On motion & Reasons shown to the Court at this term the forfetture is set aside, and it is considered by the Court that the Defendant pay all the Costs of this suit in this behalf expended & the Defendant in Mercy & C.

STATE
Vs   ) Alleas Sifa
GOODMAN TRAYWICK)

The Defendant in this case who was called out upon his Recognizance at our January term 1807 failed & forfetted, Therefore it is upon motion made to the Court & Reasons shown it Ordered that the forfetture be set aside, Therefore it is considered by the Court that the Defendant pay all the Costs in that behalf expended-

20 Deed of Conveyance John Cooke Sheriff to Henry Small was acknowledged in Open Court & ordered to be registered for two lots in Clarksville No. 12 & 15.

(p-56) Same Justices on the bench & also Samuel Smith (Esq.)

STATE
Vs   ) Presentment
REUBEN GRAYSON)
               (Jury Viz)

1 William Corbin   7 John Stewart
2 William Stroud   8 Isaac Kittrill
3 Henry Funk   9 Martin Loggans
4 Isam Mathews   10 David Outlaw
5 Stephen O'Gwin   11 John Dykas
6 Stephen Cocke   12 James Williams

Who being duly elected tried & sworn the truth to speake upon the bill of presentment do upon their Oaths say that they find the Defendant not Guilty as charged in manner & form- Therefore it is the Oppinion of the Court that the Defendant go without Day - or without Costs except his own witnesses-

On petition to the Court now sitting, it is Ordered that William Porter be appointed Guardian to Balum Bull, Jerry Bull, Beckey Bull, Molly Bull, Dempsy Bull, heirs & Orphans of Randal Bull Decd, who came here into Court & Entered into bond with William Sulivant, Samuel Smith his Securities bound in the sum of Three Thousand Dollars for the faithfull Discharges of his Duties as Guardian aforesaid-

(p-57)   Same Justices on the Bench

STATE)
Vs) Indictment
WRIGHT BONDS)

Jury (Viz)

1 William Corbin
2 William Stroud
3 Henry Funk
4 Isam Mathews
5 Stephen O'Gwin
6 Stephen Cocke

7 John Stewart
8 Isaac Kittrell
9 Martin Loggans
10 David Outlaw
11 Alexander Faith
12 James Williams

Who being duly Elected tried & sworn the truth to speake upon the bill of Indictment upon their Oath do say that they find the Defendant not Guilty as charged in Manner & form–
Therefore it is considered by the Court that the Defendant depart in peace And that said Defendant have Judgement against the prosecutor John Dikes for his Costs about his suit in this defense Expended–

Robert Sawyears a witness in the above suit proves three days attendance & four Ferriages–

Stephen Mallery a witness proves one day attendance & two ferriages–

William Hust a witness in the above suit was Solemnly called & came not. Ordered therefore that Sifa Issue to next Term–

JAMES BUNTING)
Vs) On motion of the plaintiff.
JOEL R. OLDHAM)

It is ordered that a De Po Fa Issue for said Plaintiff to take the Deposition of David Bunting De bene Esse 2 Days notice to be given to the Defendant–

(p-53) Sames Justices on the bench–

STATE)
Vs) Indictment
WILLIAM LOGGANS)

Jury (Viz) No. 1

1 William Stroud
2 Henry Funk
3 Absolam Leggett
4 Duke Josiah G.
5 James Pearce
6 Stephen Cocke

7 Isaac Kittrell
8 Stephen O'Gwin
9 David Outlaw
10 Thomas Whitledge
11 Robert Wells
12 James Bray

Who being duly Elected tried & sworn the truth to speake upon the Bill of Indictment do upon their Oaths say they find the Defendant Guilty as charged in the Bill of Indictment in Manner & form–
Motion by Defendants Attorney for New trial, argued on both sides. Motion overruled, therefore it is considered by the Court that the Defendant William Loggans be fined Twenty five cents & that the Defendant pay the costs about this suit expended–

Same Justices on the bench - State Vs Reuben Loggans & same Jury as No. 1 in the above-

Being duly elected tried & sworn the truth to Speake upon the bill of Indictment do upon their Oaths say that they find that the Defendant is Guilty as charged in the bill of Indictment. The Court therefore fines him Twenty five Cents, Therefore the Court Orders that he pay all the Costs in this behalf expended-

Jones Johnson a witness in the above suit proves one day attendance, 2 Ferriages-

John Johnson a witness proves in the above suit One Day & 2 Ferriages-

(p59). Same Justices only James Hambleton in Place of Hugh McClure, Esq.

STATE
Vs) Indictment
William LOGGANS)

The Defendant in this case comes into Court & Submitts himself. Therefore the Court Orders him fined Twenty five cents, and that the said Defendant pay the Costs of the suit in this behalf expended-

THE STATE
Vs) Indictment
JOSIAH G. DUKE)

The Defendant in this case comes into Court & Submitts- Therefore the Court Orders him fined Twenty five Cents, and it is also ordered by the Court that he pay all the Costs of this suit in this behalf expended-

STATE
Vs) Indictment
ABSOLAM LEGETT)

The Defendant in this case comes here into Court & Submitts himself. Therefore the Court orders him fined Twenty five Cents. It is considered by the Court that the Defendant pay all the Costs of the suit in this behalf expended-

(p-60) STATE
Vs)
WILLIAM LOGANS)

Alexander Faith a witness proves one day & two Ferriages-

Jones Johnston a witness One day & 2 Ferriages

John Johnston One day & 2 Ferriages

Court adjourned untill tomorrow 9 O'clock

Court met according to Adjournment

Present - the worshipfull

     Sterling Niblet)
     John H. Poston) Esquires on the bench
     James Baxter) Justices
     Abner Harris)

JOSHUA HANDLEY)
  Vs   )
SAMUEL LYONS &) Debt
JOHN MINOTT   )

On motion of the Plaintiffs Attorney for leave to amend the Declaration to suit the writ which being argued on both sides the Court is of oppinion that he have leave to amend (Sterling Niblett, Abner Harris, Thomas Smith & John H. Poston - Esquires on the bench)

MARMADUKE ONEAL)
  Vs   ) Appeal
JOHN BAXTOR   )

On motion of the plantiff at last term for a new trial argued on both sides at this term it was therefore the oppinion of the Court that the motion be overruled- Therefore it is considered by the Court that the Defendant recover against the Plaintiff his Costs about his suit in this behalf Expended & the Plaintiff in Mercy &.

(p-61) Sterling Neblett, Thomas Smith, John H. Poston Esquires on the Bench-James Hambleton Esquire-

JAMES DUNBARR)
  Vs   ) Case
BUCKNER KILLEBREW)

      Jury (Viz)

1 John Stewart   7 William Stroud
2 David Outlaw   8 James Williams
3 Stephen Cocke   9 Moses Parker
4 William Corben   10 William Nelson
5 Isam Mathews   11 James Bray
5 Stephen O'Gwin   12 Stephen Thomas

Being duly Elected tried & sworn the truth to speake upon the Issue Joined do upon their Oaths say that they find that the Defendant is not Guilty as charged in the Declaration in Manner & form - Therefore it is considered by the Court that the Defendant recover of the plantiff his Costs about his suit in this behalf expended and the Plaintiff in Mercy & that the Defendant may Depart without day-

William Bayliss a witness proves five days two ferriages in the above suit.

Curtis Gray a witness proves Three Days attendance.

John Dikes a witness proves Ten Days & four Ferriages

Needham Whitfield a witness proves Seven Days & four Ferriages

Andrew Peterson proves four days attendance.

(p-62) STATE OF TENNESSEE
MONTGOMERY COUNTY
The heirs of Benjamin McCulloch
Vs
McCLURE & ELDER

Pursuant to an order of the County Court of Montgomery issued at March Term 1808 directed to Duncan Stewart, Willie Blount & James Baxter, William Crutcher came before us Duncan Stewart, Willie Blount & James Baxter this twenty fifth day of May 1808 & being duly sworn on the Holy Evangelist of Almighty God-deposes & saith that in November 1792 he surveyed six hundred & forty acres of land represented by a plat which appears to be annexed to a grant issued by the State of North Carolina in the name of Benjamin McCulloch Assignee of Hardy Hart bearing date the 20th May 1793 situated lying & being in the County of Tennessee on the North Side of Cumberland river on the West fork of Red river, joining an entry of Benjamin Shepperds beginning at a red Oak & hickory thence South three hundred & twenty poles to a Hickory thence East three hundred & twenty poles to a stake, thence North three hundred & twenty poles to a stake: thence West three hundred & twenty poles to the beginning number of the Grant 1068 which survey he states that he made under an agreement with Robert Hays who informed this deponent that he acted as agent of Benjamin McCulloch in Superintending the surveying of lands for said McCulloch & that he made the said survey under said agreement,
Question by Benjamin McCulloch putato tree called for in the grant Issued in the name of Benjamin McCulloch did you mark this tree as a beginning corner of a survey for Ben McCulloch. Answer by William Crutcher I marked a red Oak & Hickory for the Beginning corner & believe this to be the same red Oak & the Hickory log which lies in view I believe to be the Hickory which I marked-
Question by McClure & Elder, did you at the time of marking this corner mark it for more than one tract & how many & who was in Company.
Answer by Wm. Crutcher I believe I marked it for two but do not certainly recollect who was in Company. I think it probable that John Bell or some of the fletchers were.
Questioned by McClure & Elder did you at the time you marked this corner proceed to mark any other trees on the lines of the survey?
Answer by William Crutcher. I do not recollect certainly that I did, I generally marked pointers.
Question by McClure & Elder, when did you make out your plat or return of survey & who employed you?
Answer, by William Crutcher. I do not recollect when I made out the plat of survey I was employed by Col. Robt. Hays.

(p-63) Question by McClure & Elder did you not make a number more surveys for said applicant at same time & how many?
Answer by William Crutcher, I made several surveys for Benjn. McCulloch but do not recollect making any more than one for him at that time-
Question by McClure & Elder. How many of those can you find the beginning of?
Answer by William Crutcher. I do not know unless I should turn out to look for them.
Question by McClure & Elder, did you find this corner yourself or were you

shewn it by some other person?
Answer by William Crutcher I believe I could have found it myself but did not look for it untill I was accompanied to it by Mr. Benjamin McCulloch about Novr. 1805.
Question by McClure & Elder you do not mean to swear positively to this being the corner you made for B. McCulloch in Novr. 1792, but mearly that you believe it is?
Answer by Wm. Crutcher. I believe it to be the corner
Question by Benjn. McCulloch did you at the time of marking the tree any mark or blemish other than what you made yourself.
Answer by William Crutcher I saw none-
Question by Ben McCulloch do you firmly believe this to be the tree marked as the beginning corner to a survey made for Benj. McCulloch
Answer by William Crutcher I believe it is-
Question by Wright Bonds but you will not swear positively that this is the Identical corner you made for Benjn. McCulloch now in dispute & no other-
Answer by William Crutcher. I will not swear positively but I believe it to be the corner.
And further this Deponent sayeth not-

          Wm. Crutcher

Subscribed & Sworn to before
us this 25th May 1808

D. Stewart
Willie Blount
James Barter

Court adjourned untill Monday the 27th June at 9 O'clock.

Court met according to adjournment Monday the 27th June 1808.

Hugh McClure   )
Sterling Neblett) Esquires
Thomas Smith   ) Justices
John Blair   )

(p-64) ADAM DUNCAN &)
    ALEXANDER JACKSON)
      Vs   ) Case
    HUGH MCCOLLUM   )

          Jury (Viz)

1 William Stroud   7 David Outlaw
2 Henry Funk   8 Moses Parker
3 Malchia Segrand   9 Robert Tagert
4 Stephen O'Gwin   10 James Williams
5 Isam Mathews   11 Absolam Tribble
6 Stephen Cooks   12 William Corban

Who being duly Elected tried & sworn the truth to speake upon the Issue Joined upon their Oaths do say that the defendant hath not paid the Debt in the Declaration mentioned and do assess his Damages by the Reason of the Detention thereof

Who being duly Elected tried and sworn Deligently to inquire of Damages.

On their Oaths do say that the plantiffs hath sustained Damages by Reason of the Defendants non performance of the Assumptions in the declaration mentioned to two Hundred & Thirty Nine Dollars & Fifty four Cents. Therefore it is considered by the Court that the plaintiffs recover of the Defendant the Damages aforesaid by the Jury in their Verdict aforesaid in form aforesaid assessed and also their costs about their suit in this behalf expended-

(p-65)   Same Justices on the Bench

JESSE MARTIN)
   Vs). Original Attachment
GEORGE WILLIAMS)

The Defendant being solemnly called to come into Court & Replevy the property attached came not but made Default, therefore it is considered by the Court that the plaintiff Recover of the said Defendant the sum of Eighty five Dollars the debt in the Declaration mentioned together with Two Dollars fifty cents Damage.
And also their Costs of suit in this behalf expended-

      Same Justices on the Bench

MOSES STEELE)
   Vs) Covenant & Judl. Attachment
GEORGE WILLIAMS)

The Defendant being solemnly called to come into Court and replevy the property attached came not but made Default, Therefore it is considered by the Court that the plaintiff recover of the Defendant the sum.

On motion it is allowed by the Court that the Treasurer of Montgomery County the sum of Forty Dollars for Exoficio Services up to this Term- Thomas Smith, Esq. Returns a list of Taxable property for Captain Allens Company for the present year-

(p-66)   Same Justices on the bench

JAMES M. REYNOLDS &)
JOHN R; MCFARLIN)
   Vs) Case
JOSEPH PENRICE)

      Jury (Viz)

1 John Stewart
2 James Pearce
3 Hugh McCollam
4 Andrew Tribble
5 Thomas Whitledge
6 Robert Temples
7 James Loggans
8 Thomas Bunch
9 Zebedee Dennes
10 William D. Wilson
11 Barny Duff
12 James Gillibo

Who being duly Elected tried & sworn diligently to enquire of Damages on their Oaths do say that the plantiffs hath sustained Demages by Reason of the Defendants nonperformance of the Assumption in the Declaration mentioned & assess their Damages to Seventy Three Dollars & Forty three Cents. Therefore it is considered by the Court that the plaintiffs recover against the Defendant the Damages aforesaid by the Jury in their Verdict aforesaid in form aforesaid assessed. And also their Costs about their suit in this behalf expended-

On motion it is allowed & ordered by the Court that William C. Jamison Clerk of the County of Montgomery be paid by the Treasurer of said County the sum of Forty Dollars for Exofisio Services up to this term-

Ordered also that the Treasurer of Montgomery County pay the said William C. Jamison the sum of Twenty Dollars for making tax list for last year-

(p-67) John Blair, Thomas Smith, Sterling Neblett & Samuel Gattis Esquires on the bench.

HUGH McCLURE & JAMES ELDER
Vs
AMOS BIRD

Case

Jury (Viz)

1 John Stewart
2 James Pierce
3 James Trice
4 Thomas Whitledge
5 Andrew Tribble
6 Robert Temples
7 James Loggans
8 Thomas Bunch
9 Zebedee Denness
10 William D. Wilson
11 Barny Duff
12 James Gillebo

Who being duly elected tried & sworn deligently to inquire of damages in this suit upon their Oaths do say that the Defendant did assume in Manner & form as the Plaintiffs in Declaring against him hath alledged & do assess their Damages by Reason of the nonperformance of those Assumptions to Two Hundred & ten Dollars & Sixty four Cents besides their costs about their suit in that behalf Expended- Therefore it is considered by the Court that the plaintiff recover against the Defendant the damages so assessed by the Jury in form as aforesaid as also his costs about his suit in this behalf Expended & the Defendant in Mercy & C.

Motion for appeal & appeal granted & gave Bond with George W. L. Marr & James Baxter his securities bound in the sum of four hundred & twenty one Dollars & twenty eight cents & filed his reasons for an appeal- To wit, In this case James Elder one of the plaintiffs brought into Court a book which was proven to be a book of the Defendants & in that book an Act between the Plaintiffs & Defendant was found & a Credit to the plaintiffs for _____ Dollars _____ in the hand write of one of the Plaintiffs against the Defendant & upon that with other testimony equally improper to be heard the Jury found a Verdict for the Plaintiffs which in my opinion is a sufficient reason for appealing-

           G. W. L. Marr
           Atto. for Defendant

(p-68) John Blair, Samuel Gattis, Sterling Neblett Esqrs. on the bench.

JOHN MARR Assee
RICHARD C. NAPIER
Vs
JOHN BAKER, Junr.

Debt

Jury (Viz) No. 1

1 William Stroud
2 Henry Funk
3 Stephen Cooke
4 Malicha Lagrand
5 Stephen O'Gwin
6 Isam Trotter
7 David Outlaw
8 Moses Parker
9 Robert Tagert
10 James Williams
11 William Corbin
12 Absolem Tribble

Who being duly Elected tried & sworn the truth to speake on the Issues Joined do upon their Oaths say that the Defendant hath not paid the Debt in the Declaration mentioned of One hundred & Eighty five Dollars & Forty six Cents & assess his Damages for non payment thereof to Eighteen Dollars Thirty six Cents, Therefore it is considered by the Court that the plaintiff recover of the Defendant his debt & Damages as assessed by the Jury, and also his costs about his suit in this behalf expended-

THOMAS MITCHELL)
    Vs   ) Certici & Superad.
MORGAN BROWN)

    Dismissed by a Receipt from Plaintiff therefore it is considered by the Court that the Defendant recover against the Plaintiff his Costs about his suit in this behalf Expended & the Plaintiff in Mercy &

(p-69)   Same Justices on the bench

THOS. FIGURES Assee)
RICHARD HOLLAND)
    Vs   ) Covenant
MENOAH TAYLOR   )
              Same Jury No. 1.

Who being Elected tried & sworn deligently to inquire of Damages, On their Oaths do say that the plaintiff hath sustained Damages by the Reason of the Defendants nonperformance of the Covenant in the Declaration mentioned to Fifty six Dollars sixty five Cents, Therefore it is considered by the Court that the plaintiff recover of the Defend. his Damages as assessed by the Jury in their Verdict & his costs about his suit in that behalf expended-

    Same Justices on the bench.

STEPHEN STEWART)
    Vs   )
JAMES GRANT &   ) Covenant
ISRAEL ROBINSON)
           Same Jury No. 1.

Who being duly elected tried & sworn the truth to speak upon the Issue Joined do upon their Oath do say that they find the Issue for the Plaintiff and do assess his Damages by the Reason of the nonperformance thereof to Fifty one Dollars Ninety one Cents-
Therefore it is ordered by the Court that the Plaintiff Recover against the Defendants his Damages as assessed by the Jury in their Verdict & also his Costs about his suit in that behalf expended.

(p-70) STEPHEN STEWART)
              Vs)
        JAMES GRANT &) Covenant
        ISRAEL ROBINSON)

Joseph Woolfolk a witness for the Defendants was solemnly called out on his Subpoena & failed to appear, therefore the Court orders that he be fined agreeable to Acts of the General Assembly & that Sci fa Issue accordingly to next Term-
John Blair, Samuel Gattis & Thomas Smith.

WILLIAM MORRISON) Debt
     Vs)
ADAM HARMON, Senr.)
               Jury (Viz) No. 2

1 John Stewart   7 James Loggans
2 James Pierce   8 Thomas Bunch
3 James Trice   9 James Bray
4 Andrew Tribble   10 Absolam Legett
5 Thomas Whitledge   11 Barny Duff
6 Robert Temple   12 James Gillebo

Who being duly Elected tried & sworn the truth to speake upon the Issues Joined do upon their Oaths say that the Defendant hath paid part of the Debt in the Declaration mentioned But hath not paid the sum of Ninety five Dollars Thirty seven Cents & do assess the plaintiffs Damages to seven Dollars Fifty five & a half Cents by Reason of the Detention thereof. Therefore it is ordered by the Court that Plaintiff recover against the Defendant the Debt & Damages assessed by the Jury in their Verdict and also his Costs of suit in that behalf expended.

(p-71) John Blair, Samuel Gattis & Thomas Smith Esqrs.

JOSEPH ONEAL)
    Vs) Debt
JOHN HIGNIGHT)
            Jury No. 2

Who being duly elected tried & sworn the truth to speake upon the Issues Joined do upon their Oaths say that they find that the Defendant hath not paid the Debt in the Declaration mentioned & assess his Damages to Two Dollars & Sixty Cents. Therefore it is considered by the Court that the Plaintiff Recover his Debt & Damages as assessed by the Jury in their Verdict and also his Costs in that behalf expended-

        Same Justices on the Bench

JOHN BAXTOR)
    Vs) Case
JOHN WHITLEDGE)

James M. Reynold comes here into Court & enters himself the plantiffs' Security for the prosecution of the above suit in place of James Baxtor, who is by the Court Discharged from the same-

39

JOSIAH G. DUKE Administrators of RICHD. MYRICK DECD.
Vs
PHILLIP DUKE Adminis'r. & PATSEY DUKE Admx. of JOHN DUKE, DECD.

This suit Dismissed by Plaintiffs Attoy. Therefore it is considered by the Court that Defendants Recover their Costs in this behalf expended against the plantiff about their suit in this behalf expended.

(p-72) HUGH MCCLURE & JAMES ELDER)
Vs) Debt
JOHN WHITLEDGE)

Jury Viz No. 3

1 John Stewart   7 James Loggans
2 James Pearce   8 Thomas Bunch
3 James Trice   9 James Bray
4 Andrew Tribble   10 Absolam Legett
5 Zebedee Dennis   11 Barny Duff
6 Robert Temple   12 James Gillebe

Who being duly elected tried & sworn the truth to speak upon the Issue Joined do upon their Oaths say that they find that the Defendant hath not paid the debt in the Declaration mentioned & do assess their Damages to Seven Dollars & Twenty three Cents. Therefore it is considered by the Court that the Plaintiffs recover against the Defendant the Debt and Damages as assesses by the Jury in their Verdict aforesaid & also their Costs about their suit in this behalf expended & the Defendant in Mercy &

JAMES ADKINSON by his next friend)
GEORGE ROBERTS & HENRY MINOR)
Vs) Trespass Assee & Battery
JAMES WILLIAMS)

De Po Fa to Issue to Pltff to take the Depositions of Richard Atkinson & Jane Adkinson of Fayette County, State of Pensylvania, Thirty days notice to be given to the Defendant-

(p-73) Same Justices on the Bench, James Hambleton Esq. also -

JOHN BAXTOR)
Vs) Case
JOHN WHITLEDGE)

Jury No. 3

Who being duly Elected tried & sworn the truth to speak upon the Issue Joined do upon their Oaths say that they find that the Defendant did assume as the plaintiff in manner and form hath alledged & they do assess the plaintiffs Damages by Reason of the nonperformance of these assumptions to Forty Dollars. Therefore it is considered by the Court that the plaintiff Recover of the Defendant the Damages assessed by the Jury in their Verdict in manner & form aforesaid, and also his costs about his suit in this behalf expended-
Motion for new trial by Deft. Atty.
New trial granted.

Same Justices on Bench

FREDERICK STUMP)
Vs) Debt
DIXON LOGGANS)

Jury No. 3, only Stephen Cocke in place of J. P. Loggans. Duly Elected tried & sworn the truth to speak upon the Issues Joined, do upon their Oaths say that the Defendant hath not paid the debt in the Declaration mentioned & do assess the plaintiffs Damages by Reason of the Detention thereof to Three Dollars & Sixty four Cents. Therefore it is considered by the Court that the plaintiff Recover against the Defendant his Debt & Damages as assessed by the Jury in their Verdict in manner & form and also his Costs about his suit in that behalf expended.

(p-74) Same Justices on the bench.

REUBEN LOGGANS)
Vs)
PHILLIP DUKE Executor) Debt
& Patsy Duke Executrix)
of JOHN DUKE Decd.)

Jury No. 3, only Stephen Cocke in place of J. P. Loggans- Who being duly Elected tried & sworn the truth to speake upon the Issues Joined do upon their Oaths say that they find the Issues for the Plaintiff & that the Defendants hath not paid the Debt in the declaration mentioned and do by reason of the Detention thereof assess his the Plaintiffs Damages to Twenty Eight Dollars & Seventy five Cents, Therefore it is consideration by the Court that the Plaintiff Recover of the Defendants Phillip Duke & Patsy Duke Executors of John Duke decd. the sum of two hundred & thirty three dollars & seventy five cents the Debt & Damages so assessed by the Jury in manner & form as aforesaid and also his costs by him about his suit in this behalf expended-

JOHN DEN leassee of)
ROBERT WELLS)
Vs) Ejectment
RICD. FENN &)
SPILSBY TREBBLE &)
ANDREW TREBBLE)

Andrew Tribble & Absolam Tribble came here into Court & acknowledged themselves to be indebted to the plaintiff in the sum of five hundred Dollars to be void on Condition that the said Andrew Tribble who is here admitted CoDefendant shall perform the Judgement of the Court or surrender his body in execution-

Andrew Tribble (Seal

Absalom Tribble (Seal)

Done in Open Court
A. E. Crutcher

(p-75) Same Justices on the Bench

JOSHUA WEAKLEY)
    Vs   ) Covenant
ISAAC MARTIN   )
                  Jury Viz

1 William Stroud   7 David Outlaw
2 Henry Funk   8 Moses Parker
3 Stephen Cooke   9 Robert Tagert
4 Malachia Lagrand   10 James Williams
5 Stephen O'Gwin   11 Absolam Tribble
6 Isam Mathews   12 Moses Oldham, Senr.

Who being duly Elected tried & sworn the truth to speak upon the Issue Joined do upon their Oaths say that the plaintiff hath sustained Damages by Reason of the Defendants nonperformance of the Covenant in the Declaration mentioned to one hundred & Thirteen Dollars & Thirty Cents, Therefore it is considered by the Court that the plaintiff Recover against the sd. Defendant the said Damages as assessed by the Jury by their Verdict aforesaid, and also his costs about his suit in this behalf expended & the Defendant in Mercy &

HUGH MCCLURE Esquire returns a list of Taxable property for Captain Drake's Company for the present year-

(p-76) The Court adjourns untill tomorrow 9 O'clock.

The Worshipful Court of Montgomery County have met According to adjournment Tuesday June 28th 1808
            Present

            James Hambleton)
            Hugh McClure   ) Esquires
            John Blair   ) Justices
            James Baxter   )

22 Deed of Conveyance John Cocke, Sheriff of Montgomery County to George W. L. Marr & James Baxter for one Lott in Clarksville No. 18. Acknowledged in Court & ordered to be Registered-

            Same Justices on the Bench.

WILLIAM NEWELL Assee ROBERT NELSON)
        Vs   )
        PAYTON SIMS   ) Debt

        The Defendant being solemnly called to come & defend his suit failed, Therefore it is considered by the Court a Judgment final according to Specialty be entered up against him with Interest thereon. Therefore it is considered by the Court that the Plaintiff Recover against the Defendant the sum of one hundred Dollars the debt in the Declaration mentioned as also the sum of Seven Dollars & fifty cents for his Damages by Reason of the Detention thereof, together with his Costs about his suit in this behalf expended-

(p-77) Same Justices on the Bench.

ADAM HARMON Junr)
Vs)
JAMES HUGHES &) O. Attach't.
CHARLES HENSLEY

The Defendants were solemnly called & failed to come, therefore Judgment by Default & Writ of engry. Awarded to next term-

Same Justices on the Bench-

AARON FLETCHER Assee
Vs
STERLING INGRAM

This day came the parties by their Attorneys & the matters of Law arising on the plaintiffs Demurrers to the Defendants Third & forth pleas being argued & considered by the Court it is the oppinion of the Court that the said pleas& the matters therein contained are not sufficient in law to barr & preclude the plaintiff from having his Action aforesaid against the said Defendant, Therefore it is considered by the Court that the Demurrers be sustained & the plaintiff Recover the Debt in the Declaration mentioned & the Damages by the Jury heretefore assessed - together with his Costs about his suit in this behalf expended-

James Stewart Esquire gives in his resignation as a Justice of the peace for Montgomery County which was received by the Court.

(p-78) CHARLES ANDERSON) Case
        Vs   ) Reasons in Arrest of
        ISAAC MORGAN   ) Judgem't.

At this day came the parties by their Attorneys & on Solemn Argument it is considered by the Court that the motion for arrest of Judgement be overruled and the Said Plaintiff recover & have Execution against said Defendant for ten Dollars Damages, Therefore it is considered by the Court that the Plaintiff recover against the Defendant the said sum of Ten Dollars Damages & also his Costs about his suit in this behalf Expended-

John Blair, James Hambleton & James Baxter Esquires on the Bench-

ROBERT DRAKE)
Vs   ) Case Motion to amend the Declaration.
MARTIN GOSS)

This day came the parties by their Attornies and the matter being solemnly argued, It is the oppinion of the Court that the Declaration shall not be amended-

(p-79) STATE
        Vs
        DELIRQUENT JURORS

Benjamin Cowen, Benjamin Whitehead, Nelson McDowel, William Ryburn, Senr. & Elisha Willis being legally summoned to attend at this term as Jurors was solemnly called & came not & therefore made Default. Ordered by the Court that they be fined agreeably to Acts of the Assembly.

23 Deed of Conveyance Henry Small Atty. in fact for Amos Bird To P. W. Humphries was proven in Open Court by the Oath of Duncan Stewart & James Elder subscribing witnesses thereto & ordered to Registration for 1½ Acres of land-

REYNOLDS & MCFARLAND)
        Vs   ) Case
ISRAEL ROBINSON   )

On motion ordered that the Plaintiffs have leave to alter their Declaration & make it conformable to the writ-

REYNOLDS MCFARLAND)
        Vs   ) Debt.
WILLIAM R. BELL   )

On motion ordered that the Plaintiffs have leave to alter their Declaration to make it conformable to the writ-

(p-80)   NATHANIAL A. MCNEIRY)
                Vs   )
         SPILSEY TRIBBLE &   )
         ANDREW TRIBBLE   )

On motion of the Plaintiff by his Attorney and it appearing from the return of the Sheriff that a Fire facias Issued by Henry Small Esq. Justice of the Peace in the County in favour of said Plaintiff against Said Defendant for the sum of Five Dollars Forty Cents & Costs of suit has been levied by said John Cocke Sheriff on One hundred & twenty Acres of Land the property of Andrew Tribble on the Twenty Seventh of April 1808, in this County it is ordered & considered by the Court that a writ of Vendictoni Exponas Issue to expose said tract of Land to sale to satisfy said Judgment & Costs in that behalf expended-

Deed of Conveyance Hugh McClure & James Elder to Henry Small was acknowledged in Open Court & ordered to registration for 607 Acres Land.

Deed of Conveyance Hugh McClure & James Elder to John Cocke was acknowledged in Open Court & ordered to registration for 607 Acres of Land.

(p-81)   JOHN STEELE & SAMUEL PETERS
                Vs
         BENJAMIN WEAKLY

On motion and it appearing to the satisfaction of the Court that the said John Steele & Samuel Peters were bound to Green Hill as the Securities of the said Benjamin Weakley in a Bond conditioned for said Weakley keeping the prison bound for Montgomery County to which he was committed on a Casa at the suit of said Green Hill and that Judgment has been entered up in this Court against the said John Steele & Samuel Peters on motion of the said Green Hill for the sum of Three hundred & Sixty Eight Dollars Eighty Eight & a half Cents said judgment founded on a Breech of said prison bounds by said Weakley it also appearing to the satisfaction of the Court that the said John Steele & Samuel Peters has has paid to the Sheriff of Montgomery County the full amount of the aforesaid Judgment. Therefore it is considered by the Court that the said John Steele & Samuel Peters recover against the said Benjamin Weakley the aforesaid sum of Three hundred and Sixty Eight Dollars Eighty Eight & a half Cents together with their costs with the aforesaid Judgment & their costs in this behalf expended-

(p-82) JAMES MOORE
Vs
ANDREW TRIBBLE

On motion of the Plaintiff James Moore by his Attorney & it appearing from the return of John Cocke Shrff, that a Writ of Fiere Facias Issued by Morgan Brown Esquire Justice of the peace of this County in favour of said Plaintiff Vs said Defendant for the sum of thirteen Dollars Seventy two & three fourths Cents & Costs of Suit has been Levied by said Sheriff on hundred & twenty five acres of land in this County the property of said Defendants, It is ordered & considered by the Court that a Writ Vendetioni Exponas Issue to expose said tract of land to sale to satisfy said Judgment & costs of suit in this behalf Expended-

Court adjourned untill tomorrow at 8 O'clock-

Court met according to adjournment.
Present

Hugh McClure)
John H. Poston)
James Baxter) Esquires
James Hambleton) Justices

Court adjourned untill Court in Course.

Hugh McClure J.P.
John H. Poston
James Hambleton

(p-83) The Worshipful Court of Montgomery County have met according to Adjournment Monday the 19th of September 1808.
Present

Sterling Niblett)
James Hambleton) Esquires
Joseph Woolfolk) Justices
James Moore

Grand Jury (Viz)

1 Britain Bayless, Foreman
2 Robert Biggars
3 Blodget Bird
4 Ralph Williams
5 William Williams
6 Thomas Dodd
7 John Teasley
8 David McFadden
9 Peter Oneal
10 Glidwell Killebrew
11 William McGowen
12 John Harris
13 Andrew Irwin
14 Joseph French
15 David Dupree

Who being duly Elected & sworn & C four days & was Dismissed.

John Lowther was sworn as Constable to attend the Grand Jury this Term four days.

Jacob Leech & Burwell M. Williamson Exonerated is Exonerated from serving as Jurors this term-

Joseph Price is Exonerated from serving this term as a Juror.

(p-84) Deed of Conveyance William McCroy to Charles Stewart for 200 Acres of land proven by the Oaths of Hugh McCollom a witness thereto & ordered to be Registered.

Deed of Conveyance Mathew Sellers to Charles Stewart for 500 Acres of Land proven by the Oaths of James Stewart & John Stewart witnesses thereto & ordered to be Registered-

Deed of Conveyance Thomas Tennen to Charles Stewart for 100 Acres of Land acknowledged in Court and is Ordered to Registeration.

Bill of Sale Joel R. Oldham to Connaway Oldham for four negroes proven by the Oaths of James Brantley & Marmaduke Oneal witnesses thereto & ordered to be registered.

Deed of Conveyance Robert Nelson to Charles Stewart for 129 Acres of Land acknowledged in Court & ordered to be Registered.

On petition of William Stewart White it is Ordered that the said Petitioner have leave to build a Mill on Spring Creek in Montgomery County where William Dickins formerly had a Mill on said White's land-

Deed of Conveyance for 320 Acres of Land Mathew Gilmore to Robert Peasley proven by the Oaths of William McGowen & Lewis Malone & ordered to be Registered-

(p-85) Bill of Sale Michael McNatt to James Jeffris for a Negroe boy acknowledged in Court and ordered to be Registered.

On motion of Samuel Thornton it is ordered that a Writ of Certiorari & Super Sedeas Issue Commanding James Moore Esquire to have before the Justices of the Court of pleas & Quarter Sessions on the Third Monday in December next at the Court House in Clarksville all the papers relative to an Original Attachment Obtained by Morgan Brown against the Estate of the said Samuel Thornton in order that further proceeding may then be had thereon & that all further proceeding be stayed untill then-

James Moore, Samuel Vance, Joseph Woolfolk Esquires.

JOHN STEEL & SAMUEL PETERS)
        Vs   )
BENJAMIN WEAKLEY   )

Isaac Weakley being summoned as Garnisha to declare what he ows to Benjamin Weakley being duly sworn sayeth that he owes to Benjamin Weakley Twenty one

Dollars to be paid in Good Merchantable produce at the Nashville Market price when he the said Isaac Weakley takes in his Crop.
Therefore it is considered by the Court that the said Isaac Weakley deliver unto the Sheriff of Montgomery County the Articles or trade as aforesaid to the amount of twenty one Dollars when they become due.

(p-86) Deed William Farrier to Charles Stewart for 100 acres of Land acknowledged in Court and ordered to Registeration-
Power of Attorney from Samuel Woods to John Stewart proven by the Oath of Isaac Weakley a witness thereto & ordered to Registeration.

Guthridge Lyons Exonerated from serving as a Juror this Term-

Benjamin Cowen who failed to appear as a Juror last Term came here this term & made his excuse which the Court Deemed sufficient

The Court Adjourns untill tomorrow Nine O'clock

Tuesday 20th the Court met according to Adjournment-
    Present

        Sterling Niblett)
        Joseph Woolfolk)
        Robert Prim   ) Esquires
        Thomas Smith) Justices
        James Hambleton)

SAMUEL WOOLDRIDGE)
   Vs   ) Debt
STEPHEN O'GWIN   )

   This suit is Dismissed at the plaintiffs Order & the Defendant came here into Court in proper person & Assumes all Costs-

   James H. Russell Esq. produced a License as an Attorney at Law from under the hands of John Overton & S. Powel Judges of the Superior Courts of Law who is admitted by this Court & qualified accordingly-

(p-87) Robert Whitledge, Alexander Faith, Joseph Price, Benjamin Organ, William Corbin, David Burney, Samuel Roberts, who was appointed at June term last to lay of and view a Road leading from Clarksville to Thomas Smith's Ferry as agent for Hardy Murfree and from thence to intersect Humphries Road the nearest & best way & C. have Reported that they have viewed & layed of the same agreeable to the Order-

REYNOLDS & MCFARLAND)
   Vs   ) Motion
JOHN COOPER & EDWARD LEECH)

   On motion of the plaintiffs Attorney and it appearing to the satisfaction of the Court here from the Return of Daniel Anderson Constable that a Writ of Feiri Facias Issued by James Baxter Eqqr. Justice of the peace for County in favour of said Plaintiffs Vs said Defendants for the sum of Thirty seven Dollars Thirty seven & a half Cents with lawful interest & Costs of suit has been levied by said Constable on one Hundred & Sixty four or five

Acres of Land more or less Joining Edward Leech, East boundary in this County the property of the said Defendants. It is ordered & considered by the Court that a Writ of Venditoni Exponas Issue to Expose the said tract of Land to sale to satisfy the said Judgement & Costs aforesaid & in this behalf expended & that the Defendant be in Mercy & C.

EDWARD LEACH)
  Vs) Fi fa Motion
JOHN COOPER)

On motion of the plaintiff by his Attorney and it appearing to the satisfaction of the Court here from the Return of Edward Niblett Deputy Sheriff that a Writ of Fieri Facias Issued by Thomas Smith Esqr. Justice of the peace for Montgomery County against said Defendant in favour of said plaintiff (p-88) for the sum of Thirteen Dollars Six Cents & three fourths Cents and Costs of suit in this behalf expended has been levied by said Deputy Sheriff on one hundred & fifty one acres of Land the property of the said Defendant. It is considered and Ordered by the Court that a Writ of Venditoni Exponas Issue to Expose the said tract of Land to sale to satisfy the said Judgment & costs as aforesaid & that the Defendants be in Mercy &

EDWARD LEACH)
  Vs) Fifa Motion
JOHN COOPER)

On motion of the plaintiff by his Atty. and it appearing to the satisfaction of the Court from the Return made by Edward Neblet Deputy Sheriff that a Writ of Fieri Facias Issued from Thomas Smith Esq. Justice of the peace for this County in favour of said Plaintiff Vs the said Defendant for the sum of Eight Dollars seven & one <u>forth</u> Cents and Costs of suit in this behalf expended has been levied on one <u>hundred</u> & fifty one Acres of Land on the South side of Cumberland River above the mouth of Hurrican Creek. It is Considered & Ordered by the Court that a Writ of Venditioni Exponas Issue to expose to Sale the said tract of Land to satisfy the said Judgment & Costs of suit in this behalf expended & that the Defendants be in Mercy & C.

MARTINS LOGGANS)
  Vs) Covenant
JOHN HUBBARD)

The Defendant in this Case comes here into Court and confessed Judgment for the sum of Seventy five Dollars with Interest from the 8th day Jany. 1806 untill paid. And the plaintiff by his Attorney Henry Minor stays Execution six months-

(p-89) Ordered that Charles Stewart, Senr. be appointed overseer of that part of the Road in place of Laurence Tennin from Hambleton's Ferry to Stewart's Mill.

On motion of James Fentress Esq. It is ordered that a Road be Viewed & laid out from Stewart County line leading by or near Captain West's up the Cave Spring House Bottom so as to Join or fall in with the Road to Nashville on the Ridge to the West of Benjamin Adams Plantation &

that James Fentress, William Clements, George West, Elijah Parker & Samuel McAelsyea be appointed to View the same & that James Fentress be appointed overseer thereof.

Deed of Conveyance James McCarrell to William Chisham was acknowledged in Open Court for 12 acres of land & ordered to Registeration

Joseph Bowers is appointed Constable for Montgomery County qualified accordingly gave bond & Security with James Bowers, Elisha Willis & Samuel Creswell bound as his securities-

Deed of Conveyance Hugh F. Bell to John Bird for 200 Acres of Land acknowledged in Open Court & Ordered to be registered-

Ordered that Ambrose Martin be appointed Overseer of the Road from Smith's Ferry to Humphrey's Road & that Thomas Smith Esqr. name the hands to work under him.

(p-90) Ordered that William Pennington, William D. Penny, Samuel Wilcox, Pray Whipple and William Cohoon be appointed a Jury of View on the Road from Robertson line where the Nashville Road to Port Royal intersects the same thence the nearest and best way by the Mouth of the Sulpher Fork to the Kentucky line at the 93 Miles Tree and where the Christian Road intersects this State and make Return accordingly to next Term-

Ordered that a Road be viewed and laid out from the Dickson County line below the leatherwood Fork of Yellow Creek to meet with and fall into the Road leading to Palmyra near Adam Harmon's on the East Fork and that Francis Tomkins, Adam Harmon, Benjamin Adams, James Fentress and William Clements be appointed to view and lay out said Road & that William Clements be appointed overseer thereof-

Henry Small Esquire gives into Court his Resignation as Ranger for Montgomery County-

Deed of Conveyance James Moore to James G. Whelan for one Lott in Palmyra No. 67. Acknowledged in Court and Ordered to be Registered-

Deed of Conveyance William Ross Senr. to Thomas Blackney for 13 acres of Land acknowledged in Court & Ordered to be Registered-

Deed of Conveyance William Ross Senr. to Thomas Blackney for 190 acres land acknowledged in Court & Ordered to Registeration-

(p-91) Jesse Sullivan is appointed Constable in Captain Porter's Company Gives Bond with Samuel Smith & William Porter his Securities & qualified accordingly-

Deed John Cocke Sheriff to John Blair for 1000 acres of land acknowledged in Open Court and ordered to Registeration-

Deed of Conveyance John Cocke Sheriff to Colmore Duvall & John R. McFarland for 386 acres of land acknowledged in Court and Ordered to Registeration.

Deed William Hust to Joseph Hust for 30 Acres of Land acknowledged in Court and Ordered to Registeration-

Deed of Conveyance Joseph Hust to Wm. Hust for 89 Acres of land acknowledged in Court & ordered to Registeration-

REYNOLDS & MCFARLAND)
      Vs   ) Debt
  DAVID RUDDER   )

     James Boyd comes into Court and assumes to pay unto the plaintiffs the Debt in the declaration mentioned and confesses Judgment for the same. Therefore it is considered by the Court that the plaintiffs recover of the said James Boyd the Debt in the Declaration mentioned with costs of suit & that David Rudder the Defendant be released from the payment of the same. The plaintiffs by their Attorney entered a Release in favour of the said David Reedder for the same- The plaintiffs by their Attorney stay Execution three months-

(p-92) Robert Prince, Samuel Vance, Thomas Smith, James Hambleton, Joseph Woolfolk, Samuel Smith, John Blair, Sterling Neblett, Joseph Robertson, Samuel Gattis, John Sterling-

     The Court proceeded to the Choice of a Ranger for the County of Montgomery. When James Bunting was Elected Ranger and gave Bond with Robert Wells & Samuel Creswell his securities bound in the sum of one thousand Dollars-

     Ordered that Benjamin Orgain be appointed Overseer from George Humphreys to David Pritchard's spring-

     David Pritchard is appointed Overseer from his spring to the Barron Fork of Barton's Creek and that Sterling Neblett Esq. appoint the hands that work under him-

     Ordered that Mathew Barnes be appointed Guardian to Martha Barnes & William Barnes he gives Bond with Abraham Whitehead & Britan Bayless his securities bound in the sum of fourteen Hundred Dollars for his faithfull Guardianship-

     Deed of Conveyance John Cocke Sheriff to Samuel Vance for 640 Acres of Land acknowledged in Open Court and ordered to Registeration-

     Deed of Conveyance John Cocke Sheriff to Samuel Vance for 38 acres acknowledged in Open Court & ordered to be Registered-

     Deed John Cocke Sheriff Samuel Vance for 136½ acres acknowledged in Court & Ordered to Registeration-

(p-93) Deed of Conveyance John Cocke Sheriff to Samuel Vance for 10 Acres acknowledged in Court & Ordered to Registeration-

     Deed John Cocke Sheriff to Samuel Vance for 206-1/8 Acres of Land Acknowledged in Court & Ordered to Registeration-

Deed of Conveyance John Cooke Sheriff to James C. Brown for 80 acres of Land acknowledged in Open Court and Ordered to Registeration.

Proxy William Mathews to Sterling Neblett Esqr. acknowledged in Open Court & Ordered to be Registered-

Ordered that John Nevill be appointed Overseer in the place of Benjamin Seats who has given in his resignation & was received by the Court-

Jurors to December Term 1808- Barney Duff, Thomas Whitledge, James Williams, Robertson, John Hillis, Daniel Collier, David Linch, William Allen, William Good Senr. Isaac Kittrill, James C. Brown, Peter Hubbard, Guthridge Lyons, John Smith, Elisha Willis, James Bowers, Alexander McCrabb, Henry H. Bryant, John Griffin, William Grayson, Wilson Gibson, John Shelby, John Hambleton, William Jones, James Holt, Samuel Thornton, James Trotter, William Mitchell, David Brigham, Thomas Brantley, David Rudder, Archillas Wells, Benjamin Wells, Francis Batie, John Settle, Isaac Peterson, George West (Wt. Fork) Edward Trice, Edwin Gibson.

(p-94) Ordered that the Court will take up the business of the County on Tuesday the second day of next term and the States business on the second Monday of next term and that the Clerk advertise the same at the Court House Door this term-

JAMES DIXON Senr.)
Vs) Debt
WILLIAM FARRIOR)

The Defendant in this case came into Court in proper person and confessed Judgment according to Specialty with Interest. Therefore it is adjudged by the Court that the Plaintiff recover of the Defendant his Debt in the Declaration mentioned with Interest & Costs of suit in that behalf expended- Execution stayed by the plaintiff three months. No stay to be given in this Judgment-

The Court Adjourns untill tomorrow 9 O'clock.

Wednesday 21st September 1808 the Court met according to Adjournment.
Present

James Moore) Esquires on
James Hambleton) the Bench
Samuel Vance)

Ordered by the Court that a Commission Issue to Willie Blount & Joseph Robinson Esqr. to take the privy Examination of (Mrs.) Harriet Funstall on a Deed of Conveyance from James Funstall and the said Harriet his wife to Henry H. Bryant for a tract of Land in (p-95) Martin County North Carolina-

Deed of Conveyance Minoah Taylor to Herring Taylor acknowledged in Open Court for 100 acres and ordered to be Registered-

James Hambleton, Thomas Smith, Samuel Vance, James Lockert & John Blair Esquires on the bench-

JOHN BELL)
Vs) Trespass
JAMES TRIBBLE &)
REUBEN GRAYSON)

  Continued by consent with leave to amend or add pleas & Order for taking Depositions extended-

MORGAN BROWN)
Vs) Case
THOMAS SIMMONS) Ordered for Arbitration extended & Cause continued.

JOHN DENN Lessee of NATHANIEL)
DICKINSON) Plaintiff
 Afainst) In Ejectment
JOSEPH PENRICE) Defendant

  On motion of the defendant by his attorney it is ordered that Duncan Stewart of this County do again go upon the lands in Controversy on the day of next if fair if not on the next fair day & survey & lay off the same as either party may direct having due regards to the interest of both parties & all deeds or other evidence by them or either of them produced that he report all matters of fact specially & return three fair platts & Certificates thereof to the next Court-

(p-96) WILLIAM LYTLE)
  Vs) Covent.
 SPILSBY TRIBBLE)

  The plaintiff by his attorney Dismisses his suit. Therefore it is considered by the Court that the Defendant Recover his Costs of suit as the plaintiff in this behalf expended-

JAMES W. COCKE)
 Vs) Debt
NATHANIEL SAUNDERSON Jr.)

  Dismissed by the plaintiff in proper Person & plaintiff pays one half the Costs & the Defendant assumes the other half.

THE STATE)
 Vs) Indictment
ADAM HARMAN)

  John W. Deen prosecutor to said Indictment comes here into Court and acknowledges himself bound in the sum of one Hundred & fifty Dollars to be levied off his Goods and Chattels Lands & Tenements but to be void on condition that the said John W. Deen make his personally appearance at our next Term on the Third Monday in December next then & there to give testimony in behalf of the State and not to depart the Court without leave-

Test   John W. Deen
A. E. Crutcher-

  Deed of Conveyance William R. Bell to James Hambleton Esq. for 170

Acres proven by the Oaths of Joel R. Oldham & James Brantly subscribing Witnesses thereto & ordered to Registeration-

Deed of Conveyance William R. Bell to James Hambleton Esqr. for 170 Acres proven by the Oaths of Joel R. Oldham & James Brantley subscribing Witnesses thereto & Ordered to Registeration-

Deed of Conveyance Manoah Taylor to Ralph Vicers for 245 acres of Land acknowledged in Open Court and Ordered to Registeration-

(p-97) JOSHUA HANDLEY)
            Vs   )
        SAMUEL LYONS &   )   Debt
        JOHN MINOTT   )

The Defendant Samuel Lyons & John Minott being solemnly called & failed to appear but made default, therefore it is Considered by the Court that the plaintiff recover of the Defendant agreeable to the Debt in the Declaration mentioned and Interest thereon, and also his Costs of suit in that behalf expended- Motion by Defendants attorney to set aside the Judgment by Default- Motion withdrawn-

Martin Goss to Frederick Goss Bill sale for Sundry property acknowledged in Open Court and Ordered to Registeration- Bill sale Joseph McCrabb to John Shelby was proven in Open Court by the Oath of James Lockart & Samuel Craft for three negroes & ordered to Registeration-

STEPHEN STEWART)
            Vs   )
JAMES GRANT &   )   Covenant
ISRAEL ROBINSON   )

Joseph Woolfolk who was subpoened in this case for the Defendant & failed at last term to appear & was called out upon his subpoena agreeable to Acts of assembly and sufficient reasons shewn to the Court this Term the Court set the forfiture aside by payment of Costs-

(p-98) JOHN KEATHLY   )
            Vs   )   Debt
        JAMES A. BUNTING)

John W. Lowther the security for the Defendant in this case brings into Court the Defendant & surrenders the body of said Defendant in Discharge of himself-

David Bunting comes here into Court and acknowledges himself bound as security for the said James Bunting in the place of John W. Lowther.

Test.   David Bunting (Seal)
A. E. Crutcher

Robert Prince, John Blair, James Lockart, Thomas Smith, Samuel Vanse Esquires on the Bench.

53

JOHN INSTONE)
Vs) Case
JOSIAH G. DUKE)

Jury No. 1 (Viz)

1 William Montgomery   7 Samuel Creswell
2 Benjamin Adams   8 James Trice
3 James McGowen   9 William Hightower
4 William Ross   10 Richard Whitehead
5 Reubin Bullard   11 William Whitehead
6 Alexander Carns   12 James C. Brown

Who being duly Elected tried & sworn the truth to speake upon the Issue Joined do upon their Oaths say that they find the Issues for the Defendant. Therefore it is considered by the Court that the Plaintiff take nothing by his bill but for his false Clamour be in Mercy & that the Defendant go without day & that he recover against the Plaintiff his Costs about his Defence in this behalf Expended- Motion for appeal by Plaintiffs Atty. / (p 99)

Court adjourned untill tomorrow at 9 O'clock-

The Worshipful Court of Montgomery County have met according to adjournment Thursday Sept. 22nd 1808.
    Present

            James Lockert   )
            John Blair   ) Esquires
            James Hambleton) Justices

MOSES STEELE)
Vs   ) Covenant & Juditial
GEORGE WILLIAMS) Attache. & Writ of enquiry

            Jury to wit.

1 Samuel Creswell   7 William Montgomery
2 Reuben Bullard   8 Richard Whitehead
3 Benjamin Adams   9 Alexander Carnes
4 William Ross, Senr. 10 Moses Oldham
5 William Whitehead   11 James Trice
6 Joseph Whitehead   12 James A. Bunting

Who being duly Elected tryed & Sworn the truth to speak & deligently to enquire of Damages on their Oaths do say that the Plaintiff hath sustained damages by the reason of the Defendants nonperformance of the Covenant in the Declaration mentioned to Ten Dollars besides his Costs, Therefore it is Considered by the Court that the plaintiff recover against the defendant the damages aforesaid by the Jurors in their Verdict aforesaid in form assessed and also his Costs by him about his suit in this behalf expended and the defendant in Mercy &

(P-100)   Present Robert Prince Gent.

JOHN BAXTER Plaintiff)
    AGAINST   ) In case
JOHN WHITLEDGE Defendant)

Barney Duff a witness summoned in behalf of the Plaintiff in this Cause, was solemnly called failed to appear & made default & ordered that a Scire Fasia issue against him accordingly returnable to next Court - And this day came the parties aforesaid by their Attornies and also a Jury to wit.

1	Samuel Criswell	7	William Montgomery
2	Reuben Bullard	8	Richard Whitehead
3	Benjamin Adams	9	Alexander Carnes
4	Ross Williams, Senr.	10	Oldham Moses, Senr.
5	Whitehead, William	11	Trice James
6	Whitehead, Joseph	12	Bunting James A.

Who being elected tried & sworn the truth to speak upon the issue joined upon their oath do say that the defendant did not assume upon himself in Manner and form as the plaintiff hath declared against him and as by pleading he hath alledged - And the Plaintiff by his Attorney moves the Court to set aside the Verdict & grant a new trial-

Being argued on both sides Ordered that a new trial be granted-

(p-101) Present- Robert Prince, James Lockert, John Blair, James Hambleton Esquires Justices-

SAMUEL VANCE)
WILLIAM KING &)
JOHN BRADLEY) Appeal
    Vs)
THOMAS CLINTON)
              Jury to wit

1	Samuel Creswell	7	William Montgomery
2	Reuben Bullard	8	Richard Whitehead
3	Benjamin Adams	9	Alexander Carnes
4	William Ross, Senr.	10	Moses Oldham, Senr
5	William Whitehead	11	John Trice
6	Joseph Whitehead	12	James A. Bunting

Who being duly elected tried & sworn the truth to speak upon the controversy between the parties do upon their oaths do say that they find for - On motion of the defendant and for reasons appearing to the Court. It is ordered that the Jurors aforesaid from rendering any verdict herein be discharged and that this Cause be dismissed- therefore it is considered by the Court that the Defendant recover against the Plaintiffs his costs about his suit in this behalf expended & the Plaintiffs in Mercy.

(p-102) Same Justices on the Bench, except James Lockert.

LEWIS PICKETT)
   Vs) Appeal
SEALAH PICKET, Admr.)
of CHARLES PICKETT DECD.)
              Jury to wit

1	Samuel Creswell	7	William Montgomery
2	Reuben Bullard	8	Richard Whitehead
3	Benjamin Adams	9	Alexander Carnes
4	William Ross, Senr.	10	Moses Oldham, Senr.

5 William Whitehead   11 James Trice
6 Joseph Whitehead   12 James A. Bunting

Who being duly Elected tried & sworn the truth to speak upon the Controversy between the parties upon their Oaths do say that they find for the Plaintiff & assess his damages to forty two Dollars & fifty Cents- Therefore it is considered by the Court that the Plaintiff recover against the Defendant his damages so assessed by the Jury in form aforesaid as also his costs about his suit in this behalf Expended & the Defendant in Mercy & C.

CHARLES ANDERSON)
       Vs   } Debt
JAMES A. BUNTING)

Moses Oldham, Senor, the Security for the Defendant in this Case brings into Court the Defendant & Surrenders the body of the said Defendant in discharge of himself-

Needham Whitfield comes here into Court & acknowledges himself bound as security for the said James A. Bunting in the place of Moses Outlaw.

                                                Wm. Whitfield (Seal)

(p-103) Robert Prince, James Lockert, & James Hambleton.

LOVICK VENTRESS Assee)
       Vs   } Debt
JOHN NEVILL   )

1 James McGowen   7   James Williams
2 Robert Temple   8   Lewis Pickett
3 William Hightower   9   Isam Trotter
4 Charles Murry   10 Stephen Cooke
5 Samuel Lynes   11 Andrew Tribble
6 William Ford   12 Andrew Brown

Who being Elected tried & sworn the truth to speak upon the Issue joined do upon their Oath do say that they find that the Defend. hath not paid the Debt in the Declaration mentioned but that the Defendant hath paid two hundred & Eighty Dollars & seventy two & one third cents part of the Debt in the Declaration mentioned & that there remains unpaid five hundred & twelve Dollars of said Debt & the Jury do assess the Plaintiffs Damages to Seventy nine dollars & forty-five cents by the reason of the Detention thereof-
Therefore it is considered by the Court that the Plaintiff recover against the Defendant the sum of five hundred & twelve Dollars also the damages so assessed by the Jury in form aforesaid as also his Costs about his suit in this behalf Expended & the Defendant in Mercy & C.

Motion for appeal by Defendant which was Granted and Bond Given with Joseph B. Nevill & John Edmonston Securities bound in the sum of ten Hundred & ninety one Dollars & forty five cents.

(p-104) Same Justices on the Bench.

LOVICK VENTRESS Assee)
    Vs) Debt
GEORGE NEVILL)

1 James McGowen
2 Robert Temple
3 William Hightower
4 Charles Murry
5 Samuel Lynes
6 William Ford
7 James Williams
8 Lewis Pickett
9 Isam Trotter
10 Stephen Cocks
11 Andrew Tribble
12 Adam Brown

Who being Elected tried & sworn the truth to speak upon the Issue joined do upon their Oath do say that they find that the Defendant hath not paid the Debt in the Declaration mentioned but that the Defendant hath paid two hundred & Eighty Dollars & seventy two & one third Cents part of the Debt in the Declaration mentioned & that their remains unpaid five hundred & twelve Dollars of said Debt & the Jury do assess the Plaintiff's Damages to Seventy nine Dollars & forty five Cents by the reason of the detention thereof— Therefore it is considered by the Court that the Plaintiff recover against the Defendant the sum of five hundred & twelve Dollars as also the Damages so assessed by the Jury in form aforesaid as also his costs about his suit this behalf Expended & the Defendant in Mercy & ?. Motion for appeal which was granted Bond & Security given with Joseph B. Nevill, John Edmonston & John Nevill bound in the sum of ten hundred & Nine one Dollars & forty five Cents.

(p-105)   James Lockert, Thomas Smith, Saml. Gattis

SAMUEL VANCE)
WILLIAM KING)
JOHN BRADLEY) Debt
    Vs)
ADAM HARMAN, Junr.)

Jury to wit

1 Samuel Creswell
2 Reuben Bullard
3 Benjamin Adams
4 William Ross, Senr.
5 William Whitehead
6 Joseph Whitehead
7 William Montgomery
8 Richard Whitehead
9 Alexander Carnes
10 Moses Oldham
11 James Trice
12 William Hightower

Who being elected tried & sworn the truth to speak upon the Issue joined upon their Oath do say that the Defendant has not paid the Debt in the Plaintiffs Declaration mentioned of sixty seven dollars & twenty seven cents & do assess the Plaintiffs Damages by the reason of the detention thereof to two dollars & ninety one Cents besides their costs— Therefore it is considered by the Court that the Plaintiffs recover against the Defendant the Debt in the Plaintiff's Declaration mentioned & the Damages so assessed by the Jury in form aforesaid as also their cost about their suit in this behalf Expended & the Defendant in Mercy & .

STEPHEN STEWART)
    Vs) Case
JOSEPH WIMBERLY)

Judgment by Default & a Writ of Enquirey to next Term.

(p-106) STATE)
         Vs   ) Indt.
       JAMES McFARLAND)

   John Ferguson a prosecutor in behalf of the State came into Court & acknowledged himself bound in the sum of one hundred Dollars to be levied off his goods & Chattles Lands and Tenements, But to be Void on Condition that he makes his personally appear at our next Court to be held for Montgomery County at the Court House in Clarksville on the fourth Monday in December next then & there to prosecute & give testimony in the Indictment the State Vs James McFarland & not to depart the Court without leave-

STATE)
  Vs   ) Indt.
MARVELL McFARLAND)

   John Ferguson a Prosecutor in behalf of the State came into Court & acknowledged himself bound in the sum of one hundred Dollars to be levied off his goods & Chattles Lands & Tenements to be void on condition that he makes his personal appearance at our next Court to be held for Montgomery County at the Court House in Clarksville on the fourth Monday in December next then & there to prosecute & give testimony in the Indictment the State Vs Marvell McFarland & not to depart the Court without leave-

STATE)
  Vs   ) Indt.
KELLIS McFARLAND)

   John Ferguson a Prosecutor in behalf of the State came into Court & acknowledged himself bound in the sum of one hundred Dollars to be levied off his Goods & Chattles Lands & Tenements but to be void on condition that he makes his personal appearance at our next Court to be held for Montgomery County at the Court House in Clarksville on the fourth Monday in December next then & there to prosecute & give Testimony in the Indictment the State Vs Kellis McFarland & not to Depart the Court without leave.

(p-107) Same Justices on the Bench.

STEPHEN STEWART)
       Vs   ) Case
JOSEPH WIMBERLY)

   This day came the parties by their attorneys & on motion of the Plaintiff by his attorney the defendants Plea in abatement is overruled by the Court as frivilous & it is ordered by the Court that the Defendant answer over again immediately whereupon the Defendant failed further to answer the Plaintiffs Declaration & being solemnly called came not therefore it is considered by the Court that the Plaintiff recover against the Defendant his damages sustained by the reason of the nonperformance of the assumption in the Declaration mentioned to be enquired of by a Jury at next Court-

WILLIAM LYONS)
    Vs   ) Debt
JAMES MOORE   )

The Defendant James Moore being solemnly called but came not but made Default which is final–
therefore it is considered by the Court that the Plaintiff recover against the Defendant the Debt in the Plaintiffs Declaration agreeable to the Specialty with Interest as also his Costs about his suit in this behalf Expended & the Defendant in Mercy & C–

Court adjourned untill tomorrow at 9 O'clock–

Court met according to Adjournment Friday September 23rd 1808–
    Present

                James Hambleton)
                Samuel Gattis   ) Esquires
                James Baxter   ) Justices
                John H. Poston   )

(p-108) THOMAS K. MCELRATH)
              Vs   ) Debt
          SAMUEL VANCE   )

                Jury to Wit

1 James Trice   7 William Whitehead
2 Joseph Whitehead   8 Alexander Carnes
3 Moses Oldham   9 Samuel Creswell
4 William Ross, Senr.   10 Reuben Bullard
5 Benjamin Adams   11 James McGowen
6 Isam Trotter   12 William Hightower

Who being elected tried & sworn the truth to speak upon the issues joined upon their oath do say that they find the several issues for the plaintiff and that the defendant doth owe the plaintiff the debt in the declaration mentioned and they do assess the plaintiffs damages by reason of the detention thereof to two Dollars & forty five cents besides his Costs–
Therefore it is considered by the Court that the plaintiff recover against the defendant Fifty five dollars & twenty five cents the Debt in the Declaration mentioned together with the damages aforesaid by the Jurors in their Verdict in form aforesaid assessed and also his costs by him about his suit in this behalf expended and the defendant in Mercy & C–

Ordered that William C. Jamison be allowed the sum of seven dollars for the present Minut Dockett & a book to enter the list of Taxable property in & that the County Trustee pay the same–

(p-109) JAMES ADKINSON)
          AGAINST   ) In A & B
         JAMES WILLIAMS)

Continued as on affidavit of plaintiff & the order of the last Court for taking Depositions extended untill the next term–

BURRELL BAILESS
Vs } Debt
JAMES BUNTING &
WILLIAM FARRIOR

Judgment confessed by the Defendants in person according to Specialty with Interest and Execution stayed three months-
Robert Prince, James Hambleton, James Baxter, Esquires on the bench-

Deed of Conveyance-
~~Ordered by the Court that James Baxter Esq. hold the duty Ex-~~
~~amination of Baxter Cooper as to his consent to the signing and executing-~~

(p-110) JAMES M. REYNOLDS &
JOHN R. MCFARLAND } Debt
Vs
JAMES LOGGANS

Jury No. 1

1 James Trice
2 Joseph Whitehead
3 Moses Oldham, Senr.
4 William Ross, Senr.
5 Benjamin Adams
6 Isam Trotter
7 William Whitehead
8 Alexander Carnes
9 Samuel Creswell
10 Reuben Bullard
11 James McGowen
12 William Hightower

Being duly Ellected tried & sworn the truth to speak upon the Issue Joined upon their Oaths do say that they find the Defendant has not paid the Debt in the plaintiffs declaration mentioned of Eighty seven Dollars & forty four Cents and do assess his damage by reason of the detention thereof to Two Dollars & Sixty two Cents-
Therefore it is considered by the Court that the plaintiffs recover against the Defendant the Debt declared by the plaintiffs and his Damages as assessed by the Jury in form aforesaid in Manner & form and also the Costs of suit in this behalf expended & the Defendant in Mercy & C.

Deed of Relinquishment George W. L. Marr & Bennet Searcy to each other for 250 Acres of Land proven by the Oaths of John H. Poston & William S. Bailey and ordered to Registration-

(p-111) REYNOLDS JAMES M. &
MCFARLAND, JOHN R. } Debt
Vs
JAMES BUNTING

Same Jury No. 1

Who being Elected tried & sworn the truth to speak upon the Issue Joined do upon their Oaths say they find that the Defendant has not paid the Debt in the plaintiffs Deslaration mentioned & do assess his Damage by reason of the Detention thereof to five Dollars, nineteen Cents-
Therefore it is considered by the Court that the plaintiffs recover against the Defendant the Debt declared by the plaintiffs & his damages as assessed by the Jury in Manner & form aforesaid as also his costs of suit

in this behalf expended-

REYNOLDS & MCFARLAND)
      Vs   ) Debt.
FRANCES HUBBARD   )
                  Same Jury No. 1

being elected tried & sworn the truth to speak upon the Issue Joined do upon their Oaths say that the Defendant hath not paid the Debt in the plaintiffs declaration declared and do assess his damages to two dollars sixty two cents-
Therefore it is considered by the Court that the Plaintiffs Recover against the Defendant his Debt in the Declaration and Damages as assessed by the Jury in manner aforesaid & costs of suit in that behalf expended and the Defendant in Mercy & C.

(p-112)   WILLIAM SULLIVANT Assee)
                   Vs   )
         REUBEN LOGGANS   ) Debt
         WILLIAM LOGGANS &   )
         WILLIAM MILAM   )

Same Jury No. 1 who being Elected & sworn the truth to speak upon the Issue Joined do upon their Oaths say that they find that the Defendant has not paid the debt in the plaintiff's declaration mentioned and do assess the plaintiff's damages by reason the detention thereof to two dollars and twenty five cents-
Therefore it is considered by the Court that the plaintiffs recover against the Defendants his Debt as declared by the plaintiff and their damages as assessed by the Jury & also his Costs of suit in this behalf expended & the defendants in Mercy & C.

SAME   )
VS   ) Debt
SAME   )

Same Jury No. 1 who being duly Elected tried & sworn the truth to speake upon the Issue Joined do upon their Oaths say that the Defendant has not paid the debt as the plaintiff has declared in their Declaration & do assess their damages by reason of the Detention thereof to six dollars & forty cents-
Therefore it is considered by the Court that the Plaintiff recover against the Defendant their Debt in the Declaration mentioned and the damages as assessed by the Jury as aforesaid and his costs of suit in that behalf expended & the defendt. in Mercy & C.

(p-113)   James Hambleton, Samuel Vance, John H. Poston & Samuel Gattis Esquires.

ROBERT WEAKLEY)
      Vs   ) Debt
JOHN BARTON &   )
WILLIAM BARTON   )

Same Jury No. 1 being elected & sworn the truth to speak upon the Issue

Joined do upon their Oaths say that they find that the Defendant has not paid the Debt in the Declaration mentioned by the plaintiff and do assess his damages by reason of the detention thereof to Twenty four Dollars, Therefore it is considered by the Court that the plaintiff recover against the Defendant the Debt as by the plaintiff declared with damages assessed by the Jury as aforesaid & his costs of suit in that behalf expended & the Defts. in Mercy & C.

JACOB GONTERMAIN)
    Vs   ) Debt
THOMAS GREEN)

Judgment by Default final, Therefore it is considered by the Court that the Plaintiff recover against the Defendant the Debt in the Declaration mentioned with Interest thereon according to the Specialty & his Costs of suit in that behalf expended & the Defendt. in Mercy & C.

(p-114)   Hugh McClure, Esq. Samuel Gattis & James Baxter Esquires on the bench.

SAMUEL VANCE, WILLIAM KING &)
JOHN BRADLEY   ) CASE
    Vs   )
ROBERT PRINCE)

Same Jury No. 1 being sworn & C the truth to speake upon the Issue Joined do upon their Oaths say that they find the Issues for the Defendant. Therefore it is considered by the Court that the plaintiffs take nothing by their bill but for their false Clamour & C & that the Defendant go hence without day and recover against the plaintiffs his Costs about his defence in this behalf expended at which Judgements the Plaintiffs not being contented prayed an Appeal to the Superior Court of Law for Robertson district gives Bond & C & files Reasons, To wit-

1st the Verdict & Judgement is unjust-
2nd The plaintiffs were compelled to go to trial when their material witnesses were absent or wait an unreasonable length of time for the satisfaction of their Just Claim & they prefer to seek for Justice by an appeal to an unreasonable delay which in my oppinion are sufficient reasons for the Court here to allow an Appeal to the Superior Court.

(p-115)   Same Justices only Samuel Vance Esq. on the bench.

LEWIS ELLIOTT)
    Vs   ) Debt
JAMES A. BUNTING)

Same Jury No. 1.

Who being duly Elected sworn & C the truth to speak upon their Issue Joined do upon their Oath say that they find for the plaintiff the Debt in the Declaration mentioned and do assess his Damages by Reason of the Detention thereof Two Dollars & Twenty four Cents- Therefore it is considered by the Court that the plaintiff recover against the Defendant the debt in the Declaration declared by the plaintiff and his Damages as assessed by the Jury in form aforesaid together with his Costs of suit in that behalf expended & the Defendant in Mercy & C.

Same Justices on the bench—

NICHOLAS CONRAD
    Vs   } Debt
WILLIAM MCDANIEL

    Same Jury No. 1, being Elected Sworn & the truth to speak upon the Issue Joined do say upon their Oaths that they find that the Defendant has not paid the Debt in the Declaration mentioned and do assess his Damages by Reason of the Detention to Eight Dollars & Eighty Cents, Therefore it is considered by the Court that the plaintiff recover against the Defendant the Debt in the Declaration mentioned with his Damages as assessed by the Jury as aforesaid together with (p-116) his costs as aforesaid in this behalf expended & the Defendant in Mercy & C—

Hugh McClure, James Baxter & Samuel Gattis Esquires on the Bench—

JAMES MOORE
    Vs   } Debt
GUTHRIDGE LYONS

    Same Jury No. 1.

Who being duly Elected tried & sworn the truth to speak upon the Issue Joined do upon their Oaths say that they find that the Defendant has not paid Two Hundred & three Dollars & 33 Cents of the debt in the Declaration mentioned and has paid the ballance of sd debt & do assess the damages by Reason of the Detention thereof to four Dollars Thirty nine Cents— Therefore it is considered by the Court that the plaintiff James Moore Recover against the Defendant the sum of Two Hundred and three Dollars & thirty three Cents as aforesaid by the Jury in their Verdict in form aforesaid & also his costs about his suit in this behalf expended—

LOVICK VENTRESS
    Vs   } Reasons for appeal
GEORGE NEVELL

    The Defendant files the following reasons for Appeal—

1st the Verdict was contrary to Justice.
2nd The Judgement is oppressive to the Defendant which in my oppinion are sufficient Reasons for the Court to allow an Appeal to the Superior Court—

                                            By Minor Atty. for Deft.

(p-117) BENJAMIN MASON
              Vs   } Certiorari
      JESSE WADKINS, Senr.

    The Defendant in this case comes into Court and in proper person & confesses Judgment for Eighteen Dollars & Eighty seven & a half cents, Therefore it is considered by the Court that the Plaintiff do recover against the Defendant the said sum of Eighteen Dollars as Confessed & his Costs of suit in that behalf expended & the Defendant in Mercy & C—

Court adjourned untill tomorrow @ 9 O'clock

Court met according to Adjournment 24th Sept. 1808
Present

       Robert Prince)
       Samuel Gattis)
       Samuel Vance) Esquires on the Bench
       John H. Poston)
       James Baxter)

LOVICK VENTRESS, Asses)
   Vs   ) Debt
JOHN NEVILL   )

  Reasons for an appeal to wit.

1st The Verdict was contrary to Justice-
2nd The Judgment is oppressive to the Defendant which in my opinion are sufficient reasons for the Court to allow an appeal to the Superior Court-

                 H. Minor, Atty. for Deft.

(p-118) JOHN STEWART)
     Vs   ) Appeal
   ALSIMUS KENDRICK)

     Jury(to wit) No. 2.

1 James Trice   7 Samuel Creswell
2 Joseph Whitehead   8 Reuben Bullard
3 Moses Oldham, Senr.   9 James McGowen
4 William Ross, Senr.   10 James Williams
5 Isam Trotter   11 Barnard Snelling
6 Alexander Carnes   12 James A. Bunting

Who being Elected tried & sworn the truth to Speake upon the Controversy between the parties do upon their Oaths say that they find for the plaintiff and assess his Damages to Thirty Two Dollars & forty Cents, Therefore it is adjudged by the Court that the plaintiff recover against the Defendant and his Security William Barton his Damages so assessed by the Jury in form aforesaid and also his Costs of suit in this behalf Expended-

Deed of Conveyance for one Hundred Acres of Land acknowledged in Open Court by John Cooper to John Hambleton and by the privy Examination of Easter Cooper his wife before James Baxter Esq. also acknowledged in Court & ordered to Registeration.
(State tax & Registers paid before)

(p-119) Present James Baxter, John H. Poston & Samuel Vance Esquires on the Bench & Samuel Gattis. John H. Poston withdrew from off the Bench & then returned again & Samuel Gattis withdrew.

THOMAS MARTIN & COMPY.)
          Vs   ) Appeal
JAMES McFARLAND   )

                    Jury (to wit)

1 James Trice   7 Samuel Creswell
2 Joseph Whitehead   8 Reuben Bullard
3 Moses Oldham   9 James McGowen
4 William Ross, Senr.   10 James Williams
5 Isam Trotter   11 Richard Whitehead
6 Alexander Carns   12 James A. Bunting

Who being Elected tried & sworn the truth to speake upon the controversy between the parties do upon their Oaths say that they find for the Defendant.
Therefore it is adjudged by the Court that the Defendant recover against the plaintiff his costs about this behalf expended-
Motion by Plaintiffs attorney for new trial & the cause was continued-

(p-120)   Same Justices on the bench

JAMES BUNTING   )
      Vs   ) Case
JOEL R. OLDHAM   )

         At Inst. of Plaintiff it is Ordered by the Court that De Po Fiftatum Debene Esse. Issue to take the Deposition of John R. McFarland to be Read in Evidence in sd. suit. Fifteen days notice to be given to the Defendant-

Deed of Conveyance Jonathan Stephenson to Anthony Foster was proven in Open Court by the Oath of James Williams & Jacob Prewett subscribing witnesses thereto for four half acre lots in Port Royal and ordered to registeration.

Deed of Conveyance Menoah Taylor to James Jackson was proven in Open Court by the Oath of Herring Taylor & Bright Herring subscribing witnesses thereto for one hundred acres-

Court adjourned untill Monday September 26th 1808 at 9 O'clock-

The Worshipful Court of Montgomery County have met according to adjournment Monday September 26th 1808-
Present-   James Hambleton
                  John Sterling   ) Esquires
                  John H. Poston) Justices

(p-121) Deed of Conveyance John Cocke Sheriff to Henry Minor for 447 Acres acknowledged in Open Court as also the assignment from George W. L. Marr for the same was acknowledged in Open Court & ordered to Registeration-

McCLURE & ELDER   )
      Vs   ) Debt
SIMON B. HERRING   )

The Defendant in this case was solemnly called out & failed to appear therefore Judgment by Default final was entered up according to Specialty. It is therefore considered by the Court that the Plaintiffs recover against the Defendant the Debt in the Declaration mentioned for the sum of four hundred Dollars with Interest with their Costs of suit in that behalf expended-

REYNOLDS & MCFARLAND)
         Vs   ) Debt
JAMES HAMBLETON)

The Defendant in this case was solemnly called and came not therefore Judgment by Default final for Three Hundred & fifty five Dollars Twenty seven & Three forths cents. Therefore it is considered by the Court that the Plaintiff recover against the Defendant the said sum above mentioned according to the Specialty & also his Costs of suit in this behalf expended-

(p-122) MOSELY & WATSON)
         Vs   ) O. Attachment
   JOHN WRIGHT)

The Defendant who being solemnly called and failed to appear & replevy the property so attached, therefore Judgment by Default and Writ of Enquiry was awarded to next term-

Deed of Conveyance Henry Small late Sheriff of Montgomery County to James Huling for fifty acres land proven in Open Court Samuel Peters & Drewry Pestato witnesses thereto and Ordered to Registeration-

Deed of Conveyance George W. L. Marr to William M. Marr for 106½ Acres of Land acknowledged in Open Court & ordered to Registeration-

JAMES BAXTER & CO.)
         Vs   ) Execution
JOHN COOPER)

On motion of plaintiffs attorney and it appearing to the satisfaction of the Court here from the Return of Daniel Anderson Constable-

That whereas a writ of Fieri Facias Issued from under the Hand of John H. Poston Esquire Justice of the peace for this County in favour of said Plaintiff Vs said Defendant for the sum of Eleven Dollars & Costs has been levied by said Constable on a tract of land containing One hundred & sixty acres more or less Edward Leeche's East Boundary in this County the property of the said Defendant. It is considered ordered by the Court that a Writ of Venditioni Exponas Issue to Expose said tract of Land to sale to satisfy said Judgment & Costs of suit in this behalf expended-

(p-123) James Moore, James Hambleton, John H. Poston Esqr.

Ordered by the Court that James Moore Esq. & Henry Small Esquire former Rangers for Montgomery County Deliver into the hands of James Bunting the present Ranger for said County all the Books and all other papers or Dockets thereto & his Receipt shall be good shall be good for the same-

REYNOLDS & MCFARLAND
Vs
THOMAS DUNBAR
} Debt Plea in Abatement

On motion it is considered by the Court that the plea in abatement be rejected as frivilous & the Defendant pleads payment & Issue-

Joseph B. Nevill to Robert Nelson for 640 Acres of Land proven by the Oath of John Thomas a witness thereto and ordered to Registeration.

ISAM MATHEWS
Vs
THOMAS WILLIAMS
} Covenant Demurrer

Demurrer overruled & writ of inqry. awarded to next term-

(p-124) JOSHUA HANDLEY
Vs
SAMUEL LYONS &
JOHN MINOTT
} Debt

The Defendant in this case prays a Writ of Error which was Granted & gave bond with Joel R. Oldham & Samuel Peters their Securities bound in the sum of Two Hundred & fifty Dollars-

REYNOLDS & MCFARLAND
Vs
JOSEPH ROBINSON
} LEASE Demurrer

Motion by Defendants Counsel to withdraw the Demurrer- Motion overruled-

On motion of the plaintiffs Counsel and the matters of Law arrising on the Defendants Demurrer to the Declaration being heard by the Court it is the oppinion of the Court that the said Declaration & the matters therein contained are sufficient in law for the Plaintiffs to have & maintain their action aforesaid against the Defendant- Therefore it is considered by the Court that the said Demurrer be overruled & that the plaintiff recover against the Defendants their Damages in the Declaration mentioned to be inquired off by a Jury at next term-

VANCE, KING & BRADLEY
Vs
BURRELL M. WILLIAMSON
} Debt

The Defendant being solomnly called came not therefore Judgment by Default final was entered up against the Defendant. It is therefore considered by the Court that the plaintiffs recover against the Defendant his debt in the Decleration mentioned according to specialty with Costs of suit in that behalf expended-

(p-125) REYNOLDS & MCFARLAND
Vs
WILLIAM R. BELL
} Debt

The Plaintiffs Attorney moved for leave to amend his Declaration which was granted and the Defendant has time to plead untill next term-

JOSEPH WASHINGTON)
    Vs   ) Debt
NELSON MCDOWELL)

The Defendant being solemnly called came not therefore Judgment by Default final was entered up & it considered by the Court that the Plaintiff recover his Debt in his Declaration mentioned according to Specialty with his Costs of suit in this behalf expended-

JOHN MCFARLAND)
    Vs   ) Debt
PETER LYTAKER)

The Defendant being called came not therefore Judgement by Default final was entered up therefore the Court considers that the plaintiff recover his Debt according to Specialty & his Costs of suit in this behalf expended-

The present Sheriff John Cooke enters a protest against the Goal as in insufficent-

(p-126) The Court adjourned untill Court in Course.

                                          Moore
                                          Thos. Smith
                                          James Hambleton

STATE TENNESSEE
MONTGOMERY COUNTY

The Worshipful Court of Montgomery County have met according to adjournment Monday Dec. 19th 1808-
    Present

                Hugh McClure   )
                Thomas Smith   ) Esquires
                James Baxter   ) Justices
                John Sterling   )

                    Panal for Grand Jury

1 John Shelty
2 William Good, Senr.
3 David Brigham
4 Daniel Colyer
5 Isaac Peterson
6 William Mitchell
7 John Hillis
8 Alexander McCrabb

9 David Rudder
10 James Bowers
11 Edward Trice
12 Archellis Wells
13 Barny Duff
14 James Williams
15 George West (West Fork)

Being duly Elected, sworn, charged & C. retired to inquire for the Body of the people-

Daniel Anderson sworn Constable to attend the Grand Jury proved three days attendance & is allowed agreeable to Law-

The Grand Jury served three days & was discharged-

(p-127) The Court adjourned to the House of James Carreway in the Town of Clarksville-

The Court met at the House of James Carreway agreeable to adjournment-

    Present - John Sterling, John H. Poston, James Hambleton & James Baxter Esqrs.

1. Deed of Conveyance from George Gordon to Isaac Weakley for 640 acres Land proven by the Oaths of John Stuart & Henry J. Williams & order to Registration-

Bill Sale from Allen Hunter to Isaac Weakley for one negro woman proven by John Stewart & Thos. Williams witnesses thereto & ordered to Registration.

For reason shown to the Court Francis Batie who was summoned as a Juror to this Term is Exonerated-

William Jones who was summoned to attend this term as a Juror is Exonerated on Reasons shown to the Court on affidavit-

2. Deed of Conveyance for 100 acres of Land from Robert Moore to Edwin Clifton proven in Court by the Oaths of David Cashon & Martin Cashon witnesses thereto & ordered to Registration-

(p-128)

| WILLIAM CLEMENTS SAMUEL THORNTON & HOWEL TATUM Vs ROBERT NOWLAND | } Case |

The Defendant in this case being solemnly called came not therefore made Default- Therefore it is considered by the Court that the Plaintiffs recover against the Defendant the Debt in the Declaration mentioned agreeable to Specialty with Ints. and his Costs about their suit in this behalf expended-

Court adjourned untill tomorrow 9 O'clock-

Court met according to adjournment-
    Present

	Hugh McClure	}	
	John H. Poston	}	Esquires
	Sterling Niblett	}	Justices

3. Deed of Conveyance John Cocke Sheriff Montgomery County for 272 acres to Jacob Rudolph acknowledged in Open Court & ordered to Registration.

VANCE, KING & BRADLEY)
      Vs   ) Case
ADAM HARMON   )

    The Death of William King one of the plaintiffs in this case is here sugested to the Court by plaintiffs attorney-

(p-129) KING & POSTON)
                Vs   ) Case
         ROBERT PRINCE)

    The Death of William King one of the partners is sugested to the Court by the plaintiffs Attorney-

VANCE, KING & BRADLEY)
      Vs   ) Debt
JAMES EDWARDS   )

    The Death of William King one of the partners in this case is sugested to the Court by the plaintiffs attorney-

VANCE, KING & BRADLEY)
      Vs   ) Debt
LEWIS THOMPSON   )

    The Death of William King one of the partners in this case is sugested to the Court by the plaintiffs attorney-

VANCE, KING & BRADLEY)
      Vs   ) Sifa
GEORGE HUMPHREYS)

    The Death of William King one of the partners in this case being sugested by the plaintiffs attorney-

(p-130) Obligation from Robert Nelson to Moses Steel for the Conveyance of One third part of the Southern Lott which adjoins the Public Square in Clarksville to the South West was proven in Open Court by the Oaths of John H. Poston a subscribing witness thereto and the handwriting of Robert Nelson as signed to said Obligation was proven in Open Court by John Cocke who was duly sworn & said Obligation was ordered to Rigisteration.

Robert Prince Esq. on the bench & John H. Poston & James Baxter Esq. on the bench.

KING & POSTON)
      Vs   ) Case
ROBERT PRINCE)

    Judgment confessed by the Defendant for one hundred and Ninety Dollars Sixty one & a half cents with interest from the first day of January 1808, Therefore it is considered by the Court that the plaintiffs recover against the Defendant the said sum as confessed & also their Costs about their suit in this behalf expended- Execution stay by the plaintiff untill next term-

Robert Prince, Hugh McClure, James Baxter, Sterling Neblet Esquires on the bench-

Ordered by the Court that George W. L. Marr be allowed and paid by the County Treasurer the sum of Fifty Dollars for Exoficio services as States Solicitor for this County for the last year up to this term-

5   Deed of Conveyance for Lott No. 64 to James Baxter & Company from Bennett Searcy proven by the Oaths of James Carreway and J. B. Reynolds subscribing witnesses thereto & ordered to Registeration.

(p-151)   John Sterling Esqr. on the bench.

Bill of Sale George Humphreys to Gulley Moore for a negro boy proven by the Oath of James C. Brown a subscribing witness thereto & ordered to be Registered-

Bill of Sale John Cocke Sheriff to Gulley Moore for one negro acknowledged in Open Court and ordered to be Registered-

LUNSFORD PITTS)
        Vs   ) Debt
ROBERT BIGGERS)

The Defendant in this case in proper person confessed Judgment according to Specialty with Interest. Therefore it is considered by the Court that the plaintiff recover against the Defendant his Debt as confessed with Interest and also his Costs about his suit in this behalf expended-
    Execution stayed Three months-

REYNOLDS & MCFARLAND)
        Vs   ) Debt
ALLEN ANDERSON   )

This day came the parties into Court & the Defendant in proper person confessed Judgment for Twenty six Dollars Eighty Eight & a half Cents-
    Therefore it is considered by the Court that the Plaintiff recover against the Defendant their debt so confessed as aforesaid as also their costs about about their suit in this behalf expended-
Execution stayed three months.

(p-152) Thomas Izzle an Orphan boy is bound by the Chairman of the Court to Bradshaw & Wilson Hatters in Clarksville for the Term of Three years to live in the Manner of an apprentice to the Hatters trade.

Ordered by the Court that Hugh F. Bell be allowed Letters of administration on the Estate of Robert Nelson Deceased & he entered into bond with James Huling, William R. Bell, Elisha Willis, James Hambleton his Securities bound in the sum of Twenty Thousand Dollars & he qualified accordingly.

Ordered that the Venire to June Superior Term for the District of Robertson be the following persons (to wit)

Sterling Neblett, Hugh McClure, Charles Stewart, John Blair, John McCauley, Duncan Stewart, John Smith, George West, Yellow Creek, John Sterling, Edwin Gibson, James Jeffers, Wilson Gibson- Vernire to County Court March term 1809-

John Griffin, David McFadden, John Keathly, James Williams, Thomas Travis, Senr, Zebedee Dennis, Samuel Peters, John Marshall, Peter Holt, David Burney, Jacob Leech, John Coffee, James Pearce, William Weaks, Samuel Mitchell, Robert Nowlen, Samuel Woldridge, Lewis Thompson, John Little, David Davis, Buds Creek, Henry H. Brian, John Edmonson, William R. Gibson, Robert McLaughlin, Samuel Allen, Needham Whitfield, Thomas Hunter, John Teasly, Henry J. Williams, Robert Baggers, Robert Moore, Stephen O'Gwin, Adam Harman, Senr., John King, (p-153) James Adams, Jacob Boatwright, Edmond Suter, James Gray, Reuben Pollard.

6 Deed of Conveyance, John Blair to Nathan Morris & James Yarborough for 474 Acres of Land, acknowledged in Open Court and Ordered to Registeration.

7 Deed of Conveyance Jonathan Berry to Bryan Whitfield acknowledged in Open Court for Two Acres of Land and Ordered to Registeration.

8 Power of Attorney James Maxwell, Grezy Maxwell, Leonard Hutton, Mary Hutton, William Steel, Prudence Steele, By virtue of a a probit from John Campbell Clerk of Washington County State of Virginia under hand & Seal of the said County the above Power of Attorney is admitted to Record & ordered to Registeration-

9 Power of Attorney William Berry to Samuel Berry is admitted to Record by Virtue of the Clerk's hand & Seal of Knox County in Indians Territory & ordered to be Registered-

10 Deed of Conveyance Robert Nelson to Joshua P. Vaughn for 75 Acres of Land proven by the Oaths of John Minott & Moses Parker subscribing witnesses thereto and Ordered to Registeration-

(p-154) Deed of Conveyance Joshua P. Vaughn to Barney Duff for 156 Acres of Land acknowledged in Open Court and ordered to Registeration-

Ordered that Vincent Cooper be appointed Overseer of the Road leading from John Blairs Ferry at the mouth of Yellow Creek and said Cooper shall work from blooming Grove Creek to the State line, and all the hands on the North side blooming Grove, not appointed on any other Road work under said Cooper-

Order that Samuel Craft be appointed overseer of the Road from the Furnace on Yellow Creek to John Blair's Ferry on Cumberland River at the mouth of Yellow Creek and the hands within two miles of said Road not appointed to work on any other Road to work under said Craft-

Elisha Willis is appointed Constable, he qualified & Gave Bond with

James Edwards & John Smith his Securities agreeable to Acts of the Assembly-

12 Deed of Conveyance Guthridge Lyons to Joseph Lyons for 600 Acres of Land proven by James C. Brown & Burrell M. Williamson witnesses thereto & ordered to Registration-

13 Burrell M. Williamson to Guthridge Lyons Mortguage on One Town Lott in Palmyra acknowledged in Open Court & ordered to be Registered.

(p-135) Bill of Sale Elisha James to John Brigham for a negro girl proven by the Oath of James Brigham a subscribing witness thereto & ordered to Registeration.

Ordered that David Brigham be appointed overseer of the Great Road from Palmyra Road to Shelby's Mill. And that Robert Smith be appointed from said Mill to Stewart County line and that John Blair Esq. give a list of Tithables-

WILLIAM SMITH)
  Vs   ) Tresspass
ISRAEL ROBERTSON)

This day came the parties & the plaintiff in proper person Dismissed his suit and assumed to pay his own Attorney & the Costs of the Continuance at this Term and the Defendant in proper person assumed all other Costs in this suit-

14 Deed of Conveyance William E. Williams to John Shelby for 163 Acres of Land acknowledged in Court and Ordered to Registration.

15 Burrell Bailess to William E. Williams for 200 Acres of Land acknowledged in Open Court & ordered to Registration-

STATE   )
  Vs   ) Indt.
ADAM HARMAN, Junr.)

The Defendant submits & the the Court fined the Defendant one Cent- Therefore it is considered by the Court that the Plaintiff recover against the Defendant her Costs about her suit in this behalf Expended-

(p-136) CHARLES ANDERSON)
           Vs   ) Debt
         JAMES BUNTING   )

Needham Whitfield one of the securities for the Defendants appearance came into Court and rendered the body of the Defendant in discharge of himself as security which the Court agreed to-

William R. Bell came and entered himself security for James A. Bunting in place of Needham Whitfield in the above suit which the Court accepted.

16 Covenant Bond Robert Nelson to Bryant Whitfield proven in Open Court by the Oaths of John Kethley & Needham Whitfield subscribing witnesses

thereto and Ordered to Registeration.

Francis Penrice is appointed Constable for Montgomery County and qualified accordingly gave bond with John Smith, Joseph Penrice & William Allen his securities.

Bill Sale Lewis Pickett to John Cocke for six negroes proven by the Oaths of Daniel Anderson & George Gibson witnesses thereto & ordered to Registeration.

Ordered by the Court that on the first Thursday of the March term 1809 the Court will take up the States business & the County business as usual on the second day of the term.

(p-157) JOHN BELL ）
        Vs   ） Tresspass
    JAMES TRIBBLE & ）
    REUBEN GRAYSON ）

Continued on affidavit of plaintiffs Atty. Dedimus to Plaintiff to take John Waggoner's & John S. Chapman's Deposition twenty days Notice to the Defendants as also the Deposition of Daniel McKenny all of Henderson County State of Kentucky.

Court adjourned untill tomorrow at 9 O'clock-

The Worshipful Court have met according to Adjournment Wednesday Decr. 21st 1808-
        Present-

                John Blair   ）
                Joseph Robinson ） Esquires
                John H. Poston ） Justices

ANTHONY FOSTER ）
      Vs   ） Debt
SAMUEL THORNTON ）

Dismissed by Plaintiff in proper person & the Defendant by his attorney assumes all costs - Therefore it is considered by the Court that the Plaintiff recover against the Defendant his Costs about his suit in this behalf Expended & the Defendant in Mercy &

(p-158) STATE ）
        Vs   ） Indictment
    SAMUEL PETERS ）

Mann Phillips acknowledges himself bound in the sum of Two Hundred Dollars to be levied off his goods & Chattles lands & Tenements but to be void on condition that he appear immediately & prosecute in behalf of the State against Samuel Peters on a certain bill of Indictment to be prefered by the Grand Jury-

                                                        M. Phillips

74

JAMES BRAY)
Vs) Appeal
DANIEL ANDERSON)

The Plaintiff in this case being Solemnly called came not & made Default nor is his suit further prosecuted, Therefore it is considered by the Court that the Defendant go without day and recover against the plaintiff his Costs about his suit in this behalf expended-

On motion ordered that Francis Penrice & Joseph Bowers be appointed to attend at next Term as Constables-

(p-139) Robert Prince, John Blair, James Hambleton, Sterling Neblett.

JOHN BOSLEY)
Vs) Debt
JAMES LOGGANS)

Jury (to wit)

1 James Jones   7 William Allen
2 John King   8 John Watkins
3 Igam Mathews   9 Joseph Penrice
4 Absolum Tribble   10 George Humphries
5 James Trotter   11 John Steel
6 James Holt   12 Peter Hubbard

Who being duly Elected tried & sworn the truth to speak upon the Issue Joined do upon their Oaths say that they find that fifty dollars of the Debt in the Declaration mentioned has been paid & that there remains Eighty Dollars the ballance of the Debt in the Declaration mentioned remains unpaid. Therefore they do assess his damages to Twenty four Dollars & sixty cents by reason of the detention thereof-
Therefore it is considered by the Court that the plaintiff recover against the Defendant the said Debt & Damages as assessed by the Jury in their Verdict in form aforesaid and his Costs about his suit in this behalf expended-

(p-140) STEPHEN STEWART)
Vs) Case
JOSEPH WIMBERLY)

Jury (to wit)

1 Peter Oneal   7 Jeremiah Lewis
2 Joshua P. Vaughn   8 Thomas Dunbar
3 William Lyons   9 Thomas Whitledge
4 James Edwards   10 Elisha Willis
5 William R. Bell   11 David Bunting
6 Colmore Duvall   12 Heyden Wells

Who being duly Elected tried & sworn deligently to inquire of Damages in this suit do upon their Oaths say that the plaintiff has sustained damages by reason of the nonperformance of the Assumsions in the Declaration mentioned to Ninety two Dollars Eighty two cents. Therefore it is considered by the Court that the plaintiff recover against the Defendant the Damages as aforesaid assessed by the Jury as aforesaid in manner & form and also his costs about his suit in that behalf expended-

17 Bond Robert Nelson to John Blair for 100 acres of Land the signature of said Nelson was proven by the Oaths of Robert Prince & James Elder and ordered to Registeration in Open Court-

(p-141)   Same Magistrates

THOMAS BATTSON Assee)
of MONTGOMERY BELL   ) Debt
        Vs   )
CHRISTOPHER THOMAS   )

                      Jury (to wit)

1 William Allen   7 John Wadkins
2 Peter Hubbard   8 Joseph Penrice
3 James Holt   9 Isam Mathews
4 James Trotter   10 Abselem Tribble
5 Robert Edmonston   11 John King
6 Henry Taylor   12 George Humphries

Who being duly Elected tried & Sworn the truth to speak do upon their Oath say that they find the Issues for the Defendant-
Therefore it is considered by the Court that the Defendant recover against the Plaintiff his Costs about his suit in this behalf Expended & that the Defendant be at Liberty to Depart in peace-

(p-142) Robert Prince, Joseph Robertson, James Hambleton, Esquires on the Bench-

    Samuel Vance & John Bradley surviving partners of VANCE, KING
& BRADLEY.
        Vs   ) Case
    ADAM HARMON, Junr.   )

                    Jury (to wit)

1 Moses Oldham, Senr.   7 Jeremiah Lewis
2 Haydon Wells   8 Timothy Drake
3 David Bunting   9 Peter Oneal
4 Stephen Thomas   10 Owen Perdue
5 James Jones   11 James Morris
6 Christopher Thomas   12 Elisha Willis

Who being duly Elected tried & sworn the truth to speak upon the Issues Joined do upon their Oaths say that they find that the Defendant did not assume upon himself as the plaintiff in Declaring hath alledged-
Therefore it is considered by the Court that the Defendant recover against the Plaintiff his Costs about his suit in this behalf Expended & the defendant be at liberty to Depart in peace-

Ordered that Michael Northington be appointed Overseer of the Road from Edmonstin's or the ford of Parsons Creek to the Robinson line on the Nashville Road, Joseph Robinson, Esq. give the list of hands to work on said Road-

(p-143) John Blair, James Hambleton & Joseph Robinson, Esquires on the Bench. Robert Prince Esquire.

JOHN DEN LESSEE OF
NATHANIEL DICKINSON
Vs
JOSEPH PENRICE
) Ejectmt.

Jury (Viz)

1 James Holt
2 William Allen
3 James Trotter
4 Robert Edmonston
5 Isaac Kittrel
6 James Brantley

7 Joshua P. Vaughn
8 Jedediah Hall
9 Needham Whitfield
10 John Nevill
11 John Watkins
12 John Bailey

Who being duly Elected tried & sworn the truth to speak upon their Oaths do say that the Defendt. is not Guilty of the trespass as in pleading the plaintiff hath alledged, Therefore it is considered by the Court that the plaintiff take nothing by his bill but his false clamour & that the Defendant go hence without day & recover against the plaintiff his Costs about his suit in this behalf expended & the Defendant in Mercy &c.

Deed of Conveyance John Cocke Shff. to James Williams was acknowledged in Open Court & ordered to registeration for 200 acres of Land-

(p-144)   Court adjourned untill tomorrow at 9 O'clock.

Court met according to adjournment.
Present

Robert Prince) Esquires
John Blair   ) Justices
John H. Poston)

Ordered by the Court that Joseph Woolfolk & Joseph Robinson be appointed to let the keeping of Benjamin Smith an Insane person to the lowest bidder for one year from this date-

Ordered that John Bayley who kept Benjamin Cocke Smith the last year an Insane man be allowed Sixty five Dollars & that the County Trustee pay the same-

Same Majestrates on the bench-

WILLIAM HUSTON)
      Vs   ) Petition
MARTIN GOSS   )

On motion & affidavit filed ordered that writs of Certiorari & Supersedeas Issue according to the petition of the Defendant when Security sufficient is Given-

Amos Bird by his atterney in fact Henry Small acknowledged in Open Court a Deed for part of a Lott in the Town of Clarksville No. 66 to James Williams & ordered to Registeration-

(p-145) ISRAEL ROBINSON
Vs
JAMES GRANT

On motion of Israel Robinson by his attorney and it appearing to the satisfaction of the Court that said Robinson had paid the sum of Sixty five Dollars & five cents in satisfaction of a Judgment & Costs obtained against him at the suit of Stephen Stewart as Security for James Grant at the June Sessions 1808 of Montgomery County Court.

It is ordered & devised by the Court that the said Israel Robinson recover against the said James Grant the said sum of Sixty five Dollars & five cents together with his costs & charges in this behalf expended-

On petition it is ordered by the Court that Samuel Lynes have License to keep a Tavern in his new dwelling house in the Town of Clarksville under the Restrictions of the Acts of General Assembly in such case made & provided - he gave bond with Barney Duff & Archilles Wells his securities.

JESSE COBB
Vs   ) Debt - Demurrer
STERLING INGRAM) withdraws
              Neldebet payment & sett off Issue Joined-

(p-146) Robert Prince, John Blair & James Hambleton, Esquires on the Bench-

ISAM MATHEWS
Vs   ) Covenant &
THOMAS WILLIAMS) Writ of Enquiry

Jury (to wit)

1 William Allen   7 Joseph Penrice
2 Peter Hubbard   8 Samuel Thornton
3 Isaac Kittrell   9 John Watkins
4 James Holt   10 John Bailey
5 James Trotter   11 Martin Goss
6 George Humphries   12 Moses Oldham, Senr.

Being duly Elected tried & sworn diligently to enquire of Damages in his suit upon their Oath do say that the plaintiff hath sustained Damages by occasion of the Defendants non-performance of the covenant in the Declaration mentioned to fifty one Dollars sixty eight cents besides his Costs, therefore it is considered by the Court that the plaintiff recover against the Defendant his damages aforesaid assessed in form aforesaid and his costs by him about his suit expended - & the Defendant in Mercy &

REYNOLDS & MCFARLAND)
Vs   ) Case
JOSEPH ROBINSON   )

Motion of the Defendant Counsell it is Ordered that the Interlocutory Judgt. entered at last term against the Defendant be set aside & that the Defendant have leave to plead De Novo.

(p-147)   Robert Prince, Joseph Woolfolk & James Hambleton Esquires on the bench. John H. Poston

JAMES BUNTING)
       Vs   ) Case
JOEL R. OLDHAM)

          Jury (to wit)

1 William Allen   7 Peter Hubbard
2 James Trotter   8 William Lyons
3 Isaac Kittrell   9 James Edwards
4 Elisha Willes   10 Thomas Whitledge
5 Robert Edmonston   11 Isam Mathews
6 James Holt   12 James Williams

Who being Elected tried & sworn the truth to speake upon the Issue Joined do upon their Oath say that the Defendant did assume upon himself as the plaintiff in Declaring hath alledged & do assess the plaintiffs damages by reason of the non-performance of his assomsions to Two Hundred & Ninety Eight Dollars Fifty & a half cents-
Therefore it is considered by the Court that the plaintiff recover against the Defendant his Damages so assessed by the Jury aforesaid in form aforesaid as also his costs about his suit in this behalf Expended & the Defendant in Mercy & C.

(p-148)   Court adjourned untill tomorrow at 8O'clock.

          Court met according to adjournment
                Present

                    Robert Prince   )
                    Joseph Woolfolk) Esquires
                    Hugh McClure   ) Justices
                    John H. Poston   )
                    Robert Prince Esquire withdraws

ROBERT PRINCE   )
      Vs   ) Case
JAMES EDWARDS   )
Admr. of Scott Decd.

     The Defendant in proper person comes here into Court in proper person & confessed Judgment for one Hundred & Twenty seven Dollars & fifty Cents-
Therefore it is considered by the Court that the plaintiff recovered against the Defendant the sum of one hundred & twenty seven dollars & fifty Cents together with his Costs about his suit in this behalf Expended, & the Defendant in the Mercy & C-

THORNTON & HAWKINS)
      Vs   ) Secetiorari
THOMAS GREEN   )

     Motion for Dismission of Certiorari by the plaintiffs attorney-

Robert Prince, Joseph Woolfolk, Joseph Robinson Esqrs.

The Court adjourned untill Court in Course-

       Ro Prince
      Joseph Robinson
      J. Woolfolk-

(p-149) State of Tennessee Monday March 20th 1809

   The Worshipful Court of Montgomery County have met according to Adjournment-

   Present

James Hambleton	Esquires
Thomas Smith	Justices
Sterling Niblett	
John H. Poston	

  Panal for the Grand Jury.

1 John Keathley, Foreman
2 Thomas Hunter
3 Peter Holt
4 Stephen O'Gwin
5 Thomas Travis, Senr.
6 Robert Newlen
7 William R. Gibson
8 Biggards Robert
9 John Griffin
10 James Adams
11 Needham Whitfield
12 John Coffee
13 James Pierce
14 Reuben Pollard
15 John Little

Who being sworn, & Received a charge by the Solicitor Retired- served three days & was Dismissed-

Elisha Willis was sworn as a Constable to attend the Grand Jury this Term proves three days attendance-

John H. Hyde quallified as Deputy Sheriff for the County of Montgomery he took the necessary Oaths of office & C.

(p-150) William Weeks, James Williams, Jacob Boatright & Samuel Peters who being summoned to attend this Court at this Term as Jurors are all Exonerated for Reasons shown to the Court-

1 Deed of Conveyance John Harris to Jacob Staley for 160 acres proven by the Oaths of John Rudolph and George Kirk witnesses thereto and Ordered to be Registered-

2 Deed of Conveyance William Morris to Isaac Rogers 150 Acres acknowledged in Open Court & ordered to Registeration-

3 Deed of Conveyance, John Hill, James Hill & Green Hill, by his Attorney John Hill, was proven by the Oaths of Isaac Weakley & Benjamin Mallery witnesses thereto for 640 acres & ordered to Registeration to J. & W. Berry-

Thomas Smith, James Hambleton & John H. Poston Esquires on the Bench-

(p 151) Brice Jackson records his stock mark a cross and slit in the right ear

Ordered that William Farrior have a liscense to keep a public ferry crossing Red River at the place formerly kept by James Bunting, he gives bond with JohnnSteel, Henry Small & Charles Stewart his securities bound in the sum of Two thousand dollars.

Covenant Bond, Robert Nelson to Duncan Stewart for the conveyance of land, the signature of the said Robert Nelson was proven by the oaths of Anthony Crutcher & Heydon Wells.

Court adjourned until tomorrow at 9 oclock.

The Worshipfull court met according to adjournment Tuesday March 21st 1809, Present,
    Robert Prince)
    Sterling Neblett)
    James Hambleton) Esquires, Justices
    Samuel Gattis)
    John Sterling)

Deed of conveyance John Cocks, Sheriff to William Ross Senr. for 385 acres of land acknowledged & ordered to registration.

On motion of Absolam Trible against James Moore on Petition. It is ordered by the Court that a Writ of Certiorari & Supersedias Issue agreeable to the petition of the said Absolum Tribble.

Ordered that James & William Berry have a License to keep a Public ferry across Cumberland River from the North bank thereof opposite Robert Weakley's Ferry in Dickson County they gave bond, with Paul McGraw & Cornelias McGraw Securities in the sum of Two Thousand Dollars-

(p-152) 6 Deed of Conveyance John Cocke Sheriff to Sheriff to Sterling Neblett Esq, for 45 Acres of Land acknowledged in Court & Ordered to registeration.

THOMAS DUNBAR)
Vs)
JOSEPH DOREN)

On motion of the plaintiff by his Council it is ordered that Judgment be entered up against the Defendant for the sum of Twenty Two Dollars & Ninety Three Cents for a Judgment which recovered before Squire Peston, against said Plaintiff as also his cost about his suit in this behalf Expended & the Defendant in Mercy & C-

7 Deed of Conveyance Martin Goss to Frederick Goss for 50 Acres of Land proven by Gedian Goss and Simon Miers witnesses thereto & ordered to registeration.

Power of Attorney John Moore to Thomas Moore proven by Samuel Allen & Joseph Barbee witnesses thereto & ordered to Registeration.

8 Deed of Conveyance Samuel Allen to Thomas Bunch for 40 Acres of Land acknowledged in Court & ordered to be registered-

9 Deed of Conveyance John Grey Blount by his attorney in fact Willie Blount was acknowledged in Open Court & ordered to Registeration for 1000 Acres of land-

(p-153) On motion ordered that James Moore & Samuel Vance Esquires be appointed to settle with Stephen Thomas Guardean to Hannah Cobb & make return to next Term-

VANCE, KING & BRADLEY)
Vs) Sci Fa
GEORGE HUMPHREYS)

Tuesday 21st March 1809

This day the Defendant George Humphreys brings into Court here the body of Ezekert Black in discharge of himself from this Action and he is received by the Court and ordered into the Custody of the Sheriff-

Ordered that William Hust have License to keep a Tavern at his New Dwelling house he gives Bond with William Ross, Senr. his Security bound in the sum of Five Hundred Dollars for complying with the Acts of the Assembly in that case-

Ordered that Samuel Peters have License to keep a Tavern in the House where he now lives in the Town of Clarksville he gave bond with William Farrier & Hayden Wells his securities for complying with the Acts of Assembly in such case-

10 Deed of Conveyance Brice Jackson to Robert Nolan for 200 Acres of Land proven by Samuel Woldridge & Stephen O'Gwin and ordered to registeration-

11 Deed of Conveyance Benjamin Whitehead to Joseph Whitehead proven by the Oaths of Jesse Martin & George H. Moore for 100 Acres & ordered to Registeration-

(p-154) Hugh F. Bell administrator on the Estate of Robert Nelson Deceased returned into Court an Inventory of the Estate of the said Deceased-

12 Deed William Baker to Jonathan Anderson for 50 Acres of Land was proven by Samuel Perry & Rich Anderson witnesses thereto and Ordered to Registeration-

13 Deed James Perry to Nicholas Moyer for 100 Acres of Land acknowledged in Court and ordered to registeration-

14 Deed Samuel Vance to Hawkins & Thornton for Lott No. 13 in Palmyra acknowledged in Court & ordered to registeration-

15 Deed Samuel Vance for half acre Lott No 68 in Palmyra to James G. Whaland acknowledged in Open Court & ordered to registeration-

Ordered that Anna Sugg & Mathew Morgan & John Thomas have Letters of Administration on the Estate Samuel Sugg Deceased they gave bond with Samuel Vance & Stephen Thomas their Securities bound in the sum of Two thousand five Hundred Dollars-

Deed for part Lott in Clarksville Amos Bird to James Williams proven by Colmore Duvall and Anthony Crutcher & ordered to registeration-

16 Deed Samuel Vance to John H. Hyde for one Lott in Palmyra acknowledged in Court & ordered to registeration-

(p-155) 17 Deed Robert Nelson to Charles Cherry for 285 Acres proven by William Nelson & John H. Nelson witnesses and ordered to be registered-

Power of Attorney Mathew Morgan to William B. Ross acknowledged in Court and ordered to registeration-

Deed Hugh McClure & James Elder to Colmore Duvall for 1080½ Acres acknowledged in Court & ordered to be registered-

2 Bond Robert Nelson to Britain Bayless proven by John Shelby & David Brigham & ordered to be registered-

Ordered that the administrators of Lemuel Sugg Deceased sell the Perishable property belonging to said Estate agreeable to law-

Ordered that David Brigham have a License to keep a Public ferry across Cumberland river mouth of Blooming Grove he enters into bond with Britain Bailess & William Mitchell & John Shelby his securities bound in the sum of Two thousand Dollars for his complying with the Acts of Assembly in that case made & provided.

Samuel Woods administrator to the estate of Able Jenny deceased in Orange County North Carolina produced to this Court an Inventory of the estate of the said deceased & also an amount of the sales of said estate of said deceased & also an account of the sales of said estate of said deceased certified by the Clerk of said Orange County which the Court admitted to record-

(p-156) William Hubbard is appointed Constable in Captain Drakes Company in place of Conneway Oldham, he qualified and gave bond with James Hambleton Esquire and James Williams securities.

Harbert Wheliss is appointed Constable in Captain Beaties Company he qualified and gave bond with William Barden & Elijah Ramsey his securities.

18 Deed Charles Stewart to James Stewart for 136 acres of land acknowledged in Court & ordered to be registered.

Zachariah Grant appointed Constable in Capt. Fords Company gave bond and security qualified &.

Andrew Peterson appointed Constable in Captain Fords Company gave bond & security & qualified.

19 Deed of Gift William Sullivant to Nancy Smith and husband Samuel Smith for 160 acres of land proven by Simon Helms & Jesse Sullivan witnesses thereto and ordered to registeration.

Joseph Robinson Esq. gives in his resignation as Justice of the peace.

20 Deed of Conveyance Robert Nelson to John H. Poston & wife for 300 acres of land proven by William Nelson a witness thereto and ordered to registeration & Hugh F. Bell swore he heard Robert Nelson say he had executed such a Deed.

(p-157) 21 Deed Morgan Brown to James Moore Deed for 74 acres of land acknowledged in Open Court & ordered to registeration.

Power of Attorney Mordica Johnson & Jane his wife to Samuel Vance proven by Morgan Brown and Daniel Kyle witnesses thereto & ordered to be registered.

22 Deed Morgan Brown to Samuel Thornton for Sundry Town Lotts in Palmyra acknowledged in Court & ordered to be registered.

JESSE COBB
Vs } in Debt
STERLING INGRAM

On motion it is ordered that a Commission Issue to take the Deposition of Susannah Peterson at her own house directed to James Baxter Esquire to take said Deposition it appearing to the Court that the testimony of said witness is material for said Plaintiff & that two days notice be given to the adverse party.

Hugh Harris is appointed Constable in Captain Allen's Company gave bond & security quallified & -

23 Deed of Conveyance John Cocke Shff. to Samuel Vance proven in Open Court & ordered to registeration for 1920 by the Oath of Adam Harman

Junr. & Burrell Bayliss witnesses thereto.

Bill sale Walter Wyatt to James Huling in Open Court & ordered to registeration & James Huling Esquire came into Court and acknowledged the transfer of the property to W. C. Jamison.

(P-158) Deed of Conveyance John Cooke Shff. to McClure & Elder was acknowledged in Open Court for 3950 acres of land & ordered to registeration.

24 Deed of Conveyance Isaac Morgan to Adam Harman, Junr. was proven in Open Court by the Oath of Samuel Vance & James G. Wheeler for one town lot & ordered to registeration.

25 Deed of Conveyance John Cooke Sheriff to Thomas K. McElrath & others for Sundry Town Lotts in Palmyra proven in Open Court by the Oaths of Wright Outlaw & Stephen Thomas subscribing witnesses thereto & ordered to registeration.

Bill of Sale Robert Whitlidge to Elizabeth Whitledge & others for a negro was proven in Open Court by the Oath of William Allen & Thomas Whitledge subscribing witnesses thereto & ordered to registeration.

26 Deed of Conveyance Cornelius McGraw to John Hunt was acknowledged in Open Court & ordered to registeration for 40 acres of land.

27 Deed of Conveyance Haydon Wells to Abner Harris was acknowledged in Open Court & ordered to registeration for 220 acres of land.

28 Deed of Conveyance Haydon Wells to Robert Wells was acknowledged in Open Court for 158 acres of land & ordered to registeration.

29 Deed of Conveyance Mosy Steele to John H. Poston was proven in Open Court by the Oath of James Baxter & William S. Bailey subscribing witnesses thereto for part of lot No. 58 & ordered to registeration.

Bill Sale Thomas Moore to Burrell Bayless was acknowledged in Open Court for one negro girl & ordered to registeration.

30 Deed of Conveyance William Weaks to James Trice was acknowledged in Open Court & ordered to registeration for 208 acres of land.

31 Deed of Conveyance John Cooke Shff. to Robert Nelson was acknowledged in Open Court & ordered to registeration for 640 acres of land.

(p 159) 32 Deed of Conveyance John Cooke Shff. to Robert Nelson was acknowledged in Open Court & ordered to registeration for 228 acres of land.

33 Deed of Conveyance John Cooke Shff. to Robert Nelson was acknowledged in Open Court & ordered to registeration for 590 acres of land.

34 Deed of Conveyance John Cooke Shff. to Samuel Vance was proven in Open Court by the Oath of Adam Harman, Junr. & Burrell Bayliss subscribing witnesses thereto & ordered to registeration for 243-3/4 acres.

The Administrator & Administratrix of Lemuel Sugg Deceased renders into Court an Inventory of the estate of said deceased.

35 Deed of Conveyance Guthridge Lyons to Adam Harman, Junr. was proven in Open Court by the Oaths of James Moore & Samuel C. Hawkins subscribing witnesses thereto for one lot in Palmyra.

36 Deed of Conveyance Robert Nelson to John Newell was proven in Open Court by the Oath of William Nelson & John H. Nelson subscribing witnesses thereto & ordered to registeration for 274 acres of land.

Deed Gift David Outlaw to Nancy Outlaw was proven in Open Court by Wright Outlaw & William Clements subscribing witnesses & ordered to registeration for two negroes & one bed & furniture.

Deed of Gift David Outlaw to William W. Outlaw for one negro & one bed & furniture was proven in Open Court by the Oath of Wright Outlaw & William Clements subscribing witnesses thereto & ordered to registeration.

(p-160) Ordered that Jesse Martin shall extend the road that he works on as far as Benjamin Whitehead's spring & that Thomas Smith appoint the hands to work under said Martin.

Ordered that John Lee be appointed overseer of the road leading from Palmyra to the Dixon County line & the same hands that formerly worked under Lemuel Sugg to work under the said Lee.

Ordered that David Pritchard be appointed overseer of the road from Benjamin Whitehead's to the barren fork & that Abner Harris Esquire appoint the hands to work under the said Pritchard.

Ordered that William Barton, Senr., William Morrow, Joseph Hardekin, William Bearden, John Barton, Henry Funk, Able Mann, & Absolum Tribble be appointed a Jury to review the road leading from Absolam Tribble's ferry to where it intersects Davises old road.

Ordered that Joseph Hardekins be appointed overseer of the road from Tribble's Ferry to Davises old road, in the place of Hayden Wells.

Jurors to June Term 1809

Isham Trotter, Joshua P. Vaughn, John Henderson, James Carraway, James Stewart, William Jourdan, Thomas Bunch, Henry Williams, Willis Jackson, Joseph Dickson, Edward Leech, William Corlew, Samuel Bumpass, Richard Whitehead, Joseph Edwards, Samuel Filling-imm, John Hagler, Isaac Kittrell, James C. Brown, John Russell, Samuel C. Hawkins, Thomas K. McElrath, Birch Roland, Ralph Williams, Bryan Whitfield, William Polk, William Colhoon, Hugh Tennen, William Ford, John Hignight, Ebenezer Frost, Henry J. Williams, John Trousdale, James Leggins, James Beard, William Morrow, Timothy Anderson, John Rudolph, John Dicas.

(p-161) Ordered that a road leaving the Nashville road on the South side of Red river near where the Macadoe road turns off thence the most direct way to Hornbergers old ford across Red river, thence up Jedediah Hall's Lane with Watkins & Nelson's line to the Port Royal road, thence down said road fronting Watkins House, thence the best & most direct way to White's Mill on Spring Creek & that Bright Herring, William White, John Dicas, Thomas Dunbar, Moses Oldham, Daniel Taylor, Isaac Peterson, James Bailey, John Henderson, Jedediah Hall, James Lester be a Jury to view mark & lay of said road.

Ordered that Jedediah Hall be appointed overseer of the road leaving the Nashville road to White's Mill on Spring Creek & that the hands be as follows, to work on said road, John Dicas, William S. White, Charles Cherry, Bright Herring, Watkins, Widow Nelson's (hands) Daniel Taylor, Thomas McCall, James Hambleton & all the hands convenient on the South side of Red river.

Justices to receive the list of taxable property for the year 1809.
John Blair Esquire for Capt. Frosts' Compy.

Samuel Vance	"	"	"	Penrice's	"
John H. Poston	"	"	"	The Town	"
Joseph Woolfolk	"	"	"	Bryant's	"
James Moore	"	"	"	Harman's	"
Abner Harris	"	"	"	Allen's	"
Saml. Smith	"	"	"	Porter's	"
Samuel Gattis	"	"	"	Whitfield's	"
James Lockart	"	"	"	Enlow's	"
Wm. McDaniel	"	"	"	Weakley's	"

84

(p-162) Ordered the County Tax be one half of the State Tax & that the Court House & Prison Tax be to the full extent of the Acts of the General Assembly.

On motion ordered by the Court that on the first Thursday of next June Term 1809 that they will take up the State business and on the first Tuesday of said term they will attend to the County business.

Ordered that Henry Small be appointed overseer of the road leading from Clarksville to Wine Miller's old place on the Nashville road. James Hambleton Esq. names the hands.

Ordered that Moses Oldham, Senr. be appointed overseer of the road from Clarksville to the first fork of the road beyond Farrier's ferry.

37 Deed of Conveyance John Cocke Shff. to John Blair was acknowledged in Open Court & ordered to be registered (the State Tax being paid before.)

38 Deed of Conveyance Barney Duff to Zebedee Dennis was acknowledged in Open Court & ordered to registeration for one Lott.

Ordered that James Carreway be appointed overseer of the streets of Clarksville and that all the hands in Town work under him.

(p-163) Court adjourned untill tomorrow at 9 O'clock.

The Worshipful Court of Montgomery County have met according to Adjournment Wednesday March 22nd 1809.
Present -
John Blair   ) Esquire
Hugh McClure   ) Justices
John Sterling   )

39 Deed of Conveyance for 205 acres of land Duken Grant to Archibald Edmonston proven by the Oaths of Alexander Brown & John Edmonston witnesses thereto & ordered to registeration.

Joseph Robinson & Joseph Woolfolk who was appointed to settle with Alexander Brown administrator to Nathan Ray, returns a settlement to this Court.

40 Deed Jacob Boatwright to Edmund Suter for 90 acres of land acknowledged in Open Court and ordered to registeration.

41 Deed Joseph Woolfolk to William Cohoon for 530 acres of land acknowledged in Court and ordered to registeration.

Covenant Bond Robert Nelson to Isham Trotter proven by William S. Bailey a subscribing witness & John Cocke who swore he believed it to be Nelson's hand writing.

42 Deed of Conveyance John Cocke Shff. to Morgan Brown was proven in Open Court by the Oath of Adam Harman, Junr. & Joshua Willis subscribing witnesses thereto & ordered to registeration for 427 acres of land.

(p-164) Joseph Woolfolk, John Blair, & Samuel Vance Esquires

```
     ROBERT DRAKE  )
          Vs       ) Case
     MARTIN GOSS   )
```

1 John Marshall
2 David McFadin
3 John Edmonson
4 Zebedee Dennis
5 Samuel Wooldridge
6 Samuel Mitchell
7 John Teasley
8 John King D. D.
9 Robert Akins
10 Edmond Suter D.D.
11 William Broom
12 George Humphries

Who being elected tried & sworn the truth to speak upon the Issue joined upon their Oaths do say the defendant.

The plaintiff being solemnly called came not but made Default, Therefore it is considered by the Court that a non-suit be entered against the Plaintiff & that the Defendant recover his costs about his suit in this behalf expended & the plaintiff in Mercy &.

Motion to set the non suit aside
Motion overuled.

STATE)
Vs)
DAVID WILLIAMS)

John Griffin the prosecuter in this suit acknowledges himself in the sum of one hundred dollars to be levied off his goods & Chattels lands and Tenements but to be void on conditions that he make his personal appearance at our next Court of pleas & quarter sessions to be held for Montgomery County at the Court House in Clarksville on the third Monday in June next then & there to give Testimony in behalf of the State against David Williams & not depart without leave

John Griffin (Seal)

(p-165) Robert Prince, John Blair, Abner Harris & Samuel Vance Esquires.

JOHN BAXTOR)
Vs) Case
JOHN WHITLEDGE)

1 John Marshall
2 David McFadden
3 John Edmonston
4 Zebedee Dennis
5 Samuel Woolridge
6 Samuel Mitchell
7 John Teasley
8 John King
9 Robert Akins
10 Edmund Suter
11 William Broom
12 George Humphries

Who being elected tried & sworn the truth to speak upon the Issue joined upon their Oaths do say that they find the defendant did not assume upon himself in manner & form as the plaintiff hath declared against him, Therefore it is considered by the Court that the defendant recover against the plaintiff his costs about his suit in this behalf expended & the plaintiff in Mercy &.

Power of attorney Hiram Downs to Samuel Thornton was duly proven in Open Court by the Oath of William C. Jamison who deposeth & says that he believes it to be the proper hand riting of said Hiram Downs & ordered to be recorded.

Ordered that Hugh F. Bell the administrator of the estate of Robert Nelson deceased sell all the perishable property belonging to said estate agreeable to law.

Court adjourned for half an hour.

The Worshipful Court of Montgomery County have met according to adjournment.

Present
John Blair)
Hugh McClure) Esquires
Abner Harris) Justices

(p-166) JOSEPH WOOLFOLK &) Admr's.
        DREWRY FORD)
           Vs)
        JAMES BOYD) Case

The Defendant in proper person comes into Court & confesses Judgment for sixty dollars.

Therefore it is considered by the Court that the plaintiff recover against the defendant the sum of sixty dollars as also their costs about their suit in this behalf expended & the defendant in Mercy &.

    VANCE, KING & BRADLEY)
          Vs) Original attachment
    PHILLIP HAWKINS)

Jessee Dickson came into Court after being guarnished & on Oath says that he is not indebted to the defendant any sum whatever.

Guy Smith being sworn as Mr. Dickson & on Oath says that he owes nothing to the defendant Hartwell Weaver being sworn as Mr. Smith who says on Oath that he is indebt to the defendant one spoonfull of Magnitia.

Charles Moore being sworn as before & on Oath says that he is Indebt nothing to the defendant but says that Hannah Gaskell wife of Enoch Gaskell Decd. that Hannah Gaskell was indebted to Philip Hawkins Twelve Dollars & that Evan Gaskell asknowledged himself indebted to the defendant One Dollar & fifty cents.

    JAMES ADKINSON & HIS)
    NEXT FRIENDS) Trespass
          Vs) Asst. & battery
    JAMES WILLIAMS)

The plaintiff in this case is to pay all the costs of this term.

(p-167) Hugh McClure, John H. Poston, John Blair

    REYNOLDS & MCFARLAND)
          Vs) Case
    JOSEPH ROBINSON)

1 David McFadden   7 Frederick Moody
2 John Marshall   8 Absolam Tribble
3 Samuel Wooldridge   9 John Teasley
4 Edmond Suter   10 John Edmonston
5 Samuel Mitchell   11 Samuel Allen
6 Zebedee Dennis   12 William Broom

Who being elected tried & sworn the truth to speak upon the Issue joined upon their Oath do say that the defendant did assume upon himself in manner & form as the plaintiff hath alledged & do assess the plaintiff damages to One Hundred Thirty five Dollars two & one half cents.

Therefore it is considered by the Court that the plaintiff recover against the defendant the debt in the plaintiffs declaration mentioned as also his costs about his suit in this behalf expended & the defendant in Mercy &.

Ordered that Robert Nowland be appointed overseer of the road in the place of George Ury leading from the East fork of Deason's Creek to the Elizabeth Furnace on Yellow Creek & the same hands in the bounds work thereon as heretofore.

Ordered that John Edmonston be appointed overseer of the road from Parsons Creek to the Robertson line leading towards Nashville by the way of Col. Ford's old plantation. Joseph Woolfolk Esquire notify the hands.

(p-168) ~~Joseph Woolfolk &~~
~~Drewry Ford Exors.~~   ~~Writ~~
~~of James Ford Decd.~~ ~~Debt~~   ~~Entered before.~~
         ~~Vs~~
~~James Boyd~~

~~The defendant in proper person confessed judgment for sixty dollars~~
~~due the plaintiff however three months therefore it is~~

Elias Fort Guardian)
         Vs   ) Original Attachment
LUKE DILLIARD   )

The plaintiff in this case in proper person dismisses this suit & the defendant in proper person assumes all costs - Therefore it is considered by the Court that the plaintiff recover against the defendant his costs about his suit in this behalf expended & the defendant in Mercy &.

SAME)
 Vs) Original Attachment
SAME)

The plaintiff in this case in proper person dismissed this suit & the defendant in proper person assumes all costs. Therefore it is considered by the Court that the plaintiff recover against the defendant his costs about his suit in this behalf expended & the defendant in Mercy &.

45 Deed of Conveyance Hugh F. Bell administrator of Robert Nelson Deceased was acknowledged in Open Court & ordered to registration for ½ of a Town lot No. 58 to Moses Slate.

Indenture the Cheaman of the Court to Henry Small for an Orphan Girl Mary Chumney was bound to said Henry Small.

(p-169) Court adjourned untill tomorrow at 8 O'clock.

The Worshipful Court of Montgomery County have met according to adjournment Wednesday March 23rd 1809.
Present
              JOHN BLAIR   )
              HUGH MCCLURE   ) Esquires
              JAMES HAMBLETON) Justices
              STERLING NEBLETT)

STATE   )
 Vs   ) Indictment
WRIGHT BONDS)

Griffeth Dickerson prosecutor in this suit was solemnly called & failed to appear and prosecute & therefore he forfeited his recognisance.

STATE   )
 Vs   ) Indictment N. P. Eque.
WRIGHT BONDS)

[struck through: Deed from E. ??? Administrator to Robert Nelson Deceased to John L. Jones for the sum of a Pour Pour acknowledged in Open - (Myer. entered before)]

STATE)
Vs) Indictment
JAMES MCFARLAND)

Roland Peterson, Andrew Peterson & Robert Edmonston witness for the State was solemnly called & came not, therefore they forfeited according to Act of Assembly.

Forfeiture Roland Peterson set aside.

(p-170) [struck through: STATE Vs WRIGHT BONDS / Indictment]

STATE)
Vs) Indictment
WRIGHT BONDS)

Andrew Walker & Robert Grayson witnesses in behalf of the defendant was called and failed to appear therefore they forfeited according to Acts of Assembly.

STATE)
Vs) Indictment
KILLER MCFARLEN)

Gabriel Greathouse a witness was called and came not therefore he forfeited agreeable to the Act of Assembly.

John Blair, James Hambleton, Sterling Neblett, Esquires on the bench.

STATE)
Vs) Indictment
JAMES MCFARLEN)
(Jury, No. 1)

1 John Marshell   7 Edmund Suter
2 Robert W. Temple   8 John King
3 Charles Murry   9 John Teasley
4 Zebedee Dennis   10 Peter Oneal
5 Samuel Mitchell   11 Samuel Allen
6 Samuel Wooldridge   12 William Jourdan

Who being elected tried & sworn the truth to speak upon the Bill of Indictment upon their Oaths do say that they find the defendant guilty as charged on the manner & form so declared. The Court fines the defendant Twenty five Dollars, therefore it is considered by the Court (p-171) Court that the plaintiff recover against the defendant the said sum of Twenty five Dollars so assessed and also his cost about his suit in this behalf expended & the defendant in Mercy &.

Ordered that the road from Tribble's ferry to Vaughn's Mill be shortened that is from said ferry to the first large branch below William Whiteheads and that Joseph Whitehead be appointed Overseer of said road in place of Goodman Traywick and the hands be Frederick Moody, David Leech, Josiah G. Duke, Richard Whitehead, John Allen, William Whitehead, Abner Harris, Robert Ray & Francos Neblett, and let the

ballance of the road be added to John Moore and in addition to his hands be Peter Hubbard, William Hubbard, John Hubbard & David Hubbard.
Same Justices on the bench.

STATE
Vs
MAURL MCFARLEN

Same Jury No. 1 only David McFaden in place of William Jordan, Who being sworn the truth to speak upon the Bill of Indictment do upon their Oaths say that they find the defendant not guilty as declared in manner &form so declared, Therefore it is considered by the Court that the defendant go without day & recover against the prosecutor his costs about his suit in this behalf expended.

(p-172) Court adjourned for one half hour.
Court met according to adjournment
Present
John Blair   )
Sterling Niblett) Esquires
James Hambleton) Justices
Hugh McClure   )

STATE   )
Vs   ) Indictment Non Suit
KELLIS MCFARLAND)

Therefore it is considered by the Court that the prosecutor John Ferguson pay the costs of this suit.

STATE   )
Vs   ) Indictment
SAMUEL PETERS)
(Jury Viz)

1 John Marshall   7 Samuel Mitchell
2 David McFadden   8 John King
3 John Edmonston   9 John Teasley
4 Edmund Suter   10 Samuel Allen
5 Zebedee Dennes   11 David Pritchard
6 Samuel Wooldridge   12 Samuel Roberts

Who being duly elected tried & sworn the truth to speak upon the bill of Indictment do upon their Oath say that they find the defendant guilty as in this Bill charged in manner & form & he is ordered by the Court into the custody of the Sheriff.
Motion by defendants attorney for new trial.

(p-173) William Pennington, William Cohoon, Samuel Wilcox, David C. Penny & Pray Whipple who was appointed to review a road from the Robinson line by the mouth of the Sulpher fork to the Kentucky line at the 93 mile tree do say that the present road with strating in a few short Rmas & the new road cut by the bridge on the South side of Red River to be the road. Return made March Term 1809.

Covenant Bond Robert Nelson to Robert Prince for 26 acres of land Nelson's signature proven by the Oaths of Joseph Woolfolk, Esq. & James A. Bunting & ordered to registeration.

Elizabeth Tyre Administratrix of
THOMAS TYRE, Deceased)
       Vs   ) Debt
ROBERT PRINCE)

    The defendant came into Court in proper person and confessed Judget. according to Specialty with Interest – Therefore it is considered by the Court that the plaintiff recover against the defendant agreeable to the Specialty with Interest and that she recover her Costs of suit in this behalf expended & the defendant in Mercy &.

    44 Deed James Bunting to William Farrior for 152 acres acknowledged in Court & ordered to be registered.

    45 Deed James Bunting to William Farrior to half acre Lott acknowledged in Court & ordered to be registered.

(p-174)   46 Deed Samuel Peters & John Minott for 445 acres of land to Montgomery Bell proven by the Oath of Henry Minor & James A. Bunting witnesses thereto and ordered to registeration.

    47 Deed of Conveyance Samuel Peters & John Minott to Montgomery Bell for three acres of land proven by the Oaths of Henry Minor & James A. Bunting & ordered to registeration.

    Court adjourned untill tomorrow at 9 O'clock.

    The Worshipful Court have met according to adjournment Friday March 24th 1809.
Present

               Hugh McClure   )
               James Hambleton) Esquires
               James Baxter   ) Justices

    Power of Attorney Elijah Downs vs Samuel Thornton, William C. Jamison swares that he believes it to be the said Downs hand writing & (Error) ordered to registeration.

    Ordered that James C. Brown & Sterling Niblet Esquire be appointed to settle with Abner Harris Guardian for John Pritchard an idiot.

(p-175) Hugh McClure, James Hambleton

JOSEPH PARK)
Vs) Debt
NATHANIEL SAUNDERSON)
No. 1

1 John Marshell
2 Samuel Woolridge
3 Samuel Mitchell
4 Edmond Suter
5 Zebedee Dennes
6 Samuel Allen
7 John Teasley
8 John King
9 John Edmonston
10 David McFadden
11 James Grant
12 Peter Oneal

Who being elected tryed & sworn the truth to speak upon the Issue joined do upon their oath say that the Defendant hath not paid the Debt in the Plaintiff's Declaration mentioned & do assess the Plaintiff's damages by reason of the detention thereof to three dollars & twenty five cents- Therefore it is considered by the Court that the Plaintiff recover against the Defendant the debt & damages so assessed by the Jury in form aforesaid and also his costs about his suit in this behalf expended & the Defendant in Mercy &

JOHN MCCLELLAND)
Vs) Debt & writ of Enquiry
PETER LYTAKER)
Jury No. 1

Who being elected tryed & sworn the truth to speak upon this writ of enquiry upon their Oaths do say that the Debt in the Declaration mentioned is worth 72 Dollars & 30 cents and that the Plaintiff hath sustained damages by occation of the Defendants detention of the Debt in the Declaration mentioned to Eight Dollars & thirty four cents besides his costs. Therefore it is considered by the Court that the Plaintiff recover against the Defendant the debt & damages so assessed by the Jury in form aforesaid as also his costs about his suit in this behalf expended & the Defendant in Mercy &.

(p-176) Robert Prince, James Hambleton, Hugh McClure & John H. Poston.

Same Jury No. 1

REYNOLDS & MCFARLAND)
Vs) Debt
THOMAS DUNBARR)

Who being elected tryed & sworn the truth to speak upon the Issue joined do upon their Oaths say that the Defendant hath not paid one hundred & one dollars & sixty three cents of the debt in Plaintiff's Declaration mentioned & do assess the Plaintiff damages by the reason of the detention thereof to four dollars ninety eight cents. Therefore it is considered by the Court that the Plaintiff recover against the Defendant the debt & damages so assessed by the Jury in form aforesaid as also their costs about their suit in this behalf expended & the Defendant in Mercy &

MOSELY & WATSON)
Vs) Original Attachment
JOHN WRIGHT) & Writ of Enquiry

Same Justices & Jury No. 1.

Who being elected tryed & sworn deligently to enquire of damages in this suit upon their Oaths do say that the Plaintiff hath sustained damages by occation of the Defendants non-performance to five hundred & thirty six dollars ninety seven cents besides his costs. Therefore it is considered by the Court that the Plaintiffs recover against the Defendant the damages so assessed by the Jury in form aforesaid also their costs about their suit in this behalf expended & the Defendant in Mercy &.

(p-177) James Hambleton, John H. Poston & Hugh McClure.
Same Jury No. 1.

BURRELL BAYLISS)
Vs)
STERLING INGRAM &) Debt
WILLIAM GORDON)

Who being elected tried & sworn the truth to speak upon the Issue joined upon their Oath do say to say that the Defendant hath not paid one hundred & fourteen dollars twelve & one half cents of the debt in the Plaintiffs Declaration mentioned & do assess the Plaintiffs damages by the reason of the detention thereof to four dollars & seventy five cents. Therefore it is considered by the Court that the Plaintiff recovered by the Court that Plaintiff recover against the Defendants the debt & damages so assessed by the Jury in form aforesaid and also his costs about his suit in this behalf expended & Defendants in Mercy &.

ALEXANDER FAITH)
Vs) Appeal
SIMEON B. HERRING)

Same Jury No. 1

Who being elected tried & sworn the truth to speak upon the controversey between the parties do upon their Oaths do say that they find for the Plaintiff twenty six dollars twelve & one half cents. Therefore it is considered by the Court that the Plaintiff recover against the Defendant the debt so assessed by the Jury in form aforesaid as also his costs about his suit in this behalf expended & the Defendant in Mercy &.

(p-178) Justices James Hambleton, John Poston, James Baxter.

REYNOLDS & MCFARLAND)
Vs) Debt
WILLIAM R. BELL)

1 Charles Murry
2 George Humphries
3 John Brown
4 Abram Cooks
5 Peter Lytaker
6 Moses Parker
7 Moses Ford
8 Absolum Tribble
9 Fredrick Moody
10 Joel R. Oldham
11 John Bumpass
12 Francis Long

Who being elected tryed & sworn the truth to speak upon the Issue joined do upon their Oaths say that the Defendant hath not paid the Debt in the Plaintiff's Declaration mentioned & do assess the Plaintiff damages by the reason of the Detention thereof to three dollars fifty five & three fourths cents. Therefore it is considered by the Court that the Plaintiff recover against the Defendant the debt damages so assessed by the Jury in form aforesaid as also their costs about their suit in this behalf expended & the Defendant in Mercy &.

Court adjourned for half an hour.

Court met according to adjournment.
    Present

        Robert Prince
        James Baxter   Esquires
        Hugh McClure   Justices
        John H. Poston

JAMES DIXON, Senr.
    Vs   Debt
CHARLES STEWART

The Council for the Plaintiff dismissed this suit & William Farrier in proper person assumes all costs. Therefore it is considered by the Court that the Plaintiff recover against William Farrior the Costs about his suit in this behalf expended & the said William Farrier in Mercy &.

(p-179)   ALSEMUS KENDRICK &
           WILLIAM KENDRICK
               Vs   Case
           JOHN STEWART

1 John Marshall   7 John Teasley
2 David McFadden   8 John King
3 Edmund Suter   9 Frances Hubbard
4 Samuel Wooldridge   10 Charles Murry
5 Samuel Mitchell   11 Isaac Kittrell
6 John Edmonston   12 Benjamin Wilson

Who being elected tried & sworn the truth to speak upon the Issue joined upon their Oaths do say that the Defendant did assume upon himself in manner & form as the Plaintiffs have declared against him, & they do assess the damages to the Plaintiff by reason thereof to one hundred & nineteen dollars besides their costs. Therefore it is considered by the Court that the Plaintiff recover against the Defendant the damages so assessed by the Jury in form aforesaid as also their costs about their suit in this behalf expended & the Defendant in Mercy &.

JAMES DIXON, Senr.
    Vs   Debt
JAMES BUNTING

This case is dismissed by Plaintiff Council & the Defendant in proper person assumes all costs. Therefore it is considered by the Court that the Plaintiff recover against the Defendant his costs about his suit in this behalf expended & the Defendant in Mercy & .

ROBERT SEARCY, Assee)
Vs) Cort.
GEORGE WEST)

The Plaintiff's Council dismissed this suit. Therefore it is considered by the Court that the Defendant recover against the Plaintiff his costs about his suit in this behalf expended & the Plaintiff in Mercy &.

(p-180) OLSEMUS KENDRICK &)
WILLIAM KENDRICK)
Vs) Case
JOHN STEWART)

Motion by Plaintiff attorney for an appeal which was granted and gave James Stewart & James Carreway securities bound in the sum of Two hundred & thirty eight dollars and filed the following reasons for appeal (to wit) The Verdict obtained in this case is contrary to Law & Evidence. We therefore concieve that those reasons are sufficient to authorize the said appeal.

               J. B. Reynolds.

Court adjourned untill tomorrow at 9 O'clock.

Court met according to Adjournment Saturday March 25th 1809.
 Present

     Hugh McClure)
     John H. Poston) Esquires
     Sterling Niblett) Justices
     Robert Prince)

(p-181) MORGAN BROWN)
Vs) Case
THOMAS SIMMONS)

The plaintiff in this case was solemnly called came not but made default & was non suited. Therefore it is considered by the Court that the Defendant recover against the Plaintiff his costs about his suit in this behalf expended & the Plaintiff in Mercy &.

JOHN KEATHLEY, Junr.)
Vs) Debt
JAMES A BUNTING)

This day came the parties by their attornies and the Defendant relinquishing his former plea does not deny but he owes the Debt in the Declaration mentioned & that the Plaintiff hath sustained damages by reason of the detention thereof to two dollars four & one forth cents besides his costs. Therefore it is considered by the Court that the plaintiff recover against the Defendant his debt in the Declaration mentioned and his damages as by the Jury so assess in their Verdict as also his costs about his suit in this behalf expended & the Defendant in Mercy &.

96

48 Deed of Conveyance Thomas J. Overton to James Huling two thirds of a lott in Clarksville proven by William R. Gibson & John Gibson witnesses thereto and ordered to be registered.

(p-182) Same Justices on the bench.

JAMES M. REYNOLDS & JOHN R. MCFARLAND
Vs
ISRAEL ROBINSON
} Case

Jury Viz

1 David McFadden
2 Samuel Mitchell
3 Samuel Wooldridge
4 John King
5 Edmand Suter
6 John Edmonston
7 Zebedee Dennes
8 John Marshell
9 Robert W. Temple
10 Timothy Drake
11 Samuel Lynes
12 Isaac Kittrell

Who being duly elected tried & sworn the truth to speak upon the Issue joined do upon their Oaths say that the Defendant did assume upon himself in manner and form as the plaintiffs have declared against him and do assess the damages to one hundred and twenty dollars besides their costs. Therefore it is considered by the Court that the Plaintiff recover against the Defendant the damages aforesaid by the Jurors in their Verdict in form aforesaid and also their costs about their suit in this behalf expended.

Motion for an appeal by Defendants attorney which was allowed and the Defendant gives bond with John Steele & Joseph Robinson securities bound in the sum of Two hundred and forty dolla rs and files the following reasons for an Appeal 1st Verdict of the Jury was contrary to evidence and the Judgment of the Court was contrary to law which is in my oppinion sufficient reasons for the Court to grant an Appeal.

George W. L. Marr, Atty.
for Defdt.

(p-183) Covenant Bond Robert Nelson to Robert Prince for conveyance of land proven by Henry Small & William Nelson witnesses and ordered to be registered 74 acres.

Covenant Bond Robert Nelson to Robert Prince proven by Henry Small & William Nelson and ordered to be registered 110 acres.

Robert Prince, Sterling Neblett,
James Hambleton, Samuel Mitchell
Vs
WILLIAM R. HAGLER
} Covt.

Jury (Viz) No. 1

1 John Marshell
2 Samuel Allen
3 Samuel Wooldridge
4 John Edmonston
5 Robert W. Temple
6 John Teasley
7 David McFadden
8 Edmond Suter
9 Zebedee Dennes
10 John King
11 Thomas Morris
12 Able Mann

Who being duly elected tried & sworn the truth to speak upon their Oaths do say that the Defendant did not perform his covenant as the Plaintiff have declared in his Declaration and do assess the Plaintiffs damages by reason thereof to One Cent. Therefore it is considered by the Court that the Plaintiff recover against the Defendant the damages assessed by the Jurors in their Verdict with his cost about his suit in this behalf expended.

Deed of Conveyance Morgan Brown & Samuel Vance to Stephen Hendlen 227 acres James Careway & Daniel Kyle & ordered to registration.

(p-184)   Same Justices on the bench.

HUGH MCCLURE & JAMES ELDER Assignee)
    Vs   ) Debt
HUGH F. BELL & WILLIAM R. BELL)

Same Jury No. 1

Who being duly sworn the truth to speak upon the Issue joined do upon their Oaths say that the Defendant hath not paid Ninety six dollars fifty five & a half cents part of the debt in the Declaration mentioned and do assess the Plaintiffs damages by reasons of the detention thereof to Six dollars & five cents. Therefore it is considered by the Court that the Plaintiffs recover against the Defendants the debt & damages so assessed by the Jury in form aforesaid as also their costs about their suit in this behalf expended & the Defendants in Mercy & C.

Court adjourned untill Monday the 27 of March.

The Worshipful Court of Montgomery County have met according to adjournment Monday 27th March 1809.

Present

    John Blair   )
    James Hambleton) Esquires
    Sterling Niblett) Justices
    Thomas Smith)

MORGAN BROWN)
  Vs   ) Certeorari & Supersedius
SAMUEL THORNTON)

The Plaintiff by his attorney dismisses this suit. Therefore it is considered by the Court that the Defendant recover against the Plaintiff costs about his suit in this behalf expended & the Plaintiff in Mercy &.

(p-185)   STATE OF TENNESSEE) March Session
     MONTGOMERY COUNTY) 1809

On application of John Moore who claims four hundred & fifty six acres of land on the Middle fork of Blooming Grove Creek in said County of Montgomery which land was conveyed to said John Moore by Deed from one Barnabas O. Farrell to whom the same was conveyed by one John Allison who held the same by two patants from the State of North Carolina for two hundred and twenty eight acres each the one numbered three hundred and ninety five & Dated the Fifteenth day of September in the year Seventeen Hundred and Eighty Seven and begining at two populars on the West side of the Creek above a spring & tree marked runing South 160 poles to a stake thence East East 228 poles to a popular and Black Oake North 160 poles to a Walnut West

228 poles to the begining. The other baring same date & numbered 384. Begining at two populars the North West forner of the above mentioned tract runing East with the North boundary line of said tract 228 poles to a Walnut thence North 160 poles to a stake thence West 228 poles to a stake thence South 160 poles to the begining. It is ordered by the Court that the Clerk issue a Warrant directed to Duncan Stewart, Samuel Allen & Samuel Gattis fit persons to be named Commissioners they or any two of them to attend said John Moore at his dwelling house on said land and at the boundaries called for in said patent on the third Thursday in May next there to continue or to adjourn from day to day if necessary to take the Deposition of George Bell, Senr. & to do whatever else they may dem proper for assertaining the Boundaries of said land and for perpetuating the evidence thereof in persuance of the Acts of the General Assembly passed the 23rd of October 1799 intitled an Act to ascertain the Boundaries of (p-186) land and for perpetuating testimony. And that the Clerk issue a Subpoena for George Bell, Senr. to appear at the dwelling house of said John Moore on said land to be examined by said Commissioners on said Third Thursday in May next and such succeeding day as they may adjourn to as they are above authorised.

49 Deed Conveyance Israel Robinson to John Cone was asknowledged in Open Court & ordered to registeration for 220 acres of land.

Same Justices on the bench.

JAMES MILLER
Vs
Samuel Peters &
John Minott
} Debt

Jury Vs

1 Samuel Lynes
2 Samuel Allen
3 John King
4 Zebedee Dennis
5 David McFadden
6 Samuel Mitchell
7 Samuel Wooldridge
8 Edmond Suter
9 Robert Pollock
10 John Teasley
11 George Pollock
12 Moses Parker

Who being duly elected tried & sworn the truth to speak upon the Issue joined upon their Oaths do say that the Defendants hath not paid the Debt in the Declaration mentioned & do assess the Plaintiffs damages by reason of the detention thereof to Eight dollars & forty eight cents. Therefore it is considered by the Court that the Plaintiff recover against the Defendants the D$_e$bt & damages so assessed by the Jury in form as also his costs about his suit in this behalf expended & the Defendant in Mercy &.

(p-187) Same Justices on the bench.

JOHN H. POSTON Surviving Partner
of King & Poston
Vs
WILLIAM GORDON
} Debt

The Defendant in this case waves the Issue and does not deny that he owes the Debt in the Declaration mentioned and that the Plaintiff hath sustained damages by reason of the detention thereof to ten dollars & twenty five cents. Therefore it is considered by the Court that the Plaintiff recover against the Defendant the D_bt in the Declaration mentioned &

damages as assessed by the Jury in their Verdict and also their costs of suit in this behalf expended.

Same Justices on the bench.

JOHN STEWART
Vs
JAMES A. BUNTING

The Defendant in this case does not deny that he owes the debt in the Declaration mentioned and that the Plaintiff hath sustained damages by reason of the detention thereof to ten dollars & twenty five cents. Therefore it is considered by the Court that the Plaintiff recover against the Defendant the debt in the Declaration mentioned & damages as assessed by the Jury in their Verdict and also their costs of suit in this behalf expended.

Same Justices on the bench.

(p-188) CURDWELL BREATHELL
Vs
WILLIAM FARRIOR

Case

Ordered that a D. P. T. Issue to Logan County State of Kentucky to take the Deposition of William Whitsell, Abel Brown & George Morris to be read in evidence in favour of the Plaintiff twenty five days notice to be given to the Defendant.

Same Justices

JESSE COBB
Vs
STERLING INGRAM

Debt

Jury No. 2

1 John Marshall
2 Samuel Allen
3 John King
4 Zebedee Dennes
5 David McFadden
6 Samuel Mitchell
7 Samuel Wooldridge
8 Edmond Suter
9 Robert Pollock
10 John Teasley
11 George Pollock
12 Moses Parker

Being duly elected tried & sworn the truth to speak upon the Issue joined do upon their Oaths say that they find that the Defendant hath not paid the debt in the Declaration mentioned & damages as assessed by the Jury in their Verdict in manner & form with costs of suit.

(p-189) John Blair, Sterling Neblett, Thomas Smith.

SAMUEL VANCE & BRADLEY Surviving
Partners of VANCE, KING & BRADLEY
Vs
JAMES EDWARDS

Debt

Same Jury No. 2

Being duly elected tried & sworn the truth to speak upon the Issue joined do upon their Oaths say that they that find that Defendant hath not paid the debt in the Declaration mentioned & do assess the Plaintiff damages by reason of the Detention thereof to seven dollars & forty six cents. Therefore it is considered by the Court that the Plaintiffs recover against the Defendant the debt in the Declaration mentioned and damages as assessed by the Jury in their Verdict with their costs about their suit in this behalf expended.

Court adjourned for two hours.

Court met according to adjournment.
Present

> John Blair
> Sterling Niblett   } Esquires
> James Hambleton

(p-190) CHARLES ANDERSON
Vs   } Debt
JAMES A. BUTTING

The Defendant in this case waves the Issue and does not deny that he owes the debt in the Declaration mentioned and that the Plaintiff hath sustained damages by reason of the Detention thereof to Eight Dollars twenty seven cents. Therefore it is considered by the Court that the plaintiff recover against the Defendant the debt in the Declaration mentioned with his damages with costs of suit in this behalf expended.

SAMUEL VANCE & JOHN BRADLEY
Surviving Partners of VANCE, KING & BRADLEY } Debt
Vs
LEWIS THOMPSON

The Defendant in this case waves the Issue and does not deny that, but what he owes Eighty six Dollars & Ninety cents part of the debt in the Declaration mentioned and that the Plaintiff hath sustained damages by reason of the detention thereof to Six Dollars Sixty five Cents. Therefore it is considered by the Court that the Plaintiffs recover against the Defendant part of the debt in the Declaration mentioned and the damages with their costs of suit in this behalf expended & the Defendant in Mercy.

MCCLURE & ELDER
Vs   } Case
ISAAC SHELBY

Demurrer overruled & writ of inquiry awarded to next Term.

(p-191) JAMES MOORE
Vs   } Debt
WILLIAM BENNETT

The Defendant in this case waves the Issues and does not deny that he owes the debt in the Declaration mentioned and that the Plaintiff hath sustained damages by reason of the detention thereof to Five Dollars forty seven cents. Therefore it is considered by the Court that the Plaintiff recover against the Defendant the debt in the Declaration mentioned with his damages as aforesaid and also his costs about his suit in this behalf expended & that the Defendant be in Mercy & .

BENJAMIN PORTER, Assee)
Vs) Debt
ISAAC MORGAN)

The Defendant in this case waves the Issues and does not deny that he owes part of the debt in the Declaration mentioned of One Hundred & forty seven Dollars twenty nine cents and the damages Four Dollars sixty seven cents. Therefore it is considered by the Court that the Plaintiff recover against the Defendant the debt in the Declaration mentioned as assessed by the Jury in their Verdict with his costs of suit.

(p-192) JAMES BAXTOR, JAMES JACKSON)
& WASHINGTON JACKSON)
Vs) Case
TIMOTHY DRAKE)

The Defendant in this case does not deny but that he did assume as the Plaintiff in declaring against him hath alledged & relinquishing his former agrees that the Plaintiff hath sustained damages to the amount of Three Hundred & One Dollars & Eighty six cents. Therefore it is considered by the Court that the Plaintiff recover against the Defendant the damages as he has declared in his Declaration with his costs of suit.

MCCLURE & ELDER)
Vs) Debt
TIMOTHY DRAKE)

The Defendant in this case withdraws his plea & does not deny the debt in the Declaration mentioned & that the Plaintiff has sustained damages by reason of the detention thereof to Five Dollars. Therefore it is considered by the Court that the Plaintiff recover against the Defendant the debt in the Declaration mentioned with the damages & costs about their suit in this behalf expended.

(p-193) JAMES MOORE)
Vs) O. Attachment
FRANCIS HUBBARD)

On motion of the Plaintiffs attorney & it appearing from the return of Charles Moore Constable that a writ of Fiere Facias Issued by Samuel Vance Esquire Justice of the peace for the County of Montgomery in favour of said Plaintiff against said Defendant for the sum of Twenty Seven Dollars with cost of former suit & lawfull interest being levied by said Constable on Three Hundred acres of land more or less the place where William Porter now lives on the waters of Yellow Creek this 10 day of January 1809.
It is ordered and considered by the Court that a writ of Venditioni Exponas Issue to expose to sale the said tract of land to satisfy the judgment & cost aforesaid & costs of suit.
Court adjourned untill tomorrow at 8 O'clock.

The Worshipful Court of Montgomery County have met according to adjournment Tuesday Mar. 28th 1809
Present –

John Blair
Sterling Niblett } Esquires Justices
Hugh McClure
Saml. Vance

(p-194) SAMUEL VANCE & JOHN BRADLEY } Samuel Vance Esq.
Surviving Partners of VANCE, KING & BRADLEY } withdrew
Vs } Original Attach-
FRANCIS HUBBARD } ment.

On motion of the Plaintiff's attorney and it appearing from the return of Charles Moore Constable that a writ of Original Attachment issued by James Moore Esquire Justice of the peace for the County of Montgomery in favour of said Plaintiffs against said Defendant for the sum of Fifteen Dollars Eighteen & three forths cents, with costs that he had levied the same on three hundred acres of land more or less on the waters of Yellow Creek the place where William Parker now lives 12th January 1809.

It is ordered & considered by the Court that a writ of Venditioni Exponas Issue to expose to sale the said tract of land to satisfy the said Judgement & cost of suit.

John Bailey gave bond with Augustine Lunsford his security bound in the sum of sixty nine dollars for the safe keeping & feeding Benjamin Smith an Insane person for twelve months from the date of the said Bond ordered that said John Baily be entitled to the same agreeably & that the County Trustee pay the same.

STATE
Vs } Indictment
SAMUEL PETERS

On motion of the Defendant Attorney for a new trial the case being argued & considered by the Court it is the opinion of the Court that no new trial be granted and that the Defendant be fined in the sum of Twenty five Dollars & costs of suit in this behalf expended from which Judgment the Defendant appeals & gives bond with James Hambleton & Joseph Woolfolk his securities bound in the sum of Four Hundred Dollars.

(p-195) JOHN H. POSTON, Assee }
Vs } Debt
WILLIAM GORDON }

The Defendant in this case waves his his plea and does not does not deny that he hath not paid one hundred dollars part of the debt in the Declaration mentioned and that the Plaintiff hath sustained damages by reason of the detention thereof to the sum of four dollars ninety eight cents. Therefore it is considered by the Court that the Plaintiff recover against the Defendant the sum of one hundred and four dollars & ninety eight cents with his cost of suit in this behalf expended.

Same Justices on the bench.

ISRAEL ROBINSON }
Vs } Case
WILLIAM M. BELL }
Jury No. 1.

1 John Marshell
2 David McFaden
3 John Edmonston
4 Edmond Suter
5 Samuel Allen
6 Samuel Wooldridge
7 John King
8 Samuel Mitchell
9 John Teasley
10 Robert Pollock
11 Zebedee Dennes
12 Robert W. Temple

Who being duly elected tried & sworn the truth to speak upon the Issue joined do upon their Oaths say that they find damages to the Plaintiff Seventy five Dollars. Therefore it is considered by the Court that the Plaintiff recovered against the Defendant the damages so assessed by the Jury in their Verdict and also his cost of suit in this behalf expended.

(p-196) Joseph Woolfolk is allowed License to keep a Tavern in his own dwelling house in Port royal he gives bond with James Huling his security bound for his complying with the Acts of Assembly in such case made and provided.

James Huling is allowed License to keep a Tavern at his dwelling house in Clarksville he gave bond with Joseph Woolfolk his security bound to comply with the Acts of Assembly in such case made & provided.

Same Justices on the bench.

FRANCES LONG
Vs } Ca.ss
SELAH PICKETT Admx of CHARLES PICKETT? Dd.

Jury No. 2

1 Reuben Grayson
2 John Brown
3 Jesse Cooksey
4 Isaac Kittrell
5 Absolum Tribble
6 William Gordon
7 James Loggans
8 William Mathews
9 Jesse Isaacs
10 Arthur Williams
11 James Grant
12 Israel Robinson

Who being duly elected tried & sworn the truth to speak upon the Issue joined do upon their Oaths say that they find for the Plaintiff & assess his damage to Three Hundred and One Dollars & ninety five cents. Therefore it is considered by the Court that the Plaintiff recover against the said Defendant the damages so assessed by the Jury in their Verdict and also his costs about his suit in this behalf expended & that the Defendant be in Mercy &.

(p-197) REYNOLDS & MCFARLAND) Debt. &
Vs } Ind'l.
WILLIAM BARTON) Attacht.

Same Jury No. 2

Who being duly elected tried & sworn the truth to speak upon the Issue joined do upon their Oaths say that they find that the Defendant hath not paid the debt in the Declaration mentioned & do by reason of the detention thereof assess the plaintiff damages to Nine Dollars Sixty five and a half cents. Therefore it is considered by the Court that the Plaintiff recover against the Defendant the Debt in the Declaration mentioned & damages assessed by the Jury and their costs of suit in this behalf expended.

James Baxter, John Blair & Joseph Woolfolk.

SAMUEL C. HAWKINS &
SAMUEL THORNTON } Serenarari
Vs
THOMAS GREEN

In this case the Plaintiffs Attorney moves that agreeable to the Petition that the two suits be consolidated into one which was agreed to.
The Administrators of James Ford Decd. rendered in Court on account of the sale of the property of the said Deceased. And also an additional Inventory of the said Deceased estate.

(p-198) SAMUEL C. HAWKINS
& SAMUEL THORNTON } Certiorari
Vs
THOMAS GREEN
Jury No. 2

Who being sworn the truth to speak upon the controversy between the parties do upon their Oaths say that they find for the Plaintiff Thirteen Dollars Ninety seven Cents. Therefore it is considered by the Court that the Plaintiff recover against the Defendant Thomas Green and Guthridge Lyons his security the debt so assessed by the Jury in form aforesaid and also their costs about their suit in this behalf expended.

SAMUEL C. HAWKINS &
SAMUEL THORNTON Assee } Certiorari
Vs
THOMAS GREEN
Jury No. 2

Who being sworn the truth to speak upon the controversy between the parties do say that they find for the plaintiffs Eleven Dollars & Sixty six cents. Therefore it is considered by the Court that the Plaintiff recover against the Defendant, Thomas Green & Guthridge Lyons his security the debt so assessed by the Jury in form aforesaid, and their costs about their suit in this behalf expended.

(p-199) On petition of Hugh McCollum it is ordered by the Court that writs of Certiorari & Supersedeas Issue to bring into Court all the papers in the suit George Wilson & John Easton had before Hugh McClure, Esq.

JOHN JONES
Vs } Appeal
ARTHUR WILLIAMS
Jury No. 1

Who being duly elected & sworn the truth to speak upon the controversy between the parties do say that they find for the Defendant. Therefore it is considered by the Court that the Defendant recover against the Plaintiff the his costs about his suit in this behalf expended & the Plaintiff In Mercy &.

On motion ordered that the Petition filed by Mary Waggoner, Sarah Odeneal, Thomas Joyce, Zachariah Robinson, Heirs of Adam Tate for the partition of the tract of _____ acres of land on the South side of Cumberland River granted to said Adam Tate be continued untill next Court.

DIXON LOGANS)
Vs) Si fa
JAMES LOGGANS)

The Defendant was called and failed to appear & Judgment was entered up according to Siere facias. Therefore it is considered by the Court that the Plaintiff recover against the Defendant according to Siere facias & his costs of suit in this behalf expended. The Plaintiff releases Eighteen Dollars of this Judgment.

(p-200) Court adjourned untill tomorrow at 9 O'clock.
The Worshipful Court of Montgomery County have met according to Adjournment Wednesday March 29, 1809
Present
    Hugh McClure)
    John R. Poston) Esquires Justices
    James Baxter)

STATE)
Vs) Indictment Appeal
SAMUEL PETERS) Reasons for Appeal

The Verdict was manifestly unjust and contrary to evidence and the Judgement was highly oppressive which in my oppinion are sufficient reasons for the Court here to allow an Appeal to the Superior Court.
           H. Minor Atty. for Defendt.

Robert Wells, Thompson Harris, Alexander Faith, Peter Cocke & Stephen Cocke who were appointed at January term 1799 Commissioners to run out and divide one thousand acres of land entered in the name of William Terrell, Lewis and William Terrell formally having made return thereof to the Court but having been neglected to be entered on the Minutes-
On motion to the Court it is ordered to be recorded & committed to registeration.

THOMAS MARTIN & CO.)
Vs) Appeal Motion
JAMES MCFARLAE) for new trial.

Motion overruled.

(p-201) WILLIAM CLEMENTS & JOHN H. HYDE
Vs
CHARLES MOORE & His Securities
BENJAMIN HAWKINS & ISAAC MORGAN.

On motion of the Plaintiffs by their attorney it is ordered that the Plaintiffs recover against the said Charles Moore Constable & Benjamin Hawkins, Isaac Morgan his Securities the sum of Thirty Nine Dollars & Sixty three cents the principle and Ninety Three & three fourth cents

106

costs, the amount of a Judgement recovered before Samuel Vance Esq. against Amos Rochell in favour of said Clements & Hyde, and also their costs about their motion in this behalf expended.

On motion it is ordered by the Court that the now dwelling house of Samuel Lynes be included within the parson bounds if not before included.

James Baxtor, John H. Poston, Samuel Vance Esquires on the bench.

HUGH MCCLURE & JAMES ELDER
Vs
DANIEL WILLIAMS } Debt

Demurrer overruled.

MCCLURE & ELDER
Vs
WILLIAM E. WILLIAMS } Debt Demurrer overruled and Judgment final, Therefore it is considered by the Court that the Plaintiff recover against the Defendant the sum of Seventy Dollars with Five Dollars 25 cents interest, and his costs of suit in this behalf expended.

(p-202)   State of Tennessee Montgomery County March Sessions 1809.
John Cocke Esq. Sheriff and Collector of the State and County Court House & prison taxes for the year 1808 reports to the Court that the taxes remain unpaid on the following tracts of land and he knows of no goods & chattels within this County whereon he can distress to wit.

James Perkins-100 acres not said where it is.
Dixon Loggans-200 acres Barron fork of Barton's Creek.
Alexander Tate-1280 acres a part of Adam Tate on Buds Creek. Heirs Adam Tate-2500 acres South side Cumberland River.
John Benham-550 acres Barren fork Barton's Creek.
Martin Goss-55 acres Barton's Creek
Daniel Anderson-640 acres Yellow Creek Waters,
Heirs of John Daves-3840 acres mouth Barton's Creek.
John Meares-1280 Fletcher's Fork Red River.
James McRoberts-320 acres mouth West Fork.
Bennet Searcy-150½ acres joining Clarksville & in Clarksville the following Town Lotts. No. 22, 23, 24, 25, 36, 37, 38, 64, 35 & half 74.
Thomas Tomison-640 in the Barrons.
Heirs of Seven Powell 3200 East Fork of Yellow Creek.
Amos Rochel-345 East Fork of Yellow Creek.
Thomas Waters-150 near Palmyra.
John Weakley-150 on Cumberland River by Deed.
Spencer Griffin-640 mouth West Fork
Moseley Peter-194 not said where it lies.
John Odeneal-500 West Fork

(p-203)   HUGH MCCLURE &
JAMES ELDER
Vs
DANIEL WILLIAMS } Debt

Demurrer overruled & Judgment final. Therefore it is considered by the Court that the Plaintiff recover against the Defendant Fifty three Dollars twenty eight cents with Six Dollars thirty nine cents interest

with their costs of suit in this behalf expended.
The Court adjourned for two hours.

Court met according to adjournment
Present
    Hugh McClure)
    Samuel Vance)
    John H. Poston)

Court adjourned untill tomorrow 9 O'clock.

Court met according to adjournment 20th March 1809
Present
    James Hambleton)
    John H. Poston) Esquires
    Hugh McClure) Justices
    James Baxter)

(p-204) STATE OF TENNESSEE) March Session
    MONTGOMERY COUNTY) 1809.

  John Cooke Esq. Sheriff and Collector of the State and County Tax for the year 1806, 1807, 1808 & 1809, reports to the Court that 136 acres of land on Macadoo Creek supposed to belong to the Heirs of William Perry, Deceased was not given in for taxation for the year 1808 also that 5840 acres near Palmyra on the South side of Cumberland River was not given in for taxation for the year 1808. Also that 640 acres on Parsons Creek supposed to belong to John McFerson was not given in for taxation for said year of 1808 also that 160 acres on Red River supposed to belong to the Heirs of Charles Brantley Decd. was not given in for taxation for the said year 1808. Also that 1417 acres on Parsons Creek supposed to belong to the Heirs of Thomas Parsons Deceased was not given in for taxation for the said year 1808. Also that 228 acres on Parsons Creek supposed to belong to the Heirs of Thomas Parsons was not given in for taxation for the year 1808. Also that 25 acres on Spring supposed to belong to Robert Young was not given in for taxation for the year 1808. Also that one Town Lott in Portroyal supposed to belong to John Dunn or James McFarland was not given in for taxation for the year 1808. Also that 640 acres supposed to belong to John McFerson lying on Parsons Creek was not given in for taxation for the year 1808. Also that 1428 acres on Red River supposed to belong to Doct. Samuel Cooley was not given in for the year 1808. Also that 640 acres granted to Elijah Robertson by Patent No. 1649 was not given in for taxation for the year 1808. Also that 640 acres granted to John Nelson & Alexander Nelson by Patent No. 1650 was not given in for taxation for the year 1808. Also that 151 acres a part of a large tract granted to Thomas Molloy by Patent and lying next the begining corner of said tract No. 2988 was not given in for taxation for the year 1808.

(p-205) On motion ordered that John Cooke Shff. have a credit with the District Treasurer & the County Trustees & Commissioners of the Publick Buildings for the year 1807 on the following persons as being Insolvent, to wit.
 William Hogan one white poll - $0.43-3/4
 Charles Smith " " " - .43-3/4

Joseph Moss	one white poll	$0.43-3/4
Willis Holland	" " "	.43-3/4
John Henderson	" " "	.43-3/4
James Burnes	" " "	.43-3/4
John Dean	" " "	.43-3/4
Eli Smith	" " "	.43-3/4
George Thomas	" " "	.43-3/4
Evan Gaskell	" " "	.43-3/4
Allen Morgan	" " "	.43-3/4
Nathaniel Blackwell	" " "	.43-3/4
Joseph Baker	" " "	.43-3/4
John Fletcher	" " "	.43-3/4
Edwin Gore	" " "	.43-3/4
Robert Norman	" " "	.43-3/4
Job Wallace	" " "	.43-3/4
Ezekiel Black	" " "	.43-3/4
Thomas Wallace	" " "	.43-3/4
William Baker	" " "	.43-3/4
Pleasant Cashen	" " "	.43-3/4
Nathan Blackwell	" " "	.43-3/4
Vinson Ennis	" " "	.43-3/4
Shadrick Gardner	" " "	.43-3/4
William McClure	" " "	.43-3/4
John McClure	" " "	.43-3/4
Jonathan Stephenson	" " "	.43-3/4
Herring Taylor	" " "	.43-3/4
Thomas Flack	" " " & one black	1.31¼
John Whitledge	" " "	.43-3/4

(p-206) On motion ordered that John Cocke Sheriff have a credit with the District Treasurer the County Trustees & the Commissioners of the Public Buildings for the year 1808 on the following persons as being insolvent, to wit.

Isiah Gattis	One white poll	$0.43-3/4
Reuben Chisenhall	" " "	.43-3/4
William Woods	" " "	.43-3/4
Isaac Gattis	" " "	.43-3/4
Nicholas Green	" " "	.43-3/4
John Keathley, Junr.	" " "	.43-3/4
James McKee	" " "	.43-3/4
Saunders Moore	" " "	.43-3/4
Andrew Murphy	" " "	.43-3/4
John Ross	" " "	.43-3/4
Thomas Watkins	" " "	.43-3/4
James Graves	" " "	.43-3/4
Robert Saunderson	" " "	.43-3/4
John Whitledge	" " "	.43-3/4
Andrew Walker	" " "	.43-3/4
Ashel Duncan	" " "	.43-3/4
Philip Duff	" " "	.43-3/4
William Jones	" " "	.43-3/4
William Moore	" " "	.43-3/4
John Mitchell	" " "	.43-3/4

David Morris	one white poll		$0.43-3/4
James Nicholas	" " "		.43-3/4
Roland Vick	" " "		.43-3/4
William Justice	" " "		.43-3/4
Joseph Montgomery	" " "		.43-3/4
Philip Henderson	" " "		.43-3/4
John Minn	" " "		.43-3/4
Robert Rushing	" " "		.43-3/4
William Trice	" " "		.43-3/4
Thomas Dean	" " "		.43-3/4
Daniel Tucker	" " "		.43-3/4
Joseph Hall	" " "		.43-3/4
Peter Hubbard, Junr.	" " "		.43-3/4
William Knight	" " "		.43-3/4
John Lockener	" " "		.43-3/4
Eli Senny	" " "		.43-3/4
Lewis Thomas	" " "		.43-3/4
John D. F. Campbell	" " "		.43-3/4
George Murphy	" " "		.43-3/4

(p-207)

Richard Acoff	" " "		.43-3/4
Henry Bivel	" " "		.43-3/4
John McLandon	" " "		.43-3/4
Asa Briggs	" " "		.43-3/4
George Robertson	5 black "		2.42-3/4

John H. Poston Esq. withdrawn.

John H. Poston surviving Partner of
    KING & POSTON   }
          Vs   } O. Attachment
    DAVID SLOCUMB }

On motion of the Plaintiffs attorney and it apearing from the return of Charles Moore Constable that a writ of original attachment issued by James Baxter Esq. Justice of the peace for the County of Montgomery, in favour of said Plaintiffs against said Defendant for the sum of Eighteen Dollars Eighty three cents with costs that he had levied the same on a tract of land in Montgomery County one hundred and sixty acres it being a part of a tract granted to James Berry by the State of North Carolina this 22d March 1809. Therefore it is considered by the Court that a writ of Venditioni Exponas Issue to expose to sale the said tract of land to satisfy the said Judgement & costs of suit.

Samuel Vance & John Bradley,)surviving Partners of
    VANCE, KING & BRADLEY)
           Vs   )
      EDMOND SUTER   )

On motion of the Plaintiffs attorney and it appearing from the return made by Charles Moore Constable a writ of Fiere Facias issued by Sterling Neblett Esq. a Justice of the peace for Montgomery County in (p-208) favour of said Plaintiff against said Defendant for the sum of Thirty eight

Dollars Ninety one & one forth cents and costs of suit I have livied on one hundred acres of land more or less in this County the place where he now lives. It is considered by the Court that a writ of Venditioni Exponas Issue to expose to sale the said tract of land to satisfy the Judgment and costs of of suit in this behalf expended.

SAME)
Vs)
SAME)

On motion of Plaintiffs attorney and it appearing from the return made by Charles Moore Constable that a Writ of Fieri Facias issued by James Moore Esq. Justice of the peace for Montgomery in favour of said Plaintiffs against said Defendant (p-209) for the sum of Forty Six Dollars three cents and costs of suit. I have levied on one hundred acres of land the place where he now lives this 16th Jany. 1809. It is therefore considered by the Court that a writ of Venditioni Exponas Issue to expose to sale the said tract of land to satisfy the Judgement and costs of suit in this behalf expended.

Samuel Vance & John Bradley, Surviving partners of
VANCE, KING & BRADLEY)
Vs)
ROBERT RUSHING & BENJAMIN HAWKINS his Security)

On motion of the Plaintiffs attorney and it appearing by the return of Charles Moore Constable that a Writ of Fiere Facias issued from James Moore Esq. Justice of the peace for Montgomery County in favour of said Plaintiff against said Defendant for the sum off Thirty Dollars Twenty five cents and cost of suit. I have levied the same on three hundred acres of land more or less the place where B. Hawkins now lives this 10th March 1809. It is therefore considered by the Court that a Writ of Venditioni Exponas Issue to expose to sale the said tract of land to satisfy the Judgment & costs of suit in this behalf expended.

Vance & Bradley Surviving partners of
VANCE, KING & BRADLEY)
Vs) O. Attachment
MARTIN GOSS)

On motion of the Plaintiffs attorney and it appearing from the return of Jesse Sullivant (p-210) Constable that a Writ of original attachment issued by Samuel Smith Esq. Justice of the peace for Montgomery County in favour of said Plaintiff against said Defendant for the sum of Twenty four Dollars four & a half cents with costs.

I have levied on a certain tract of land lying on the South side of the middle fork of Barton's Creek supposed to be the property of Martin Goss adjoining or bound on Mr. William Sullivan's line & Mr. James Trotter's line, Mr. William Hightower's line supposed to be fifty acres or upward I say levied upon by me this day and date above written. Therefore it is considered by the Court that a writ of Venditoni Exponas issued to expose to sale the said tract of land to satisfy the said debt with costs of suit in this behalf expended.

Samuel Vanse & John Bradley, surviving partners of
VANCE, KING & BRADLEY
     Vs   } O. Attachment
JOHN C. THOMAS

On motion of the Plaintiffs attorney and it appearing from the return made by John H. Hyde Depy. Sheriff for Montgomery County that an original attachment issued from James Moore Esq. Justice of the peace for the said County for the sum of Twenty seven Dollars fifteen & three forths cents with costs. I have levied on the tract of land whereon James Bagget now lives at the head waters of the West fork of Bud's Creek containing 100 acres more or less also summoned Stephen Thomas as Garneshee to appear in Palmyra Saturday next. Therefore it is considered by the Court that a writ of Venditioni Exponas Issue to expose to sale the land levied on to satisfy the Judgment and costs of suit in this behalf expended.

(p-211)   WILLIAM CLEMENTS
          SAMUEL THORNTON &
          HOWEL TATUM   } Fi fa
              Vs
          BENJAMIN HAWKINS

On motion of the Plaintiffs attorney and it appearing by the return of Charles Moore Constable that a Writ of Feiri facias issed from James Moore Esq. Justice of the peace for Montgomery County for the sum of Twenty five Dollars & twenty five cents in favour of the Plaintiffs against the Defendant with costs of suit.

I have levied on 300 acres of land more or less the place where he now lives this 15th March 1809. Therefore it is considered by the Court that a Writ of Venditioni Exponas issue to expose to sale the said tract of land to satisfy the Judgment & costs of suit in this behalf expended.

        MCCLURE & ELDER
            Vs   } O. Attachment
        JOHN C. THOMAS

On motion of the Plaintiffs attorney and it appearing from the return of John H. Hyde D. Shff. for Montgomery County that an Original Attachment issued from John H. Poston Esquire Justice of the peace for Montgomery County for the sum of Sixty nine Dollars eighty two cents & interest with costs of suit.

I have levied on a plantation whereon James Bagget now lives at the head of the West fork of Budds Creek containing of 100 acres more or less 7th Feby. 1809. Therefore it is considered by the Court that a Writ of Venditioni Exponas issue to expose to sale the land levied on to satisfy the Judgment with the costs in this behalf expended.

(p-212)   HUGH MCCLURE & JAMES ELDER
                Vs   } Fi fa
          GEDEON MILLS & TIMOTHY DRAKE

On motion of the plaintiff attorney and it appearing from the return made by Daniel Anderson Constable for Montgomery County that a Fiere facias as issued from James Hambleton Esquire Justice of the peace for Montgomery County for the sum of Thirty seven Dollars nineteen & three forths cents with lawfull interest in favour of the Plaintiffs against the said Defendant with cost of suit.

I have levied 10th Inflant. on house & lott in new addition of Clarksville property of Timothy Drake. Therefore it is considered by the Court that a Writ of Venditioni Exponas issue to expose to sale the said lott & house to satisfy the Judgement & costs of suit in this behalf expended.

  WILLIAM CLIFTON
    Vs
  MARTIN GOSS

On motion of the Plaintiffs attorney and it appearing from the return of Jesse Sullivan Constable for Montgomery County that a Fiere facias issued from Samuel Smith Esquire Justice of the peace for Montgomery County for the sum of Forty seven Dollars eighteen and one forth cents.

I have levied the execution on one certain tract of land lying on the South side of the middle fork of Barton's Creek supposed to be the property of Martin Goss adjoining or bounding on Mr. Sullivans line and Mr. James Trotter's line, Mr. William Hightower's supposed to be fifty acres or upwards I say levied on by me this day & date above written,

(p-213) Therefore it is considered by the Court that a Writ of Venditioni Exponas issue to expose to sale the said land to satisfy the Judgment and costs aforesaid in this behalf expended.

  GEORGE WESTNER
    Vs
  MARTIN GOSS

On motion of the Plaintiffs attorney and it appearing from the return made by Jesse Sullivan Constable for Montgomery County that a Feire facias issued from Samuel Smith Esquire a Justice of the Peace for Montgomery County for the sum of Forty one Dollars twenty seven cents.

I have levied this execution upon one certain tract of land lying on the South side of the middle fork of Barton's Creek supposed to be the property of Martin Goss adjoining on William Sullivan line & Mr. James Trotter line & Mr. William Hightower line supposed to be fifty acres or upwards I say levyed by me. Therefore it is considered by the Court that a Writ of Venditioni Exponas issue to expose to sale the said tract of land to satisfy the Judgment & costs of suit in this behalf expended.

  SAMUEL PETERS & JOHN MINOTT
    Vs   Debt
  MARTIN GOSS

On motion of the Plaintiff's attorney and it appearing by the return made by Jesse Sullivan Constable that a Feire facias issued from Smith Esquire Justice of the peace for Montgomery County for the sum of Forty three Dollars sixteen cents,

I have levied this execution on one certain tract of land lying on the South side of the middle fork of Barton's Creek supposed to be the property of Martin Goss adjoining or bounding on Mr. William Sullivan's line & Mr. James Trotter's line & Mr. William Hightower's line supposed to be fifty acres or (p-214) upward. It is considered by the Court that a Writ of Venditioni Exponas issue to expose to sale the said land to satisfy the Judgment and costs of suit in this behalf expended.

REYNOLDS & MCFARLAND)
Vs)
WILLIAM BARTON)

Motion for new trial which was granted gave bond with William Bearden & John Barton his securities bound in the sum of Four hundred & forty eight Dollars fifty three cents.

Reasons for appeal that the Defendant is not ready to pay the money which in my oppinion is sufficient reasons why an appeal at his request should be granted.

On motion ordered that James Carraway have license to to keep a Tavern at his dwelling house in Clarksville he gave bond with James Hambleton & his securities bound in the sum of five hundred Dollars for his complying with the Acts of the Assembly in such case.

PETER BRAWNER & JOHN H. HYDE) Debt
Vs) Juditial
SAMUEL HANDLEY) Attacht.

Dismissed by the Plaintiffs attorney. Therefore it is considered by the Court that the Defendants recover against the Plaintiffs his costs of about his suit in this behalf expended & the Plaintiff in Mercy &.

WILLIAM JONES & COMPANY)
VS) Case
DANIEL MCCAULEY)

Dismissed by Plaintiffs attorney. Therefore it is considered by the Court that the Defendant recovered against the Plaintiffs his costs about his suit in this behalf expended.

(p=215) THOMAS MARTIN & CO.)
Vs) Debt
RALPH WILLIAMS)

Dismissed by Thomas Martin one of the partners. Therefore it is considered by the Court that the Defendant recover against the Plaintiffs his costs of suit in this behalf expended.

CLEMENTS & HYDE Assee)
VS) Covenant
SAMUEL LYNES)

Dismissed by Plaintiff the Defendant assumes all costs. Therefore it is considered by the Court that the Plaintiff recover against the Defendant their costs of suit in this behalf expended.

VANCE, KING & BRADLEY)
Vs) Debt
JOSEPH PEBRICE)

Two cases both dismissed by Plaintiffs attorney & Defendant assumes all costs. Therefore it is considered by the Court that the Plaintiffs recover their costs of suit in this behalf expended.

JAMES BAXTER & CO.)
Vs) Debt
JOSEPH PEBR CE)

The Plaintiff dismissed the suit & Defendant assumes all costs. Therefore it is considered by the Court that the Plaintiffs recover against the Defendant their costs of suit in this behalf expended.

DIXON LOGGINS)
Vs) Sci fa
JAMES LOGGINS)

The Defendant being solemnly called but made default therefore Judgment according to Seirie facias. Therefore it is considered by the Court that the Plaintiff recover against the Defendant his debt agreeable to Sci fa amounting to Thirty Dollars & seventy five cents & Thirty Dollars forty three & one half cents as former costs as also his costs about his suit in this behalf expended & the Defendant in Mercy &.

(p-216) Court adjourned untill tomorrow 9 O'clock.
Court met according to Adjournment 31st March 1809.
Present

James Hambleton)
Hugh McClure) Esquires
James Baxter)

JOHN H. POSTON, Surviving partner of
KING AND POSTON)
Vs)
TIMOTHY DRAKE)

On motion of the Plaintiffs attorney and it appearing from the return of Henry Small Deputy Sheriff that a Fieri Facias issued from James Baxter Esquire a Justice of the peace for Montgomery County for the sum of Forty Dollars three and three fourths cents. Levied on two Town lotts in now addition to Clarksville where said Drake now lives number seventeen and Eighteen. Therefore it is considered by the Court that a Writ of Venditioni Exponas issue to expose to sale the said lotts to satisfy the Judgment and costs of suit in this behalf expended.

(p-217) SAMUEL VANCE & JOHN BRADLEY, Surviving partners of
VANCE, KING & BRADLEY)
Vs) O. Attaht.
PHILLIP HAWKINS)

On motion of the Plaintiffs attorney and it appearing to the Court that from a return made by Charles Moore, Constable that an Original Attached from James Moore Esq. and that he had levied the same on Sundry Articles the property of the Defendant. It is therefore ordered by the Court that a Writ of Venditioni Exponas issue to expose to sale the said property so attached to satisfy the debt of the Plaintiffs and their costs of suit in this behalf expended.

50 Deed of Conveyance Hugh McClure & James Elder to James Baxter & Co. for 353 acres acknowledged in Court & ordered to registeration. Court adjourned until Court in Course.

        James Baxter
        James Hambleton
        Hugh McClure J. P.
        John H. Poston

(p-218) The Worshipful Court of Montgomery County have met according to Adjournment Monday the 19th June 1809.
Present

     Thomas Smith   )
     Sterling Neblett) Esquires
     John McCauley   ) Justices
     James Hambleton)
     Samuel Gattis   )

Panal for the Grand Jury

1 Bryan Whitfield, Foreman 9 Hugh Tennen
2 John Dikas 10 John Henderson
3 William Folk 11 Henry Williams
4 John Hignight 12 William Cohoon
5 William Curlew 13 James Stewart
6 William Ford 14 Isaac Kittrell
7 John Trousdale 15 William Morrow
8 Joshua P. Vaughn

Who being elected & sworn retired to enquire for the body of the County served four days & was dismissed.

Daniel Anderson sworn Constable to attend the Grand Jury proved four days attendance & is allowed agreeable to law.

William R. Gibson produced a Commission as a Justice of the peace for Montgomery County from under the hand and seal of his excellency John Sevier Govenor of this State he took the Oath of qualification and also the Oath of office as Justice of the peace.

1 Deed of Conveyance Edmond Suter to John Lindsey was proven by the Oath of Richard Whitehead & Isham Trotter witnesses thereto & ordered to be registered 100 acres.

(p-219) Power of attorney James Dickson Senr. to William Dickson was proven by the Oath of Michael Dickson a subscribing witness thereto who also proves that Edward McGowin and John McGowen the other witness thereto does reside in North Carolina as he believes. The Court ordered it to registeration. This day came Rebecca Downs widow of William Downs and filed her petition prayin this Court to direct their writ to the Sheriff of this County commanding him to summon a Jury according to the Acts of the General Assembly in such case made & provided to set off her Dower in one hundred & twenty acres of land as described in her petition and it appearing to the satisfaction of the Court that the said Rebecca had give notice ten days previousu to filing her petition to the heir and administrator of said interstate. It is therefore ordered by the Court that the Clerk of the County direct his writ to the sheriff of said County commanding him to summon twelve free holders neither connected by affinity or consanguanity and entirely disinterested to go upon the premises and set apart to said Rebecca her dower in said land in said petition mentioned and put her in possession of the same and make a return thereof said Writ and proceedings at our next term.

Ordered that William Neblett be appointed overseer of the Road in place of James Jones.

The Court adjourned until tomorrow 9 O'clock.

(p-220) Court met according to adjournment Tuesday June 20, 1809.
Present

    John Sterling   )
    Sterling Niblett) Esquires
    William R. Gibson) Justices

William Cohoon is appointed overseer of the road leading from Robertson County line through Portroyal to the Kentucky line in place of William Pennington & Joseph Woolfolk Esq. to name the hands to work under him.

Ordered that Isham Trotter be appointed overseer of the road from the forks of the road leading to Nelson's ferry to the ferry and that Isral Robinson hands Prestly Pollock & George Pollock work under him.

Ordered that William Trigg be appointed overseer of the road in place of William Gibson Esqr. & that William Gibson Esq. name the hands to work under him.

2 Deed of Conveyance Peter Oneal to John Highnight for ten acres of land acknowledged in Oppen Court & ordered to be registered.

Henry H. Bryan Esq. produced a Commission from under the hand and Seal of the Govenor of this State as a Justice of the peace for Montgomery County. He took the Oaths of qualification & the Oath of office.

(p-221) Bryan Whitfield Esq. produced a commission as a Justice of the peace for Montgomery County from under the hand & Seal of the Govenor of the State, he took the Oaths of qualification and also the Oath of Office.

Deed of Conveyance Amos Bird to Louisa Ann Duvall for a Town lott No. 1 in the addition to Clarksville proven by Anthony Crutcher & Zebedee Dennes. witnesses thereto and ordered to be registered.

Covenant Bond Robert Nelson to John Shelby the 2nd proven by the Oath of Alexander Trousdale a witness and ordered to be recorded.

Jacob Leech who was summoned to attend as a Juror at March term and failed is exonerated by the Court on reason offered.

James Moore & Samuel Vance Esquires Commissions who were appointed Commissioners to settle with Stephen Thomas Guardian to Hanah Cobb redered into Court an account of said settlement which is allowed.

Bond Robert Nelson to Reuben Bullard was proven by the Oaths of Samuel Peters & Thomas Brantley subscribing witnesses thereto and ordered to be recorded.

3 Deed of Conveyance Heydon Wells to Victor Harris for one hundred acres of land acknowledged in Open Court and ordered to registeration.

Benjamin Hawkins Esq. produced a Commission from under the hand and Seal of the Govenor as Justice of the peace for Montgomery & qualified.

(p-222) Adam Harmon is allowed license to keep a Tavern in the Town of Palmyra in dwelling house he gave bond with Samuel C. Hawkins & Joseph Edwards his securities.

4 Deed of Conveyance Heydon Wells to Charnell Corben for Ninety six acres of land acknowledged in Open Court & ordered to be registered.

5 Deed of Conveyance Amis Bird to William C. Jamison for a Town lott in Clarksville new addition No. 29 proven by Colmore Duvall & Anthony Crutcher witnesses thereto & ordered to be registered.

James Lockert Esq. returned a list of taxable property for Capt. Goodman's Company for 1809.

John Blair Esq. returns a list of taxable property for Capt. Frost's

Company for the year 1809.

James Hambleton Esq. is appointed to receive the list of taxable property in Capt. Batie's Company for the present year.

6 Deed of Conveyance Heydon Wells to Mathew Morgan for Three hundred & forty acres of land acknowledged in Open Court & ordered to registeration.

7 Deed of Conveyance Heydon Wells to Abner Bone for thirty acres of land acknowledged & ordered to registration.

8 Deed of Conveyance Heydon Wells to Obediah Magbee for Thirty two acres acknowledged & ordered to registration.

(p223) Ordered by the Court that the County business shall be taken upon the first Monday of the next term & the States business on the first Thursday & that the Clerk advertise the same at the Court House Door.

Ordered that the Venire to December Superior term for the District of Robertson be the following person, to wit

Henry H. Bryant, Abner Harris, Sterling Neblett, James Hambleton, William R. Gibson, Bryan Whitfield, William Lyons, Samuel Smith, Stephen Cooke, Samuel Northington, Thomas Smith, John H. Poston, and that the Veneri to September term 1809 for the County Court be the following persons, to wit.

Robert McGlaughlen, Jonathan Johnson, Thomas C. Minor, Luke Dilliard, Joseph Robinson, Alexander Carns, John Rudolph, Jr. James Morrow, John Hogan, Samuel Bumpass, Stephen Cooke, David Linch, Peter Hubbard, Joseph Dickson, Willis Jackson, Jacob Leech, Victor Harris, Benjamin Cowen, Stephen Hendlin, Joshua Weakley, George Ury, Wright Outlaw, Stephen Thomas, Guthridge Lyons, Burrell Bailess, Brittain Bailess, David Brigham, John McCarrell Senr. William Goodin, John French (West Fork) David Duprey, Nedham Whitfield, Samuel Allen, John Keathley, Bright Herring, Isaac Peterson, John Teasley, Mathew Rybourn, Francis Smith.

Thomas Brantley is allowed administration on the Estate of James Brantley Decd. he gave bond with John Edmonston, Andrew Peterson securities bound in the sum of One Thousand Dollars he qualified accordingly.

(p-224) Covenant Bond Robert Nelson to Vincent Cooper proven by Burrell Bailess a witness thereto & ordered to be recorded.

9 Deed of Conveyance Peter Oneal to Harden Oneal for 58 acres land acknowledged in Open Court and ordered to registeration.

Robert Prince, Samuel Gattis, John McCawley, Abner Harris, Sterling Niblett, James Hambleton, Thomas Smith, John Blair, Hugh McClure, Samuel Smith, John Sterling, William R. Gibson, Joseph Robertson, James Lockart, Esquires Justices on the bench.

Ordered by the Court that a tax be levied to wit, One cent on each white poll, one cent on each black pole & one cent on each and every hundred acres of land to be levied & collected for the support off the poor in Montgomery County.

Ordered by the Court that Robert W. Temple be allowed the sum of Seventeen Dollars sixty two & a half for erecting stocks and Sundry other services rendered to the County as pr. Acct. exhibited to be paid out of the Treasury of said County.

Ordered by the Court that William C. Jamison Esq. be allowed the sum of Forty Dollars for Exoficio services for the last year & also the sum Twenty Dollars for making tax list to be paid out of the Treasury of said County of Montgomery.

Ordered that John Cocke Sheriff be allowed Forty Dollars for Exoficie services rendered to the County the last year to be paid out the County Treasury.

Covenant Bond Robert Nelson to Robert Prince was proven by William Nelson a subscribing witness thereto and ordered to be recorded.

(p-225) Ordered that Joshua P. Vaughn be appointed overseer of the road from Smith's Ferry to Clarksville and that Barney Duff hands work with Vaughn.

William Barton, Joseph Hardeman, William Bearden, John Barton, Abel Man, Absolom Tribble, Henry Funk, who was appointed at last term of View & lay off a road leading from Absolum Tribble's Ferry to where it intersects Davises old road made return as follows, leaving the old road at the foot of the Bluff, thence runing up the first Holler so as to intersect the old road again near the Cross Road leading from Joseph Hardican's to Jacob Rudolph's.

Samuel Norrington & William Beorden Esqrs. produced Commissioners from under the hand & Seal of the Govenor of this State as Justices of the peace for Montgomery County they took the Oaths of qualification and also the Oath of Office as Justice of the peace.

Ordered that the road leading by John Frenshe's & Robert Searcye's be discontinued as a useless road.

Ordered that George West (West Fork) be appointed oversear of a road leading from Smith's Old Cabbins to Noah's Spring at the State line give him all the hands within five miles that is not on any other legal laid out road.

Joseph Woolfolk Esq. returns a list of taxable property for Capt. Bryant's Company for 1809.

Samuel Smith Esq. returns a list of taxable property for Capt. Porter's Company for 1809.

(p-226) STATE)
       Vs) Indictment
   ROBERT WELLS)

William Barton came here into Court and acknowledges himself bound in the sum of One Hundred Dollars to be levied off his goods & Chattels lands and Tenements, but to be void on condition that the said William Barton does make his personally appearance immediately then & there to prosecute the suit State against the said Robert Wells, and not to depart the Court without leave.

Sealed & acknowledged in Open Court.

                                                 Willis Barton (Seal)

Henry Ford records his stock mark Swallow Fork in each Ear.

Moses Ford records his stock mark a cross off the left ear & Hole in the Right.

Hugh F. Bell Admr. of Robert Nelson Decd. renders into Court an additional list of property that has come into his possession.

(p-226) STATE)
       Vs) Indictment
   ROBERT WELLS)

William Barton comes here and acknowledges himself bound in the sum of One Hundred Dollars to be levied off his goods & Chattels lands &

Tenements but to be void on condition that he make his personally appearance immediately & prosecute the Indictment the State against the said Robert Wells and not depart the Court without leave.

William Barton (Seal)

Mathew Morgan, John Thomas & Anne Sugg, Admrs. & Admrx. of of Samuel Sugg Decd. Renders into Court an Inventory of the Estate of said Deceased.

(p-227)   Anne Sugg is appointed Guardian for Lucinda Sugg, Elizabeth Sugg, Martha Sugg, Milton B. Sugg, Howell Sugg, Noah Sugg. She gives bond and security with Stephen Hendlen bound in the sum of One Thousand Dollars.

John Blair, Sterling Neblett, John McCauley Esq. on the Bench.
Court adjourned untill tomorrow at 9 O'clock.
Court met according to adjournment June 21st 1809.
Present

Sterling Niblett	Esquires
Abner Harris	Justices
John McCauley	

JOHN BELL Vs JAMES TRIBBLE & REUBEN GRAYSON	Trespass

This day came the parties by their attorneys & a Jury of good and lawful men, to wit,

Samuel Hawkins, Henry J. Williams, John Hagler, Burch Roland, Thomas Bunch, Robert W. Temple, Luke Dillard, Isam Trotter, James C. Brown, William Mathews, Edward Leech, Israel Robinson,

Who being duly elected tried & sworn the truth to speak upon the Issue joined do upon their Oaths say that they find the Issues for the Defendants. Therefore it is considered by the Court that the Defendant go without day & recover against the Plaintiff his costs about his defense in this behalf expended.

(p-228) WM. CLEMENTS & JOHN H. HYDE Vs WILLIAM BURNES	Case

Dismissed by the Plaintiffs attorney. Therefore it is considered by the Court that the Defendant recover against the Plaintiffs his costs about his defence in this behalf expended.

AARON FLETCHER Assee Vs WILSON GIBSON	Debt

Dismissed by the Plaintiff in proper person and the Plaintiff assumes all costs. Therefore the Court considers that the Defendant recover against the Plaintiff his costs about his defence in this behalf expended.

10 Deed of Conveyance John Niblett to Samuel Roberts was acknowledged in Open Court for 330 acres of land & ordered to registeration.

11 Deed of Conveyance John Neblett to Edward Niblett was acknowledged in Open Court & ordered to registeration for 119-3/4 acres of land.

Covenant Bond Robert Nelson to Isaac Shelby was proven in Open Court by the Oath of William Lyons a subscribing witness thereto & ordered to registeration.

(p-229) Sterling Neblett, Samuel Smith & Benjamin Hawkins Esquires on the bench.

Easter Cooper widow of John Cooper Decd. is allowed letters of Administration on the Estate of John Cooper Deceased. She gave bond with Abner Harris & David Burney her securities bound in the sum of Five hundred Dollars and was qualified accordingly. The Admx. returned an Inventory of the Estate.

```
MICAJAH PICKETT )
      Vs        ) Certiorari
JOSEPH ONEAL    )
```

Diminution of the records suggested by the Pltff. and ordered that an Alias Certiorari Issue.

Samuel Gattis Esq. returned a list of taxable property for Capt. Whitfields Company for the year 1809.

Abner Harris, Samuel Smith & John McCauley Esqrs. on the bench.

12 Deed of Conveyance Barnabas O. Ferrell to John Moore proven by the Oath of Thomas Moore a subscribing witness thereto who also proves that he knew Barnabas O. Ferrell to be the person who executed the same Deed, that it was executed in his presence & in the presence of C. Campbell & Samson Moore at the time the said Deed bares date and that he believes Samson Moore resides in the State of North Carolina & that he knows not where the other witness resides tho is convinced he does not live in this State. 456 acres & ordered by the Court to registeration.

(p-230) Robert Prince, Benjamin Hawkins, Abner Harris, John McCauley, Esquires on the bench & Samuel Gattis.

```
James Adkinson by his next friends )
GEORGE ROBERTS & HENRY MINOR       )
            Vs                      ) Trespass
        JAMES WILLIAMS              ) Asslt. & Batty.
```

This day came the parties by their attornies and a Jury of good and lawfull men, to wit,

1 Adam Harmon
2 John Watkins
3 John Rudolph
4 Richard Whitehead
5 John Prance
6 Joseph Edwards
7 Adam Harmon, Junr.
8 Christopher Thomas
9 Ralph Williams
10 James Sullinger
11 Charles Anderson
12 Alexander Faith

Who being duly elected tried and sworn the truth to speak upon the Issue joined do upon their Oaths say that they find the Issues for the Plaintiff and assess his damages to Twenty five Dollars. Therefore it is considered by the Court that the Plaintiff recovered against the Defendant the damages by the Jury in their Verdict assessed and also his costs about his suit in this behalf expended & the Defendant in Mercy &.

(p-231) Court adjourned untill tomorrow 9 O'clock.

Thursday 22nd June 1809 Court met according to adjournment. Present
Robert Prince, John McCauley & Benjamin Hawkins Esquires on the bench.

13 Deed of Conveyance Parry W. Humphrey Esq. & John Cooke Shrff. to Henry Minor for lotts in Clarksville No. 87 & 88 proven by the Oaths of William Smith & Drewry Pistol witnesses thereto and ordered to registeration.

    MORDICA JOHNSON & JANE HIS WIFE)
                  Vs   ) Case
        JESSE DENSON   )

The Plaintiffs in this case were so solemnly called came not but made default. Therefore it is considered by the Court that the Defendant recover against the Plaintiffs his costs about his defence in this behalf expended. Motion by Plaintiff to set aside the non pross.

Non suit set aside & continued untill next term for want of Dist.n-

Covenant Bond Robert Nelson to William Ross proven by the Oaths of William S. Bailey to James Hambleton & ordered to registeration.

Bond Robert Nelson to William Lyons & James Moore the hand writing proven by Robert Prince & William Ross & ordered to registeration.

Mary Waggoner & Others Petition continued.

(p-232) Ordered that John Watkins be appointed overseer of the road in place of Alexander Trousdall and that the hands of David Lamb, Oswell Potts, Thomas Potts, Peter Matheny, John Lamb, James Lamb, John Darnald, Wright Tyre, Samuel Phillingham, Mr. Robertson, Alexander Trousdale & Son and all the hands living within the bounds of those already named, work under him.

    THE STATE   )
       Vs   ) Indictment
    JESSE COOKSEY)

Joseph Hardecan comes here and acknowledges himself bound in the sum of One Hundred Dollars to be levied of his goods & Chattels, land & Tenements but to be void on condition that he appear immediately and prosecute the Indictment the State against Jesse Cooksey & not depart the Court without leave.
                                                his
Test   Joseph X Hardican   (Seal)
A. E. Crutcher   Mark

    STATE   )
      Vs   ) Indictment
    REUBIN DICKSON)

Robert Rushing acknowledges himself bound in the sum of One Hundred Dollars but to be void on condition that he appear immediately and prosecute the Indictment the State against Reubin Dickson & not depart the Court without leave.
Test.
A. E. Crutcher   Robert Rushing (Seal)

(p-253) STATE
        Vs   } Indictment
        REUBIN DICKSON

Reubin Dickson was solemnly called and failed to appear but made default. Therefore it is considered by the Court he has forfeited agreeable to the Acts of Assembly.

STATE
Vs   } Indictment
REUBIN DICKSON

Jesse Dickson who was security for Reubin Dickson in his recognizance bond for his appearance at this term being solemnly called failed to bring in the body of the Defendant in discharge of himself, therefore made default. Therefore it is considered by the Court that he has forfeited agreeable to the Acts of Assembly.
Motion to set aside the forfiature.
Forfiture set aside on payment of cost.

14 Deed of Conveyance Wm. H. Davis to Drury H. Cross for One hundred & ten acres of land proven by the Oath of Stephen O'Gwin & Daniel O'Gwin witnesses thereto and ordered to registeration.

(p-254) JAMES ADKINSON
        Vs   } Trespass, Agst. & B.
        JAMES WILLIAMS

Braxton Sims who was summoned as a witness was solemnly called and came not but made default. Therefore it is considered by the Court that Sci fa Issue.

THOMAS SHELBY, Assee
Vs   } Debt
BRIGHT HERRING

The Defendant in this case comes in proper person and confesses a Judgment according to Specialty with interest. Therefore it is considered by the Court that the Plaintiff recover against the Defendant his debt agreeable to the Specialty with lawfull interest and also his costs of suit in this behalf expended. Execution stayed untill next term.

Ordered that Henry J. Williams be exonerated from any further attendance as a Juror this term.

Bright Herring, William White, John Dikas, Thomas Dunbar, Moses Oldham, Daniel Taylor, Isaac Peterson, James Bailey, John Henderson, Jedediah Hall & James Lister, who was appointed at March Term a Jury at last term to view & lay off a road from leving the Nashville Road on the South side Red near where the McAdoe Road to White's Mill on Spring Creek has made return to this term.

(p-255) Deed of Conveyance David Rudder to James Boyd for seventeen acres of land acknowledged in Open Court and ordered to registeration.

Abner Harris Esq. renders into Court a list of taxable property for Captain William Allen's Company for the year 1809.

```
STATE      )
   Vs      )  Presentment
JOSEPH RAY )
```

Motion to quash the presentment. Motion overruled.

Court adjourned untill tomorrow 8 O'clock,
Court met according to adjournment.
Present

```
                Robert Prince   )
                John Blair      )
                Benjamin Hawkins)  Esquires
                Samuel Gattis   )  Justices
                Sterling Neblett)
                John McCauley   )
```

On motion ordered that the blank book purchased by this Court for William C. Jamison for the use of his Office be delivered to Robert Prince the present Register of Montgomery for the use of his office and the Alphabet belonging thereto.

```
(p-236)  VANCE, KING & BRADLEY )
                  Vs            )
         CONEWAY OLDHAM         )
```

On motion by the Plaintiffs Counsell is ordered by the Court that Judgment be rendered up against said Defendant Constable and his securities for his delinquency in not making & rendering the monies on an Execution issued by John H. Poston Esq. at the instance of the said Vance, King & Bradley against a certain James Bunting for the sum of Sixteen Dollars & forty cents & 1/4 of a cent and it appearing to the Court on investigation that said Defendant did not make his return on said Execution within twenty days agreeable to law also appearing to the Court that no stay was prayed by the said James Bunting. It likewise appearing to the Court that the said Execution is *is* credited with Six Dollars.

```
STATE         )
   Vs         )  Indict.
JAMES WILLIAMS)
```

The Defendant in this case was solemnly called & came not but made default. Also James Hambleton security for James Williams was solemnly called and failed to appear or bring in the body of the said James Williams, but made default.

```
(p-237)  STATE       )  Indictment
            Vs       )  for Assl.
         ROBERT WELLS)  on John Barton
```

The Defendant in this case comes into Court and submitts himself to the Court. Therefore it is considered by the Court that the Defendant Robert Wells be fined Twenty five Cents and that he pay the costs of suit.

Samuel Vanse, John McCauley, Sterling Niblett Esqrs. on the Bench.

```
THE STATE    )
   Vs        )  Indictment
JAMES WILLIAMS )
```

The Defendant in this case submitts himself to Court and pleads guilty, Therefore it is considered by the Court that the said Defendant be fined Six Dollars & pay the Costs of this suit.

William McDaniel Esq. renders into Court a list of taxable property for Capt. John Weakley's Company for the year 1809.
Ordered that Sterling Niblett and Abner Harris Esquires be appointed to settle with Isham Trotter Guardian to Robert Trotter an Insane person & make return thereof.
James Moore Esquire returns the list of taxable property for Capt. Harmon's Company for 1809.

(p-238) Deed of Mortgage, Sterling Ingram to James Baxter for negro boy proven in Court by the Oaths of James B. Reynolds & J. E. Jinkins subscribing witness and ordered to registeration.
Ordered that that Thomas Smith Esq. take the privy examination of Silvey Whitehead, wife of Benjamin Whitehead concerning the Execution of a Deed of relinquishment & interest to Abner Harris Esqr. The relinquishment was duly acknowledged in Open Court by Benjamin Whitehead and on examination of Silvey Whitehead declares that she did make her relinquishment freely & of her own accord and not forced to do so & ordered to be Certifyed.   dd to A. Harris.

```
STATE        )
  Vs         )  Indictment
ROBERT WELLS )  Wm. Barton Prosecutor
```

The Defendant in this case submitts himself to the Court, therefore the Court considers that he be fined the sum of Seventeen Dollars and that he pay all costs of this suit.

```
STATE        )
  Vs         )  Indictment Wm. for Robert Barton.
ROBERT WELLS )
```

The Defendant in this case submitts, and it is considered by the Court that he be fined in the sum of Fifty Cents and pay the costs of this suit.

(p-239)   John Blair, Thomas Smith, John McCauley Esqrs. on the Bench.

```
STATE       )
  Vs        )  Presentment
JOSEPH RAY  )
```
              Jury to wit   Jury No. 1

1 John Hagler   7 John Rudolph
2 William Bogard   8 Thomas Bunch
3 Edward Leech   9 James C. Brown
4 Joseph Edwards   10 Ralph Williams

5 Isham Trotter   11 Burch Roland
6 Richard Whitehead   12 Willis Jackson

Who being elected tried & sworn the truth to speak upon the bill of presentment do upon their Oaths say that they find the Defendant not guilty as charged in the bill of presentment.

```
STATE        )
Vs           ) Presentment
JOSEPH PENRICE )
```

The Defendant comes into Court & submitts himself to the Court. Therefore it is considered by the Court that he be fined Twenty five Cents and pay the costs of this suit.

Ordered that John Steel be appointed overseer in place of Joseph Penrice over that part of the road.

```
(p-240)  STATE           )
         Vs              ) Indictment
         SAMUEL C. HAWKINS )
```
Jury No. 1

Only Joseph Penrice in place of James C. Brown who being duly elected & sworn the truth to speak upon the bill of Indictment do upon their Oaths say that they find that the Defendant is not guilty as charged in the bill of Indictment. Therefore it is considered and it appearing to the Court that the Indictment was malicious that the prosecutor in this case pay all costs of this suit.

```
STATE        )
Vs           ) Indictment
SAMUEL C. HAWKINS )
```

Peggey Green the prosecutor in this case was solemnly called & came not but made default therefore it is considered by the Court that she has forfeited her recognizance & that Sci fa Issue to next Term.

```
STATE                              )
Vs                                 ) Indictment
SAMUEL C. HAWKINS, John D. Scott   )
John Whealand                      )
```
Same Jury No. 1 on Adam Harmon, Junr. in place of Joseph Penrice who being elected & sworn the truth to speak upon the bill of Indictment do upon their Oaths say that they find that the Defendants are not guilty as charged in manner & form. Therefore it is considered by the Court that the Defendants go without day & that the prosecutor pay all costs about his bill of Indictment.

```
(p-241)  STATE              )
         Vs                 )
         SAMUEL C. HAWKINS, ) Indictment
         John D. Scott &    )
         John Whealand      )
```

Guthridge Lyons the Prosecutor in this case was solemnly called to appear & prosecute but came not and made default. Therefore it was considered by the Court that the prosecutor in this case pay all costs of this suit.

The Court adjourns untill tomorrow 8 O'clock.

Saturday June 24th the Court met according to their adjournment. Present

    Sterling Neblett)
    John McCauley   ) Esquires
    Hugh McClure   ) on the Bench.
    James Hambleton)

RICHMOND CROSWELL)
  Vs   ) Appeal
GUTHRIDGE LYONS)

The Plaintiff in this case was solemnly called and came not but made default. Therefore it is considered by the Court that a non suit be entered & that the Defendant recover against the Plaintiff his costs about his Defense in this behalf expended.

1d Deed John Cooke Sheriff to Edward Leech for 269 acres of land acknowledged in Open Court and ordered to registration.

(p-242) Same Justices on Bench only H. McClure Esq.

ISAAC KITTRELL)
  Vs   ) Trespass
ROBERT WELLS)

This day came the parties by their attorneys and also a Jury of good and lawfull men, to wit,

1	John Rudolph	7	Edward Leech
2	Duroh Roland	8	Thomas Bunch
3	Richard Whitehead	9	Isham Trotter
4	Samuel C. Hawkins	10	William Love
5	James C. Brown	11	John Barnes
6	Ralph Williams	12	John Hagler

Who being duly elected tried and sworn the truth to speak upon the issue joined do upon their Oath say that they find the Defendant guilty as charged in the declaration & do assess the Plaintiffs damages to Twenty nine Dollars & seventy five cents. Therefore it is considered by the Court that the Plaintiff recover against the Defendant the damages so assessed by the Jury in manner and form aforesaid, and also his costs about his suit expended & the Defendant in Mercy &.

Motion by Defendants Attorney for arrest of Judgment and reasons filed the same day.

  Deed of Conveyance John Cook Sheriff to James Moore for Nineteen Hundred and Twenty Acres of land acknowledged in Open Court and ordered to registeration.

dd to A. Bunting

 Deed of Conveyance John Cooke Sheriff to James Moore for 914 acres of land acknowledged in Open Court and ordered to registration.

(p-243)   James Moore, James Hambleton & John McCauley on the Bench.

```
JOHN COUTS              )
    Vs                  )
SAMUEL PETERS & JOHN MINOTT )  Debt No. 17
```

No. 2

This day came the parties by their attorneys & also a Jury of good & lawfull men, to wit.

1 David Burney
2 Isaac Starr
3 William Good
4 James Williams
5 Adam Harmon
6 Robert Wells
7 Robert Jackson
8 William Bogard
9 Absolam Tribble
10 Adam Harmon, Jr.
11 Robert Mann
12 Mason Bennett

Who being duly elected tried & sworn the truth to speak upon the Issue joined do upon their Oath say that they find that the Plaintiff hath not paid the debt in the declaration mentioned do assess the plaintiff.

Damages by reason of the detention thereof to Three Dollars & Sixty Cents. Therefore it is considered by the Court that the Plaintiff recover against the Defendants the debt in the declaration mentioned and the damages as assessed by the Jury in their Verdict in form aforesaid, and his costs of suit in this behalf expended.

Same Justices on the Bench

```
SAME  )
 Vs   )  Debt No. 19
SAME  )
```
Jury No. 2

Who being duly elected tried and sworn the truth to speak upon the Issue joined do upon their Oaths say that they find that the Defendant has not paid the debt in the declaration mentioned and do assess the Plaintiff damages by reason of the detention thereof to Eight Dollars forty cents. Therefore it is considered by the Court that (p-244) the Plaintiff recover against the Defendants the Debt in the declaration mentioned and his damages as assessed by the Jury in their Verdict in manner & form assessed and also his costs about his suit in this behalf expended.

Same Justices on the Bench.

```
SAME  )
 Vs   )  Debt No. 18
SAME  )
```
Jury No. 2

This day came the parties by their attorneys and also a Jury of good and lawfull men, who being duly elected tried & sworn the truth to speak upon the Issue joined do upon their Oath say that they find that the Defendant has not paid the debt in the declaration mentioned and do by reason of the detention thereof to Seven Dollars & sixty six cents. Therefore it is considered by the Court that the Plaintiff recover against the Defendants the debt in the declaration mentioned and the damages as assessed by the Jury in manner & form and also his costs about his suit in this behalf expended.

James Hambleton, Hugh McClure & John McCauley Esqrs. on the Bench.

```
WM. PORTER    )
    Vs        ) Appeal
SIMON HOMES   )
                Jury No. 2
```

Who being duly elected tried & sworn the truth to speak upon the matter of controversy between the parties do upon their Oaths say that they find for the Defendant. Therefore it is considered by the Court the Defendant go without day, and that the Defendant recover against the Plaintiff his costs about his defence in this behalf expended.

(p-245) Ordered that Easter Cooper widow and Admr. of John Cooper, Decd. sell the perishable property of the said Decd. giving nine months credit with bond & sufficient security given.

An assignment for a platt & Certificate of Survey for 228 acres of land from James McCarrell & Zelpha his wife, Jeremiah Walker & Zebe his wife and George Elliott, heirs of John Elliott Decd. being produced into Court. It is ordered by the Court that Dedamus Potis tatum. Issue to take the privy examination of the said Zelpha & Zebe, seperate and apart from their husband.

Robert Prince, Thomas Smith, Hugh McClure, James Baxter & Samuel Smith Esquires on the Bench.

Charles Anderson moves for a Judgement to be entered up against Adam Harmon, Junr. for Sundry Monies which he has failed to account to said Plaintiff for & for not returning Sundry Executions put into his hand.

Motion overruled by the Court. Therefore it is considered by the Court that the Defendant Adam Harman recover against the Plaintiff the costs about his suit in this behalf expended & the Plaintiff in Mercy &.

(p-246) James Hambleton, John McAuley, William Bearding Esquires on the Bench.

```
JANE WATT     )
    Vs        ) Appeal
JESSE COOKSEY )
```

This day came the parties by their attorneys and also a Jury of good and lawfull men, to wit,
                Same Jury No. 2

Who being duly elected tried & sworn the truth to speak upon the controversy between the parties do upon their Oath say that they find for the Plaintiff and assess her damage to Forty one Dollars & fifty cents. Therefore it is considered by the Court that the Plaintiff recover against the Defendant the same assessed by the Jury in their Verdict, and her costs of suit in this behalf expended.

Court adjourned untill Monday 10 O'clock.

Monday 26th June 1809 Court mett according to adjournment.
Present

       Robert Prince)   Esquires
       Hugh McClure   )   on the Bench
       Thomas Smith   )

17 Deed of Conveyance John Trotter to Jacob Leech for two acres of land proven by the Oath of Edward Leech & James Matlock subscribing witnesses thereto & ordered to registration.

(p-247) Robert Prince, Hugh McClure, Thomas Smith & Samuel Smith Esquires on the Bench.

   MARK HARWELL & NEVILL GEE, Administrators of
      STERLING HARWELL)
        Vs   )   Debt
      GEORGE HUMPHREYS)

On motion of Plaintiffs attorney to amend the writ founded upon a affidavit of the attorney filed of record. It is ordered by the Court that the Plaintiffs attorney be allowed to proceed in this cause. Mark Harwell & Nevill Gee administrators of Sterling Harwell by the additional words executors of the last will & Testament of Sterling Harwell, Decd.

Same Justices on the Bench only Robert Prince.

   SAUNDERS MOORE)
      Vs   )   Case
   ROBERT PRINCE   )

This day came the parties by their attorney and a Jury thereon, to wit,

1   John Rudolph   7   John Nevill
2   James C. Brown   8   George W. Nevill
3   Thomas Bunch   9   Richard Glover
4   Edward Leech   10   Simeon Holmes
5   Joseph Edwards   11   William Love
6   Isam Trotter   12   Richard Whitehead

Who being duly elected tried & sworn the truth to speak upon the Issue joined upon their Oath do say that they find that the Defendant did assume upon himself as the Plaintiff in declaring hath alledged.

Miss trial by consent of parties.

(p-248)   THOMAS MCENTRE & CO.)
       Vs   )   Debt
     WILLIAM SMITH   )

The Plaintiff in this case was solemnly called and failed to appear. Therefore it is considered by the Court that a non suit be entered up & that the Defendant go without day & recover against the Plaintiff his costs about his defense in this behalf expended.

Hugh McClure, Thomas Smith & Samuel Smith Esquires on the Bench, Robert Prince & James Baxter Esqrs.

Elisha Willis quallifyed as Deputy Sheriff for the County of Montgomery &.

FOSTER ALEXANDER Assee)
     Vs   ) Case
JOHN MINOTT   )

The Defendant in this case comes by his attorney and confesses Judgment according to Specialty & the Plaintiff by his attorney agrees to stay Execution untill December Term next. Therefore it is considered by the Court that the Plaintiff recover against the Defendant his debt in the declaration mentioned & his costs about his suit in this behalf expended.

Court adjourned untill tomorrow 9 O'clock.

Court met according to adjournment June 27th 1809.
Present

                        Robert Prince   ) Esquire
                        Hugh McClure   ) Justices
                        Sterling Neblett)

(p-249)   SAUNDERS C. MOORE)
               Vs   ) Case
           ROBERT PRINCE   )

The parties in proper person comes here into Court & dismisses the suit each pays his own witness & own attorney and the Clerks and Sheriffs fees they divide.

GREEN HILL   )
   Vs   )
JOHN COOKE, Sheriff)

The Defendant John Cooke confesses Judgment for Two hundred & Eighteen Dollars eighty eight & a half cents monies collected by him in the suit Green Hill against Samuel Peters & John Steel securities for Benjamin Weakley for prison bounds. Therefore it is considered by the Court that the Plaintiff recover against the Defendant the aforesaid sum so confessed for, as also his costs about his suit in this behalf expended, & the Defendant in Mercy &

CLEMENTS & HYDE   )
     Vs   ) Debt
BURRELL M. WILLIAMSON)

The Defendant in this case was solemnly called and came not but made default. Therefore it is considered by the Court the Plaintiffs recover against the Defendant according to the Specialty with interest and also their costs of suit in this behalf expended. Execution stayed three months.

JOHN H. POSTON Surviving Partner)
         Vs   ) Debt
JAMES HAMBLETON   )

The Defendant in this case was solemnly called and came not but made default. Therefore it is considered by the Court that the Plaintiffs recover against (p-250) the Defendant according to Specialty with interest and their costs of suit in this behalf expended.

JOHN H. POSTON, Surviving Partner)
        Vs) Debt
JAMES HAMBLETON)

The Defendant in this case was solemnly called & came not but made default. Therefore it is considered by the Court that the Plaintiffs recover against the Defendant his debt according to Specialty with interest and their costs about their suit in this behalf expended.

Thomas Smith, John Sterling, Samuel Smith, Sterling Neblett Esquires on the Bench.

HUGH McCLURE & JAMES ELDER)
        Vs) Case
ISAAC SHELBY)

This day came the parties by their attorneys and also a Jury of good and lawfull men, to wit

1 John Rudolph
2 Edward Leech
3 John Hagler
4 James C. Brown
5 William Love
6 Richard Whitehead
7 Isham Trotter
8 Richard Glover
9 Charles Anderson
10 Thomas Bunch
11 William Moore
12 Darden Brown

Who being duly elected tried and sworn the truth to speak upon the Issue joined do upon their Oath say that the Defendant did assume upon himself as the Plaintiffs in declaring hath alledged against him and do assess the Plaintiffs damages to Three Hundred & sixty two Dollars & ten cents by reason thereof. Therefore it is considered by the Court that the Plaintiff recover against the Defendant the damages assessed by the Jury in their Verdict and their costs about their suit in this behalf expended.
Same Justices.

(p-251) HENRY SMALL)
        Vs) Debt
JAMES HAMBLETON) No. 40 on Docket

The Defendant in this case was solemnly called and came not but made default. Therefore it is considered by the Court that the Plaintiff recover against the Defendant his debt according to the Specialty with interest and his costs of suit in this behalf expended.
Same Justices

HENRY SMALL Assee)
        Vs) Debt No. 41
JAMES HAMBLETON)

The Defendant in this case was solemnly called and came not but made

default. Therefore it is considered by the Court that the Plaintiff recover against the Defendant his debt according to Specialty with interest and his costs about his suit expended.
   Same Justices

    HENRY SMALL   )
        Vs   ) Debt   No. 42
    JAMES HAMBLETON)

The Defendant in this case was solemnly called but came not but made default. Therefore it is considered by the Court that the plaintiff recover against the Defendant his debt according to Specialty with interest and his costs of suit in this behalf expended.
   Same Justices.

    JAMES BAXTER & CO.)
        Vs   ) Debt
    THOMAS TRAVIS   )

The Defendant in this case was solemnly called but came not and made default. Therefore it is considered by the C(p=252) Court that the Plaintiff recover against the Defendant, ~~recover against the Defendant~~ according to Specialty with interest and their costs of suit in this behalf expended & the Defendant in Mercy &
   Same Justices

    JAMES BAXTER & CO.)
        Vs   ) Debt
    JAMES HAMBLETON)

The Defendant in this case was solemnly called and came not but made default. Therefore it is considered by the Court that the Plaintiff recover against the Defendant his debt accord to Specialty with interest and their costs of suit in this behalf expended.
   Same Justices.

    JOSHUA P. VAUGHN)
        Vs   ) Debt
    THOMAS WHITLEDGE)

The Defendant in this case being solemnly called came not but made default. Therefore it is considered by the Court that the Plaintiff recover against the Defendant his debt accord- to the Specialty with interest and his costs of suit in this behalf expended.
   Same Justices on the Bench.

    WILLIAM TAIT Assee)
        Vs   ) Debt
    JOSHUA P. VAUGHN)

The Defendant in this case being solemnly called came not but made default. Therefore it is considered by the Court that the Plaintiff recover against the Defendants his debt according to the Specialty with interest and also his costs of his suit in this behalf expended.

(p-253)   Same Justices.

    BENJAMIN THOMAS)
        Vs   ) Debt
    DARDEN BROWN   )

This day came the parties by their attornies and also a Jury, to wit.

1 Joseph Edwards   7 John Rutledge
2 Simeon Holms   8 William Porter
3 William Bogard   9 Absolam Tribble
4 James Williams   10 George W. Nevell
5 George Grace   11 Alexander Brown
6 George Trotter   12 John Nevell

Who being duly elected tried and sworn the truth to speak do upon their Oath say that they find the Issue for the Plaintiff and assess his damages by reason of the Defendants non-performance of the condition of the writing obligatory in the declaration mentioned to Three Hundred & fifty Dollars. It is therefore considered by the Court that the Plaintiff recover of the Defendant One Thousand Dollars the debt in the declaration mentioned to be discharged by the payment of Three Hundred & Fifty Dollars the damages aforesaid by the Jury aforesaid in form aforesaid assessed with his costs of suit in this behalf expended.

Same Justices on the Bench.

    MCCLURE AND ELDER)
        Vs   ) Debt
    ANDREW BEATIE   )

The Defendant in this case being solemnly called came not but made default. Therefore it is considered by the Court that the Plaintiffs recover against the Defendant their debt according to the Specialty with interest and also their costs of suit in this behalf expended.

(p-254) James Hambleton John Sterling, Sterling Neblett Esqrs. on the Bench.

    JOHN H. POSTON Surviving P.)
    of KING & POSTON   )
        Vs   ) Debt
    ALEXANDER FAITH   )

This day came the parties by their attornies and a Jury of good and lawfull men , to wit,

1 John Rudolph   7 Isham Trotter
2 Darden Brown   8 Henry Starr
3 Edward Leech   9 Thomas Rynch
4 James C. Brown   10 David Williams
5 William Farrior   11 Willis Jackson
6 Richard Glover   12 Charles Anderson

Who being duly elected tried & sworn the truth to speak upon the Issue joined do upon their Oath say that they find that the Defendant has not paid the debt in the declaration mentioned and assess the Plaintiffs damages by reason of the detention thereof to Five Dollars thirty seven & a fourth cents. Therefore it is considered by the Court that the Plaintiffs recover against the Defendant their debt in the declaration and his damages as assessed by the Jury in their Verdict aforesaid and their costs of suit in this behalf expended.

```
RICHARD WHITEHEAD      )
        Vs             )  Trespass, V. A.
JESSE SAUNDERSON &     )
WM. BARNES             )
```

The Plaintiff in proper person came into Court and dismissed his suit. One of the Defendants Jesse Saunderson assume all costs but the Plaintiffs attornies. Therefore it is considered by the Court that the Plaintiff recover against Defendant his costs about his suit in this behalf expended.

```
(p-255)  ADAM HARMON, Sr.  )
              Vs           )  Debt
         JAMES MOORE       )
```

By consent of the parties this case is left to John Bailess & Francis Tompkins and if they should not agree that they shall choose a third person whose award shall be the decision of this Court at next term.

18 Deed of Conveyance James Moore to Samuel Lynes for a Town Lott in the new addition to Clarksville No. 24.
Acknowledged in Court and ordered to registeration.

D. D. to   Deed of Conveyance John Cocks Sheriff to Colmore Duvall for
C/ Duvall 1538 acres of land was acknowledged in Open Court and ordered
           to registeration.

```
JOSIAH FORT & ELIAS FORT EXECUTORS  )
              Vs                    )  Debt
         HUGH F. BELL                )
```

This day came the parties by their attornies and a Jury, to wit,

John Rudolph, Richard Whitehead, Edward Leech, James C. Brown, William Farrier, Richard Glover, Isham Trotter, Joseph Edwards, Thomas Bunch, David Williams, Willis Jackson, Charles Anderson. Who being duly elected tried & sworn the truth to speak upon the Issue joined do upon their Oath say that they find that Defendant has not paid the debt in the declaration mentioned and do assess the Plaintiffs damages by reason of the detention thereof to Fifteen Dollars & thirty six cents. Therefore it is considered by the Court that the Plaintiffs recover against the Defendant (p-256) the debt in the declaration mentioned and the damages as assessed by the Jury in their Verdict as assessed in manner & form aforesaid & his costs of suit in this behalf expended.

19 Deed of Conveyance William Farrier to David Bunting for 200 acres of land acknowledged in Open Court and ordered to registeration.

Price Arnold a minor is bound by the Court to Samuel Lynes to learn the Art and History of a sadler to live untill he comes to the age of Twenty one years of age the said apprentice is said to be Seventeen years of age.

WILLIAM BOGGARD, JOSEPH BOGARD & CHARLES BOGARD
Vs
JOHN SEELEY
} Detenue

The Plaintiffs in this case were solemnly called & came not but made default. Therefore it is considered by the Court that the Defendant go without day & recover against the Plaintiff his costs about his suit in this behalf expended.

On motion of Plaintiffs Counsel Non pros set aside.

John Hagler a Juror to this term & sufficient reasons shewed to the Court is Exonerated from attending any longer at this term.

Covenant Bond Robert Nelson for 320 acres to Samuel Craft proven in Court by the Oath of William Nelson & Hugh F. Bell witnesses thereto and ordered to registration.

(p-257)   Same Justices on Bench.

JOHN McALLISTER
Vs
WILLIS JACKSON
} Covenant

This day came the parties by their attornies & a Jury of good & lawfull men, to wit. John Rudolph, Richard Whitehead, Edward Leech, James C. Brown, William Farrior, Richard Glover, Bright Herring, Joseph Edwards, Thomas Bunch, Absolum Tribble, Robert W. Temple, Charles Anderson. Who being duly elected tried & sworn the truth to speak upon the Issue joined upon their Oath do say that they find the Issues for the Defendant. Therefore it is considered by the Court that the Defendant recover against the Plaintiff his costs about his suit in this behalf expended & the Plaintiff in Mercy &

Court adjourned untill tomorrow at 9 O'clock.

Court met according to adjournment Wednesday June 28th 1809.
Present

John Blair
Hugh McClure
John H. Paston
} Esquires
Justices

Isham Trotter records his stock mark a smooth crop off the left Ear & an overslope in the right Ear.

Deed of Conveyance Colmore Duvall to James B. Reynolds for 320 acres acknowledged in Open Court and ordered to registration.

(p 258)
WILLIAM PORTER
Vs
SIMON HOMES
} Appeal

Motion for Appeal by Plaintiffs attorney which was allowed and the Plaintiff gives bond with William Sullivan & Elisha Willis his securities bound in the sum of One Hundred Dollars. And the reasons for Appeal filed, to wit. 1st That the Court improperly rejected testimony offered by the Plaintiff. 2nd the Verdict was contrary to evidence which in my oppinion are sufficient reasons for the Court here to grant an appeal.

Minor for Pltff.

CLEMENTS & HYDE)
    Vs)
THE ADMINISTRATORS & ADMX)
OF SAMUEL SUGG)

This case continued for declaration & leave given to amend Original Writ.

Same Justices on the Bench.

JAMES M. REYNOLDS &)
JOHN R. MCFARLAND) Debt
    Vs)
STEPHEN STEWART)

This day came the parties by their attornies and also a Jury of good & lawfull men, to wit, Thomas Bunch, Edward Leech, James C. Brown, Isham Trotter, George W. Newell, William Bogard, Benjamin Whitehead, William Love, Moses Oldham, Christopher Owens, Lewis Malone, William Farrier,

Who being duly elected tried and sworn the truth to speak upon the Issue joined do upon their Oath say that they find that the Defendant has not paid the debt in the declaration mentioned and do assess the Plaintiffs damages by reason of the detention to Five Dollars & fifteen cents. Therefore it is considered by the Court that the Plaintiffs do recover against the Defendant the debt in the declaration mentioned, amounting to Two Hundred ten Dollars & 35½ cents. The damages assessed by the Jury in manner & form and also their costs about their suit in this behalf expended.

(p-259) Hugh McClure, John Sterling, John H. Poston Esquires on the Bench.

THOMAS DUNBAR)
    Vs) Demurrer
ANTHONY CRUTCHER)

Demurrer overruled & Execution stayed by Plaintiffs attorney until next term.

Same Justices on the Bench.

REYNOLDS & MCFARLAND)
    Vs) Debt
THOMAS WEAKLEY) Plea in Abatemt.

On motion plea in Abatement set aside the Defendant not pleading and the Defdt. being solemnly called came not but made default. Therefore it is considered by the Court that the Plaintiff recover against the Defendant their debt according to Specialty & Interest and also their costs of suit in this behalf expended.

Motion to set aside the Judgment by Defendants attorney. Motion overruled.

Same Justices on the Bench.

JOHN MACKEY Exr.)
Vs) Debt Jury No. 3
STEPHEN STEWART)

This day came the parties by their attornies and a Jury of good and lawfull men, to wit.

Thomas Bunch, Edward Leech, James C. Brown, Isham Trotter, George W. Newell, William Bogard, Benjamin Whitehead, William Love, David Williams, Christopher Owens, David Bunting, Andrew Dikas.

Who being duly elected tried and sworn the truth to speak upon the Issue joined do upon their Oath say that they find that the Defendant has not paid the debt in the declaration mentioned and does assess the Plaintiffs damages to Three Dollars & twenty seven cents. Therefore it is considered by the Court that the Plaintiff recover against the Defendant the debt in the declaration mentioned amounting to Fifty Seven Dollars & also his damages in form aforesaid as also his costs about his suit in this behalf expended & the Defendant in Mercy &

(p-260) James Hambleton, John Sterling, James Baxter Esquires on the Bench.

Mark Harwell & Nevell Gee Executors
of the last Will & Testament of
STERLING HARWELL)
Vs) Debt
GEORGE HUMPHRIES)

On motion of the Plaintiffs attorney that the Defendant plead to the Declaration as amended and try immediately and that if he fail to do so Judgment by default final be entered against him, the Defendant not being ready it is ordered by the Court that a final Judgment by default according to Specialty with interest be entered against him, the said Defendant. Therefore it is considered by the Court that the Plaintiffs recover against the Defendant according to the Specialty with interest, and their costs of suit in this behalf expended.

Therefore the Defendant prays a writ of error, which is granted he gives bond with Absolam Tribble & James Hambleton Esq. Securities bound in the sum of Sixteen Hundred Dollars.

Same Court & Jury No. 3

JAMES & WASHINGTON JACKSON,)Assee
Vs) Debt
ADAM HARMON, Senr.)
Same Jury No. 3

Who being duly elected tried & sworn the truth to speak upon the Issue joined do upon their Oaths say that they find the Issue for the Plaintiffs & that the Defendant hath not paid the sum of Two Hundred & Two Dollars 18 cents part of the debt in the declaration mentioned and do assess the Plaintiffs damages by reason of the detention thereof to Twelve Dollars. Therefore it is considered by the Court that the Plaintiffs recover the sum assessed by the Jury & their damages so assessed in manner & form with their costs about their suit in this behalf expended.

New trial by consent of parties.

(p-261) Same Justices on the Bench

ELIAS FORT, Junr. Guardian)
    Vs   ) Debt
JOHN BAKER, Junr. &)
JOSEPH ROBINSON   ) Same Jury No. 3, only John Dikas in place of Christopher Owens.

Who being duly elected tried and sworn the truth to speak upon the Issue joined do upon their Oaths say that the Defendants hath not paid Four Hundred & Seventy Eight Dollars twenty & a half cents part of the debt in the declaration mentioned and do assess the Plaintiff damages by reason of the detention thereof to Forty Nine Dollars & twenty three cents. Therefore it is considered by the Court that the Plaintiffs recover against the Defendants the sum assessed by the Jury in their Verdict in manner & form and also their costs about their suit in this behalf expended.

Same Justices on the Bench.

JAMES BOWERS)
    Vs   ) Debt
VINCENT COOPER)

The Defendant in this case was solemnly called came not but made default. Therefore it is considered by the Court that the Plaintiff recover against the Defendant his debt according to Specialty with interest and also his costs about his suit in this behalf expended.

(p-262) Ordered by the Court that the Jurors be discharged for this Term.

DAVID WILLIAMS)
    Vs   ) Covenant
JOHN GRIFFIN)

Motion to set aside a Judgment at last term had and that the Defendant be allowed to plead & the cause continued.

An assignment of platt & Certificate of Survey from James McCarrell & Zelphia his wife, Jeremiah Walker & Zebe his wife and George Elliott which said Zelpha was the widow and(which said George & Zebe are the heirs of John Elliott) ~~do here by convey over to William Farrier the within~~ to William Farrier proven by the Oaths of James Huling & George Gibson witnesses thereto & ordered to registeration.

COLMORE DUVALL)
    Vs   ) O. Attachment
WILLIAM WILSON &)
JONATHAN BRADSHAW)

Ordered by the Court that the Clerk issue a Venditions Exponas to sell the property so attached. Therefore it is considered by the Court that the Plaintiff recover against the Defendant his debt agreeable to the attachment so declared as also his costs about his suit in this behalf expended.

(p-263) JAMES & WASHINGTON JACKSON) Asses.
                    Vs   ) Debt
            ADAM HARMAN, Senr.   )

Thereupon the Defendant prays a writ of error which is granted he gives Adam Harman, Junr. & Elisha Willis security in the sum of Four Hundred & Four Dollars & thirty six cents.

Motion for writ of error withdrew by Defendants attorney.

John H. Poston Esq. returns a list of taxable property for Capt. Drakes Company for the year 1809.

Capt. Vance returns a list of taxable property for Capt. Penrises Company for the year 1809.

                                              Jno. Stirling
                                              Hugh McClure, J. P.
                                              John H. Poston

(p-264) The Worshipful Court of Montgomery County have met according to adjournment Monday September 18th 1809.

Present

                John Blair   )
                John Sterling   )
                Sterling Neblett) Esquires
                James Hambleton   ) Justices
                Abner Harris   )

Pannel for the Grand Jury.

1 Joseph Robinson, Foreman   9 Wright Outlaw
2 Guthridge Lyons   10 Joseph Dickson
3 Stephen Cocke   11 Victor Harris
4 Stephen Hamblin   12 Joshua Weakly
5 David Dupree   13 Jonathan Johnson
6 John French   14 William Goodwin
7 Needham Whitfield   15 Stephen Thomas
8 John Rudolph, Jr.

Who being elected & sworn retired to enquire for the body of the County the Grand Jury served four days & was dismissed.

Harbert Wheelis sworn as Constable to attend the Grand Jury proves four days attendance.

Ordered that William McElrath be appointed overseer of the road leading from James Huling the same down as far as Capt. Trigg worked. That the hands living at said Hulings & all below that belonged to said Trigg that worked under him work under said McElrath.

(p-265) Ordered that Bryen Whitfield & Bright Herring be appointed to settle with William Farrier administrator & the Heirs of George Sims, Deceased & make return of the same to next Court.

        STATE   )
        Vs   )
        JOHN H. HYDE)

Avery Lambert acknowledges himself indebted to the State in the sum of One Hundred Dollars to be void on condition he appears prosecute & give evidence on behalf of the State against John H. Hyde. Acknowledged in Open

Court Sept. Term 1809.
Teste W. C. Jamison Clk.

1 Deed of Gift William Chisholm, Senr. to William Chisholm, Junr. & others for a negro girl & was acknowledged in Open Court & ordered to registration.
2 Deed Henry J. Williams to Mathew Ryburn was acknowledged in Open Court & ordered to registration for 22½ acres of land.
3 Deed John Moseley to Philmore Whitsworth was duly proven in Open Court by the Oath of Mathew Rybourn & Henry J. Williams subscribing witnesses thereto & ordered to registration for 77-3/4 acres of land.
4 Deed of Conveyance Joel R. Oldham to Thomas H. Oneal was acknowledged in Open Court & ordered to registration for 80 acres of land.

(p-266) Thomas Brantly Administrator of James Brantly Deceased renders an Inventory of the said Deceased Estate into Court.
5 Deed of Conveyance William McDaniel to Edwin Clifton was acknowledged in Open Court & ordered to registration for 83 acres of land.
6 Deed of Conveyance William McDaniel to Mark Chambles was acknowledged in Open Court & ordered to registration for 100 acres of land.
7 Bill Sale William Chishim to John Cheshim for one negro boy was acknowledged in Open Court & ordered to registeration.
8 Bill Sale William Chishem to Joseph Bogard for one negro was acknowledged in Open Court & ordered to registration.
9 Bill of Sale William Chishim to Charles Bogard for one negro was acknowledged in Open Court & ordered to registration.
10 Deed of Conveyance William Chishim to Taylor Chishem was acknowledged in Open Court & ordered to registration for 100 acres of land.

On affidavit of Brittain Bayliss the Court Exonirates said Bayliss from attending as a Juror this Term.

Ordered that Walter Wyatt be appointed overseer of that part of the road that Richd. Fowler formerly worked upon & that William R. Gibson Esquire give the list of hands to work thereon.

(p-267) JAMES BAXTER & CO.)
     Vs   )
   THOS. TRAVIS)

On motion of the Defendant by his Council it is ordered that the Execution in this cause be quashed & that the Judgment upon which it was sued & which was entered by default at last Court be set aside for cause shewn by Affd. of the Defendant & the Defendant have leave to plead at this term.

Ordered that Joseph Woolfolk be appointed Guardian of Francis Prince Pennington Heir of John Pennington Decd. & give Bond & Security for $200.

Ordered that John Coffee be appointed overseer of the road in the place of Benjm. Organ.

Ordered that Thomas Brantly Administrator of James Brantly Deceased sell all the perishable property of said Estate of the said Decd. on a credit of nine months.

11 Deed of Conveyance John Cooke Shff. to Thomas Martin was acknowledged in Open Court & ordered to registration, for 500 acres.

(p-268) Deed of Conveyance John Cooke Shff. to James Matlock for 125 acres of land was acknowledged in Open Court & ordered to be registered.

Deed of Conveyance John Gray Blount by his attorney Willie Blount to John George Rinor was duly proven in Open Court by the Oath of John Cooke & James M. Reynolds subscribing witnesses thereto 640.

Deed of Conveyance John G. Blount by his attorney Willie Blount to James Steele was proven in Open Court by the Oath of James B. Reynolds & John Cooke Shff. subscribing witnesses thereto for 232.

Deed of Conveyance John G. Blount by his his attorney Willie Blount to John Steele was proven in Open Court by the Oath of James B. Reynolds & John Cooke Shff. subscribing witnesses thereto 232.

Ordered that Rowlan Peterson be appointed overseer of the road in the place of John Chisholm.

Ordered that James Huling Esquire the County Trustee have a credit of Thirty Dollars on account of a extray house proven by John Weathers as his property & that Thomas Williams be discharged from the payment as required by law as said Williams was the poster. The Jury of View that was appointed to view a road leading from Davidles Ferry at the mouth of half pone reports to Court their proceedings.

(p-269) The Venire to December Term 1809 James Wilson, Junr. Benjamin Wilson, Edward Clifton, John Stewart, half pone, Brittain, Bayliss, Ebenezer Frost, William Lyons, William Weaks, John Brigham, Abraham Whitehead, John Trousdale, Joseph Edwards, Thomas Doyle, Joseph Penrice, Peter Holt, Samuel Thornton, Adam Harman, William Ford, Samuel Allen, James Boyd, Henry Funk, William M. Man, William Corlew, William Whitehead, James Loggins Edwin Gibson, William Grayson, John Hillis, James Williams, Thomas Collier, Samuel Pillingim, Thomas Moore, Daniel Mitchell, Benjamin Adams, Benjamin Cowen, Jessee Sibley, Samuel Wooldridge, David Davis, Benjam Organ.

Court adjourned untill tomorrow at 9 O'clock
Court met according to adjournment Tuesday Sept. 19th 1809.
Present

     Robert Prince) Esquire
     John Blair   ) Justices
     Hugh McClure)

(p-270) Ordered by the Court that the County business be taken up on the first Monday of next term & the States business on the first Thursday.

13 Covenant Bond Robert Nelson to Jonathan Chandler proven by the Oath of Sam'l Scott subscribing witness thereto & John McCarrell, Senr. proves the handwriting of Robert Nelson.

Robert Prince, John Blair & Bryan Whitfield Esquires on the Bench.

MICAJAH PICKETT)
  Vs   ) Certiorari & Supersedias
JOSEPH ONEAL)

This day came the parties by their attornies & a Jury of good & lawfull men to wit,

1 Alexander Carns   7 Samuel Bumpass

2 Burrell Bailess
3 Leech Jacob
4 Rybourn Mathew
5 Herring Bright
6 Leech David
8 John McCarrell
9 Robert McGloughlin
10 James Morrow
11 Thomas C. Minor
12 John Teasley

Who being duly elected tried and sworn the truth to speake upon the matter of Controvercy do upon their Oaths say they find for the Plaintiff & assess his damage to Ten Dollars. Therefore it is considered by the Court that the Plaintiff recover against the Defendant & his Security (p-271) Thomas H. O'Neal the damages so assessed by the Jury & his costs about his suit in this behalf expended & the Defendant in Mercy &

JOHN DEN Lessee of)
ISAAC KITTRELL   )
Vs   ) Ejectment
BARNET SNELLING   )

Isaac Kittrell the Plaintiff in this case being solemnly called failed to appear & prosecute his suit. Therefore it is considered by the Court that the Defendant go without day, and the Defendant recover against the Plaintiff his costs about his suit in this behalf expended.

14 Deed of Conveyance John G. Robins to Thomas C. Minor for 100 acres land proven by the Oath of Anthony Crutcher & John W. Lowther witness thereto & ordered to registeration.

Bill Sale James Ross to James James Jeffris for one negroe proven by James Lockart & William Ross, Sr. & ordered to registeration they being subscribing witnesses thereto.

(p-272) Same Justices on the Bench.

HUGH F. BELL, Admr. of)
ROBERT NELSON, Decd.   ) Debt
Vs   )
WILLIAM GORDON   ) No. 2

This day came the parties by their attornies and a Jury of good & lawfull men (to wit)

1 Isaac Peterson
2 Peter Hubbard
3 John Keathley
4 Peter Oneal
5 William Ross
6 Benjamin Organ
7 George Humphries
8 John Coffee
9 Francis Beatie
10 James Trice
11 Andrew Beatie
12 Jehue Hoskins

Who being duly elected tried & sworn the truth to speak upon the Issue joined do say that they find that the Defendant hath not paid the debt in the declaration mentioned & do assess the Plaintiffs damages by reason of the non payment to Six Dollars twenty two & a half cents. Therefore it is considered by the Court that the Plaintiff recover against the Deft. his debt in the declaration mentioned & his damages as assessed by the Jury in their Verdict, and his costs about his suit in this behalf expended & the Defend't. in Mercy &

James Hambleton Esquire rendered into Court a list of taxable property for Capt. Beaties Company for the present year.

(p-273) Robert Prince, James Lockart, Samuel Gattis & Samuel Smith Esquires.

```
GEORGE W. NEVELL  )
       Vs         )  Case
ROBERT AKINS      )
```

This day came the parties by their attornies & Jury No. 2 only John Brown in place of John Keathley & Thomas Hunter in place of John Hoskins
Who being sworn the truth to speak upon the Issue joined do upon their Oath say-
The case being argued by the Counsel on both sides, it is considered by the Court that the Plaintiff be be nonsuited & that the Defendant recover against the Plaintiff his costs of suit ~~about his suit~~ in this behalf expended & the Plaintiff in Mercy &

15 Bill Sale Rich'd. Lee to William Hust for one negroe, proven in Court by Wright Bond & John Hust & ordered to registeration.
16 Deed Conveyance John Cooke Sheriff to John P. Vaughn 150 acres acknowledged in Court & ordered to registeration.
17 Deed of Conveyance Jesse Oldham to Thomas Brantley for 58 acres acknowledged in Court & ordered to registeration.

(p-274) Thomas Smith, Sam'l. Smith & James Lockart Esquires on the Bench.

```
ADRIN DEVENPORT &   )
EMANUEL ENSMINGER   )  Debt
       Vs           )
JAMES D. DAVIS      )
```

This day came the parties by their attornies & the same Jury No. 2,
Who being duly elected & sworn the truth to speake upon the Issue joined do upon their Oath say that they find that the Defend't. hath paid Twenty Dollars part of the debt in the declaration mentioned, but that he hath not paid Seventy Nine Dollars sixty & a half cents & do assess the Plaintiff damages by reason of the detention thereof to Five Dollars Ninety Six & a forth cents. Therefore it is considered by the Court the Plaintiff recover against the Defendant the sum of Seventy Nine Dollars Sixty & a half cents part of the debt in the declaration mentioned & his damages as assessed by the Jury in their Verdict as aforesaid, also his costs about his suit in this behalf expended & the Defendant in Mercy &

18 Deed of Conveyance Haydon Well to William Corbin was proven in Open Court by the Oath of William Corlew & Richard Whitehead, subscribing witnesses thereto for 292 acres of land & ordered to registeration.

(p-275) Same Justices on the Bench

```
JAMES & WASHINGTON JACKSON  )
            Vs              )  Debt
PETER MOSELEY               )
```

This day came the parties by their attornies & Jury No. 1,
Who being duly sworn the truth to speak upon the Issue joined do upon

their Oath say that they find that the Defendant hath not paid the debt in the declaration mentioned & do assess the Plaintiffs damages by reason of the detention thereof to Four Dollars fifty cents. Therefore it is considered by the Court that the Ptff. recover against the Defendant the debt in the declaration mentioned, and his damages by the Jury assessed also his costs about his suit expended.

19 Deed of Conveyance Willie Blount to Thomas L. Carney for 160 acres land proven by the Oaths of Elisha Gossett & Daniel Huff subscribing witness thereto & ordered to registeration.

Bill of Sale David Collins to P. W. Humphries for a negro was proven in Open Court by the Oath of George West & Robert West subscribing witness thereto & ordered to registeration.

(p-276) Same Justices

```
EBENEZER FROST  )
     Vs         ) Debt
DAVID DAVIS     )
```

This day came the parties by their attornies & Jury No. 1 only Jehus Hoskins in place of Burrell _____

Who being duly sworn the truth to speak do upon their Oaths say that the defendant hath not paid Eighty Dollars part of the debt in the declaration mentioned & do assess the Plaintiff damages by reason of the detention thereof to Four Dollars sixty cents. Therefore it is considered by the Court that the Plaintiff recover against the Defendant the sum of Eighty Dollars part of the debt in the declaration mentioned & his damages as assessed by the Jury in their Verdict, also his costs about his suit in this behalf expended.

Same Justices

```
WILLIAM LYTLE, Junr.  )
     Vs               ) Debt
THOMAS TRAVIS         )
```

This day came the parties by their attornies & same Jury No. 1

Who being duly sworn the truth to speak upon the Issue joined do upon their Oath say that they find that Defendant hath not paid the debt in the declaration mentioned & do assess the Plaintiffs damages by reason of the detention thereof to Six Dollars & Seventy Cents. Therefore it is considered by the Court that the Plaintiff recover the debt in the declaration mentioned & his damages as assessed by the Jury in their Verdict. Also his costs about his suit in this behalf expended.

(p-277) Same Justices

```
JAMES BAXTER & CO.  )
     Vs             ) Debt
JOHN BARTON         )
```

This day came the parties by their attornies & thereupon No. 1.

Who being duly sworn the truth to speak upon the Issue joined do upon their Oath do say that they find that the Defendant hath not paid the debt in the declaration mentioned & do assess the Plaintiffs damages by reason of the detention thereof to Three Dollars Seventy Six Cents. Therefore it is considered by the Court that the Ptff. recover against the Defendant the debt in the declaration mentioned of $88 Dollars & 74 cents and the damages so assessed by the Jury & his costs of his suit in this behalf expended.

Same Justices

JAMES BAXTER & CO.)
Vs   ) Debt
WILLIAM BARTON   )

This day came the parties by their attornies & also same Jury No. 1 Who being duly sworn the truth to speak upon the Issue joined do upon their Oaths say that they find that the Defendant hath not paid the debt in the declaration mentioned & do assess the Plaintiffs damages by reason of the detention thereof to Three Dollars Sixty Eight & a half cents. Therefore it is considered by the Court that the Plaintiff recover against the Defendant their debt in the declaration mentioned with his damage assessed by the Jury also his costs of suit in this behalf expended.

(p-278) 20 Deed of Conveyance
Robert Akins to John Rudolph was proven in Open Court by the Oath of John Hoskins, Thomas Yarborough subscribing witnesses thereto for 84 acres land.

25 Deed of Conveyance John Come to Richard Carney was proven in Open Court by the Oath of Elisha Gossett & Thomas L. Carney subscribing witnesses thereto & ordered to registeration 229 acres.

ROBERT AKINS   )
Vs   ) Debt
ISAAC KITTRELL)

The Defendant in this case comes in proper person & confesses Judgment according to Specialty with all costs with lawfull Interest. Therefore it is considered by the Court that the Plaintiff recover against the Defendant the debt in the declaration mentioned with lawfull Interest & his costs about his suit in this behalf expended.

Same Justices

SAMUEL PETERS   )
Vs   ) O. Attachment
ADRIAN DAVENPORT)

B. M. Williamson Garnishee appears in Court & declares upon Oath that he ows nothing to Adderine Davenport but that: there is six barrells of salt in his possession belonging to Marmaduke Davenport in his possession.

(p-279) John Blair, James Hambleton, James Lockert, William Gibson Esquires on the Bench.

REYNOLDS & MCFARLAND)
Vs   ) Debt
SAMUEL CRAFT   )

This day came the parties by their attorneys & also Jury No. 1, only ~~of~~ ~~George~~ ~~in~~ ~~place~~ ~~of~~ John Keathly in place of Burrell Bailess, Who being duly sworn the truth to speak upon the Issue joined do upon their Oath say that the Defend't. hath not paid the debt in the declaration mentioned & do assess the Plaintiffs damages by reason of the detention thereof to Two Dollars sixteen & a half cents. Therefore it is considered by the Court that the Plaintiffs recover against the Defendant the debt in the declaration mentioned & his damages assessed by the Jury in their Verdict also his costs of suit in this behalf expended.

22 Deed of Conveyance for Lott in Clarksville No. 58 Henry Small to Robert Nelson proven by James Hambleton & William S. Bailey witnesses thereto & ordered to be registered.

(Copyise Note) (Page 280 was omitted in this Record)

(p-281) Same Justices only William Gibson.

ROBERT AKINS)
Vs) Debt
LAMUEL PETERS)

This day came the parties by their attorneys & also Jury No. 1 Who being sworn the truth to speake upon the Issue joined do upon their Oaths say that they find that the Defendant hath not paid the debt in the declaration mentioned and do assess his damages by reason of the detention thereof to Five Dollars Sixty two cents. Therefore it is considered by the Court that the Plaintiff recover against the Defendant the debt in the declaration mentioned with his damages as assessed by the Jury in their Verdict also his costs about his suit in this behalf expended.

23 Deed of Conveyance for 320 acres from Cuthbert Powell to Seven Powell ordered to registeration by virtue of the Clerks Seal of District of Columbia.

The above Deed was acknowledged before Judge Cranch & ordered to registeration.

24 Deed of Conveyance Alexander Faith to John Gaynor acknowledged in Court for 66 acres & ordered to be registered.

(p-282) Court adjourned untill tomorrow at 9 O'clock.

Court met according to adjournment Wednesday Sept. 20th 1809.
Present

Robert Prince)
John Blair) Justices
John Sterling) Esquires
Henry H. Bryant)

James G. Jinkins & George W. Jinkins Orphens comes into Court chooses Thomas W. Jinkins their Guardian and the Thomas W. Jinkins gives bond in the sum of Ten Thousand Dollars with Joseph Gray, Senr. Joseph Gray, Junr. his securities which was received by the Court.

Same Justices

THOMAS HICKMAN)
Vs) Case
PLEASANT ROACH)

Jury No. 3

This day came the parties by their attornies & thereupon a Jury of good & lawfull men, to wit,

1	Alexander Carns	7	John McCarrell
2	Mathew Rybourn	8	Samuel Bumpass
3	David Linch	9	Thomas C. Minor
4	Bright Herring	10	John Teasley
5	Robert McLaughlin	11	James Morrow
6	John Keathley	12	Jacob Leach

Who being duly elected tried & sworn well & truly to enquire what damages the Plaintiff hath sustained by reason of the non performance of the Assumpsets (p-283) in the declaration mentioned upon their Oath do say that they assess his damages to Fifty Seven Dollars Nineteen cents. Therefore it is considered by the Court that the Plaintiff recover against the Defendant his damages as assessed by the Jury in their Verdict aforesaid, also his costs of suit in this behalf expended & the Defendant in Mercy &

Same Justices

NANCEY SCOTT
Vs
JAMES EDWARDS Admr.
SOLOMON SCOTT Decd. } Case

The Plaintiff in this case was solemnly called and came not but made default. Therefore it is considered by the Court that the Defendant go without day & recover against the Plaintiff his costs about his suit in this behalf expended.

Samuel Vance & John Bradley Surviving Partners of

VANCE, KING & BRADLEY
Vs
PHILLIP HAWKINS } O. Attacht.

The Defendant being solemnly called failed to appear & replevy the property. Therefore it is considered by the Court that a Writ of Venditioni Exponas Issue commanding the Officer to sell the property so attached.

(p-284) Same Justices on the Bench.

JAMES & WASHINGTON JACKSON
ASSIGNEE
Vs
WILLIAM CUNNINGHAM } Debt

This day came the parties by their attornies & a Jury No. 3
Who being duly elected and sworn the truth to speak upon the Issue joined do upon their Oath say that they find that the Defendant hath not paid the debt in the declaration mentioned and do assess the Plaintiffs damages by reason of the detention thereof to Nine Dollars Forty three cents. Therefore it is considered by the Court that the

Plaintiff recover against Defendant his debt in declaration mentioned and his damages as assessed by the Jury & his costs about his suit in this behalf expended.

Same Justices

EBENEZER FROST
    Vs   } Debt
JAMES D. DAVIS

This day came the parties by their attornies & thereof a Jury of lawfull men to wit Jury No. 3

Who being duly elected tried & sworn the truth to speak upon the Issue joined do upon their their Oaths say that they find that the Defendant hath not paid Eighty Dollars part of the debt in the declaration mentioned and do assess the Plaintiffs damages by reason of the detention thereof to Four Dollars. Therefore it is considered by the Court that the Plaintiff recover against the Defendant the Verdict of the Jury in form aforesaid as also his costs about his suit in this behalf expended & the Defendant in Mercy &

(p-285)   Robert Prince, John Blair & Henry H. Bryant.

HENRY DOUGLASS
    Vs   } Covenant
JAMES D. DAVIS

This day came the parties by their attornies & a Jury of good & lawfull men No. 3

Who being duly elected & sworn ~~the truth to speak upon the issue joined to upon their oath do say~~ delegently to inquire of damages upon their Oath do say that the Plaintiff hath sustained damages by the reason of the Defendants non performance of the Covenant in the declaration mentioned to Fifty Two Dollars Sixteen & two thirds cents. Therefore it is considered by the Court that the Plaintiff recover against the Defendant the debt in the declaration mentioned and the damages so assessed by the Jury in form aforesaid as also his costs about his suit in this behalf expended & the Defendant in Mercy &

Samuel Vance & John Bradley,) Surviving Partners of
  VANCE, KING & BRADLEY   )
    Vs   ) Trespass Vi et Armes
  SAMUEL THORNTON   )

The Plaintiff in this case failing to prosecute this suit for the want of witnesses it is ordered by the Court that the Plaintiff be non suited. It is considered by the Court that the Defendant recover his costs about his suit in this behalf expended & the Plaintiff in Mercy &

Deed of Conveyance John Cocke Shff. to William T. Lewis was acknowledged in Open Court & ordered to registeration for 1000 acres.

Same Justices

(p-286)   Elijah Willis resigned his commission as Constable in Montgomery

County, and in his place the Court appointed Joseph Edwards, who gave bond with Elisha Willis his security bound in the sum of Six Hundred & Forty Dollars & qualified accordingly.

James Lockart, Henry H. Bryant, John McCauley-Esquires-Hugh McClure Esq.

MANN PHILLIPS
   Vs   } Case
SAMUEL PETERS

This day came the parties by their attornies & thereupon a Jury of good and lawfull men, to wit, Jury No. 3, only Peter Hubard in place of Thos. C. Miner.

Who being duly elected tried & sworn the truth to speake upon the Issue joined do upon their Oath say that they find ~~damages for the plaintiff four hundred dollars~~ that the Defendant did assume upon himself in manner & form as the Plaintiff hath alledged and do assess the Plaintiffs damages to Four Hundred Dollars. Therefore it is considered by the Court that the Plaintiff recover against the Defendant his damages so assessed by the Jury also his costs about his suit expended.

The Defendant not being satisfied with the Verdict of the Jury prayed & obtained an Appeal, gave bond with James Huling & John Edmonston his securities bound in the sum of Eight Hundred Dollars & filed the following reasons the said Defendant by his attorney prays an appeal to the Superior Court of Law & for Robertson District for the following reasons to wit, because the Verdict is contrary to law & evidence.

                                                    J. B. Reynolds
                                                         Atty.

(p-287)   Same Justices on the Bench.

Rebecca Downs widow of William Downs at appearing to the Court that the Jury summoned by the Sheriff to lay off the Dower specified in a writ directed to the Sheriff at the instance of Rebecca Downs have made an incompleat return to said writ, therefore it is ordered by the Court here at September term 1809 that an alias writ issue directed to the Sheriff of Montgomery returnable to December term next commanding him to summons a Jury to lay off said Dower as he was heretofore commanded.

Ordered that James Walker be appointed overseer of the road in the place of Joseph Wray & that James Lockart Esquire give the list of hands to work thereon.

25 Deed of Conveyance Willie Blount attorney for John Gray Blount to James Huling for 520 acres proven in Court by the Oath of James Elder & James M. Reynolds subscribing witnesses thereto & ordered to registeration.

James Trice records his stock mark a swallow fork in the left ear & a hick under the right ear.

(p-288)   Same Justices on the Bench

WILLIAM ROSS, Senr.
   Vs   }
WILLIAM GORDAN & STERLING INGRAM

On motion of the Plaintiffs attorney and it appearing by the return made by John Lowther Constable that a Fiere Facias issued from James Lockert Esquire Justice of the Peace for Montgomery County for the sum of Forty Nine Dollars & Sixty Two & a half cents. I have levied this Execution upon Six Hundred and Forty acres of land at the mouth of Red River on the 15th day of July 1809. ~~Supposed to be by the property of~~ Therefore it is considered by the Court that a Writ of Venditioni Exponas Issue to expose to Sale the said tract of land to satisfy the Judgment and costs suit in this behalf expended.

Court adjourned untill tomorrow at 9 O'clock.

Court met according to adjournment.
Present

      John H. Poston
      John McCauley
      William R. Gibson   Esquire
      Henry H. Bryant   Justices
      James Hambleton

John Cocke Esquire is appointed collector for the public taxes for the present year and gave bond with Henry H. Bryant & Stephen Cocke his securities bound in the sum of Five Thousand Dollars.

(p-289)   STATE
             Vs   Indictment
         JOHN TRIBBLE

The Defendant in this case submitted to the Court. Therefore it is considered by the Court that he be fined Eleven Dollars forty cents with costs of suit in this behalf expended and that he continue in custody untill he pay the same.

Ordered that William Watkins, Junr. be appointed overseer of the road from William Farriers Ferry five miles on the road leading towards Portroyal & that Bryan Whitfield Esquire give a list of the hands to work thereon.

       JAMES MALLERY
           Vs   Case
       BURRELL BAYLISS

The parties dismiss their suit, the Defendant confesses to pay to the Plaintiff Five Dollars. The Plaintiff assumes half the costs and the Defendant the other half. Therefore it is considered by the Court that the Plaintiff recover against the Defendant the Five Dollars & half the costs of the suit in this behalf expended.

26 Covenant Bond Robert Nelson to Joseph & Charles Bogard proven by John Nelson a subscribing witness thereto & Anthony Crutcher proves Robert Nelson hand writing & ordered to registeration.

(p-290)   JOHN MCCLAIN
            Vs   Debt
        THOMAS COLLIER

The Defendant in proper person comes into Court & confesses Judgment agreeable to Specialty with Interest.

The Plaintiff stays Execution untill Decr. 1st. next. Therefore it is considered by the Court the the Plaintiff recover against the Defendant his debt & interest as also his costs about his suit in this behalf expended & the Defendant in Mercy &

27 Proxy Joseph French to Duncan Stewart proven in Open Court by the Oaths of William Goodwin & David Dupree & ordered to registeration.

James Hambleton, Thomas Smith, John McCauley, Henry H. Bryant, William R. Gibson, Samuel Gattis.

```
STATE     )
Vs        ) Indictment
DAVID WILLIAMS )
```

This day came the parties by their attornies & thereupon a Jury of good & lawfull men to wit,

1 Mathew Rybourn
2 Burrell Bailiss
3 Alexander Carnes
4 Bright Herring
5 John Keathley
6 Robert McLaughlin
7 James Morrow
8 John Teasley
9 Samuel Bumpas
10 David Linch
11 Jacob Leach
12 Peter Hubbard

Who being duly elected tried & sworn the truth   (p-291)   to speak upon the bill of Indictment do upon their Oath say that they find the Defendant not guilty, as charges in the bill of Indictment. Therefore it is the oppinion of the Court that Defendant go without day.

Ordered that Sterling Nibblet & Abner Harris be appointed to settle with Isam Trotter Guardian to Robert Trotter & make return to next term.

```
STATE     )
Vs        ) Presentment
WILLIAM R. GIBSON )
```

The Defendant submitted & the Court fined him Twenty five cents & also his costs of suit in this behalf expended.

Court adjourned untill tomorrow 9 O'clock.

Friday 22nd. Court met according to adjournment.
Present

```
          Henry H. Bryant    )
          William R. Gibson  ) Esquires
          Sterling Niblett   )
```

Mathew Rybourn records his stock mark an overslope & under Reel in each ear.

(p-292) On petition ordered D. P. T. Issue to John H. Poston Esq, to take the Deposition of James Carrew in behalf of Stephen Hendlen in a suit Samuel Vance against sd. Hendlen.

```
STATE     )
Vs        ) Indictment
JOHN DAVIDSON )
```

The Defendant in this case was solemnly called to appear and defend his suit came not but forfeited his recognizance. Therefore it is the oppinion of the Court that the State recover against the Defendant the sum of Two Hundred Dollars the amount of his recognizance & the costs of

suit in this behalf expended.
Robert Prince, Sterling Neblett, William R. Gibson, Esquires.

```
STATE      )
Vs         ) Indictment
WILLIAM DAVIDSON )
```

The Defendant submits himself to the Court & prays Mercy. Therefore it is the oppinion of Court that the Defendant be fined Fifteen Dollars & costs of suit & that he remain in the hands of the officer untill paid.

28 Covenant Bond Robert Nelson to Moses Pierce & James Pierce was proven in Open Court by the Oath of William Pearce a subscribing witness thereto & Anthony Crutcher proved the hand wrighting of Robert Nelson & ordered to registeration.

(p-293) 29 Deed of Conveyance Adam Harmon Senr. to John Harmon for 113 acres acknowledged in Oppen Court & ordered to registeration.
Robert Prince, Sterling Niblett, William R. Gibson Esquire.

```
STATE      )
Vs         ) Indictment
JOHN DAVIDSON )
           Jury #4.
```

This day came the parties by their attornies & a Jury of good & lawfull men to wit.

1 Mathew Rybourn   7 James Morrow
2 Burrell Bailess   8 John Teaslsy
3 Alexander Carnes   9 Samuel Bumpass
4 Bright Herring   10 David Linch
5 John McCarrell Senr.   11 Jacob Leach
6 Robert McLaughlin   12 Peter Hubbard

Who being duly elected & sworn the truth to speak upon the bill of Indictment do upon their Oath say that they do find the Defendant guilty as charged in the Bill of Indictment. Therefore it is the oppinion of the Court that he be fined Five Dollars & costs of suit & remain in the hands of the Officer untill paid.
Same Justices

```
SAME  )
Vs    ) Indictment
SAME  )
```

The Defendant submitts to the Court. Therefore it is the oppinion of the Court that he be fined Three Dollars with costs & remain in the hands of the Officer untill paid.

```
(p-294)   FRANCIS TOMPKINS )
              Vs           ) Case
          MORGAN BROWN     )
```

This day came the parties by their attornies & Jury No. 4
Who being elected tried & sworn the truth to speake upon the Issue joined do upon their Oath say that the Defendant did assume upon himself

in manner & form as the Plaintiff hath declared against him & they do assess the damages to the Plaintiff by reason thereof to Three Hundred Dollars. Therefore it is considered that the Plaintiff recover against the Defendant his damages as assessed by the Jury in their Verdict aforesaid, also his costs of suit in this behalf expended.

Hugh McClure, Sterling Neblett, John H. Poston Esquires on the Bench.

```
JAMES M. REYNOLDS &
JOHN R. MCFARLAND     )
         Vs           )  Debt
HUGH F. BELL, Admr.   )
ROBERT NELSON? Dec'd. )
```

This day came the parties by their attorneys & a Jury Viz. No. 4. Who being duly elected tried & sworn the truth to speak upon the Issue joined do upon their Oath say that they find that the Defendant hath not paid the debt in the declaration mentioned and do assess the Plaintiffs damages by reason of the detention thereof to Twenty Six Dollars forty five cents. Therefore it is considered by the Court that the Plaintiffs recover agst. the the Defendant the debt in the declaration and damages as assessed by the Jury with costs of suit in this behalf expended.

(p-295)   Same Justices

```
HUGH F. BELL Admr, of  )
ROBERT NELSON Decd.    )
         Vs            )  Debt
ISAAC SHELBY           )
```

This day came the parties by their attorneys & a Jury (Viz) No. 4. Who being elected tried & sworn the truth to speak upon the Issue joined do say that they find that the Defendant hath not paid part of the debt in the declaration mentioned of One Hundred & Sixty Six Dollars Eighteen cents & do assess the Plaintiffs damages by reason of the detention thereof to Sixteen Dollars Twenty One cents. Therefore it is considered by the Court that the Plaintiff recover his debt in the declaration mentioned & his damages as assessed by the Jury & his costs of suit in this behalf expended.

Same Justices

```
JAMES STEWART &
HUGH F. BELL Exr. Charles Brantley Decd.)
         Vs                              )  Debt
ISAAC SHELBY                             )
```

This day came the parties by their Attornies & Jury No. 4. Who being elected tried & sworn the truth to speak upon the Issue joined do say upon their Oath say that the Defendant hath not paid the debt in the declaration mentioned & do assess the ptff. damages by reason of the detention thereof to Twenty Dollars Ninety & half cents. Therefore it is considered by the Court that the Plaintiffs recover against the Defendant their debt in the declaration mentioned & damages assessed by the Jury and their costs about their suit expended.

(p-296) Same Justices

HUGH F. BELL Admr.
ROBERT NELSON Decd.
Vs
SAMUEL CRAFT

This day came the parties by their Attornies & a Jury of lawfull men to wit, No. 4.

Who being duly elected tried & sworn the truth to speaks upon the Issue joined do upon their Oath say that they find that the Plaintiff hath not paid the debt in the declaration and do assess the Plaintiffs damages by reason of the detention thereof to Twenty One Dollars Eighty Seven & a half cents. Therefore it is considered by the Court that the Plaintiff recover against the Defendant the debt in the declaration mentioned and his damages assessed by the Jury & also his costs of suit expended.

Appeal prayed & granted gave Brice Jackson & George Humphries securities bound in the sum of One Thousand Forty three Dollars 75 cents.

Same Justices

SAMUEL CRAFT
Vs   } Debt
BENJAMIN HAWKINS

This day came the parties by their Attornies & a Jury of good & lawfull men to wit, Jury No. 4.

Who being duly elected tried & sworn the truth to speak upon the Issue joined do upon their Oath say that they find that they find that the Plaintiff hath not paid the debt in the declaration mentioned & do assess the Plaintiffs damages by reason of the detention thereof to Eleven Dollars Eighty Nine cents. Therefore it is considered by the Court that the Plaintiff recover against the Defendant the debt in the declaration mentioned, and his damages assessed by the Jury & also his costs of suit expended.

(p-297) ABEL OLIVER
Vs   } Debt
ISAAC SHELBY

This day came the parties by their Attornies and also a Jury to wit, No. 4. Who being duly elected tried & sworn the truth to speaks upon the Issue joined do upon their Oaths say that they find that the Defendant hath not paid the debt in the declaration mentioned and do assess the Plaintiffs Damages by reason of the detention thereof to Four Dollars and Twenty five cents. Therefore it is considered by the Court that the Plaintiff recover his debt in the declaration mentioned amounting to One Hundred Dollars and his damages as assessed by the Jury in their Verdict and his costs about his suit in this behalf expended.

Francis Penrice comes into Court & gives in his resignation as Constable which was received by the Court.

William Penrice comes into Court & gives Bond with Francis Penrice Burrell Bayliss his secutities bound in the sum of Six Hundred & Forty Dollars & quallified as Constable for the County in the place of Francis Penrice.

Court adjourned untill tomorrow at 9 O'clock.

Court met according to Adjournment Saturday Sept. 23, 1809.
Present

Hugh McClure }
John H. Poston } Esquires
James Baxter } Justices
Bryan Whitfield }

(p-298) THOMAS HICKMAN }
Vs } In Case
PLEASANT ROACH }

The Defendant in this cause having been surrendered by his security to the Court in discharge of themselves. Whereupon it was ordered by the Court that the said Pleasant Roach should remain in custody of the Sheriff of Montgomery County, on motion of the Defendants Attorney that the said Defendant be prayed in custody of the Sheriff the Plaintiffs Counsel, and the said Defendant not being prayed in custody, it is ordered by the Court that he be discharged from his imprisonment &

H. F. BELL & WILLIAM BELL }
Vs } Case
ANDREW LYTLE }

The Plaintiff in proper person dismissed this suit. The Defendant in proper person assumes all costs. Therefore it is considered by the Court that the Plaintiff recover against the Defendant their costs about their suit in this behalf expended & the Defendant in Mercy &

(p-299) Hugh McClure, John H. Poston & Bryan Whitfield, Esquires.

JOSEPH BAXTER & }
JOHN MORELL }
Vs } Case
JOHN EDMONSTON }

This day came the parties by their Attornies and also a Jury of good and lawfull men, to wit,

1 Mathew Rybourn
2 Bright Herring
3 Peter Hubbard
4 Samuel Bumpass
5 Robert McLaughlen
6 James Morrow
7 John Teasley
8 Jacob Leach
9 David Linch
10 Burrell Bailess
11 Alexander Carnes
12 John Keathley

Who being duly elected tried & sworn the truth to speake upon the Issue joined do upon their Oath say that they find that the Defendant did assume upon himself as the Plaintiffs in declaring hath alledged and do assess the Plaintiffs damages by reason of the non performance of the assumpsets to One Hundred & Fourteen Dollars Ninety Seven & a half cents. Therefore it is considered by the Court that the Plaintiff recover against the Defendant the damages as assessed by the Jury in their Verdict and their costs about their suit in this behalf expended.

Motion for appeal which was granted he gave bond with James Elder & James Huling securities bound in the sum of Three Hundred Dollars & filed the following reasons. The Verdict in this case is against evidence & against Justice & so is the Judgment of the Court which in my opinion is a sufficient reason why an Appeal should be granted to the Defendant.

           G. W. L. Marr
           Atty. for the Defendant

(p-300) Deed of Conveyance John Cooke Shff to Isham Trotter was acknowledged in Open Court & ordered to be registered for 150 acres of land.

30 Deed of Conveyance John Cooke Shff. to John Nevill was acknowledged in Open Court & ordered to registration for 596 acres.

James Baxter, John H. Poston, Bryant Whitfield Esquires on the Bench.

   PETERS & MINOTT)
     Vs   ) Debt
   ISAAC SHELBY)

This day came the parties by their Attornies & a Jury to wit, No. 4 only William Farrior in *in* place Mathew Rybourn & Isam Trotter in place John Teaseley.

Who being sworn the truth to speake upon the Issue joined do upon their Oath say that the Defendant does owe the debt in the declaration mentioned & do assess the Plaintiffs damages by reason of the detention to Four Dollars Thirty five Cents. Therefore it is considered by the Court that the Plaintiffs recover against the Defendants the debt in the declaration mentioned and their damages as assessed by the Jury in their Verdict aforesaid also their costs about their suit in this behalf expended.

(p-301) Hugh McClure, James Baxter, Bryant Whitfield Esquires on the Bench.

   Alexander Richardson, surviving partner of
   Guy S. Trigg, William King & Alexander Richardson, Assee of)
   WM. L. LEWIS   ) Debt &
     Vs   ) Demurrer
   ROBERT WELLS   ) Demurrer

overruled.

The Defendant in this case being solemnly called failed to appear but made default. Therefore it is considered by the Court that the Plaintiffs recover against the Defendant according to the Specialty with Interest and their costs of suit in this behalf expended.

On motion of the Defendants Counsel the Judgment by default is set aside, and the said Defendant is allowed to demur, whereupon the parties appeared this day by their Counsel and on solemn argument heard thereon it is considered by the Court that the said demurrer be overruled. It is therefore considered by the Court that the Plaintiffs recover against the Defendant according to Specialty with Interest & costs of their suit in this behalf expended.

Deed of Conveyance for 1600 acres of land acknowledged in Oppen Court to William Bogogard ordered to be recorded.

31 Bill Sale William Chism to William Bogard proven Timothy Drake & J. Dun Davis for one negroe & ordered to registeration.

(p-302) EBENEZER FROST)
          Vs) Debt
     THOMAS SIMMINS)

The Defendant in this case was was solemnly called & came not but made default. Therefore it is considered by the Court that the Plaintiff recover against the Defendant according to Specialty amounting to Ninety Eight Dollars & Seventy five cents with interest and also his costs about his suit in this behalf expended.
    Same Justices

    REYNOLDS & MCFARLAND)
          Vs) Debt
    JAMES BOWERS)

This day came the parties by their Attornies & Jury No. 4
Who being duly sworn the truth to speak upon the Issue joined do upon their Oath say that the Defendant hath not paid Fifty Two Dollars Seventy Seven & three forth cents and do assess the Ptfs. damages by reason thereof to Five Dollars Twelve & a half cents. Therefore it is considered by the Court that the Plaintiffs recover against the Defendant ~~hath not paid~~ Fifty Two Dollars part of the Debt in the declaration mentioned and ~~assess the Plaintiffs damages and~~ & his damages as assess'd. by the Jury & their costs of suit in this behalf expended.

(p-303) Hugh McClure, James Baxtor, James Hambleton Esquires.

    BRYANT WHITFIELD)
          Vs)
    HUGH F. BELL Admr. of)
    Robert Nelson, Decd.)

This day came the parties by their attornies & a Jury of good & lawfull men to wit,

1 William Farrior   7 Isam Trotter
2 Bright Herring   8 Jacob Leach
3 Peter Hubbard   9 David Lench
4 Samuel Bumpas   10 Burrell Bailess
5 Robert McLaughlen   11 Alexander Carnes
6 James Morrow   12 Jacob Rudolph

Who being duly elected tried & sworn deligently enquire of damages upon their Oath do say that the Plaintiff hath sustained damages by reason of the non performance of the Covenant in the declaration mentioned to Four Hundred & Sixty Nine Dollars. Therefore it is considered by the Court that the Plaintiff recover against the Defendant the damages assessed by the Jury in their Verdict & also his costs of suit in this behalf expended.

(p-304) Court adjourned untill Monday at 10 O'clock.
The Worshipfull Court of Montgomery County have met according to Adjournment Monday September 25th 1809

Present

	Hugh McClure	) Esquire
	James Hambleton	) Justices
	John H. Poston	)

JOHN DEN Lessee, of)
JOHN MOORE   ) Ejectment
    Vs   )
BRITAIN BAILESS   )

On motion & by consent of the parties it is ordered by the Court that Duncan Stewart be appointed surveyor to survey & make out Three just & fair platts of the land in dispute & return the same to next term & that ten days notice be given to the Defendants.

JOHN DEN Lessee, of)
JOHN MOORE   ) Ejectment
    Vs   )
JOSIAH HORN   )

On motion by consent of the parties it is ordered by the Court that Duncan Stewart be appointed surveyor to survey the lands in dispute & make out three fair platts thereof & return the same to next Court ten days notice to be given to the Defendant.

(p-305)   Same Justices

ROBERT SEARCY Assee)
    Vs   ) In Debt
SAMUEL LYONS   ) Demurrer

Argued by the Counsel on both sides It is the oppinion of the Court that the Demurrer be overruled. Therefore it is considered by the Court that the Plaintiff recover against the Defendant his debt according to Specialty with interest & his costs of suit in this behalf expended & the Defendant & the Defendant in Mercy &
    Same Justices

SAMUEL THORNTON)
    Vs   ) Sci fa Demr.
AMOS ROCHAL   )
ADAM HARMON, Senr) & Stephen Handlin

Being argued it is the oppinion of the Court that the Demurrer be overruled. Therefore it is considered by the Court that the Plaintiff recover against the the Defendant according to Siere facias & his costs about his suit in this behalf expended.
    Same Justices

HUGH MCCOLLOM)
    Vs   ) Debt
WM. FARRIOR   ) Demr.

The Demurrer overruled. Therefore it is considered by the Court that the Plaintiff recover against the Defendant his debt according to

Specialty with interest & his costs of suit in this behalf expended &
the Defendant in Mercy &

(p-306)　Same Justices

```
DAVID WILLIAMS  )
     Vs         )  Covent.
JOHN GRIFFEN    )
```

Ordered by the Court that the Judgment by default had at March term
last be set aside & that the Defendant in this case have leave to plead.
　　　　Same Justices

```
JAMES MILLER    )
     Vs         )  Debt
LEMUEL PETERS   )
```

This day came the parties by their attornies and the matters of law
therein arrising upon the Defendants Demurrer upon the Plaintiffs declaration being argued it is the oppinion of the Court that the the said declaration & matters therein contained are not sufficient in Law to bar
prevent the said Plaintiff from having his action aforesaid for the Plaintiff to have his said action against the Defendant. Therefore it is considered by the Court that the Plaintiff recover against the Defendant
agreeable to Specialty with interest as also his costs about his suit in
this behalf expended & the Defendant in Mercy &

(p-307)　Hugh McClure, James Hambleton & James Baxter, Esq.

```
FREDRICK STUMP   )
     Vs          )
REUBIN LOGGANS & )  Sci fa
WILLIAM LOGGANS  )
```

The Defendant being solemnly called & came not but made default.
Therefore it is considered by the Court that the Plaintiff recover against
the Defendants according to Sciere facias with interest and also his costs
of suit in this behalf expended & the Defendants in Mercy &
　　　　Same Justices on the Bench.

```
SAMUEL VANCE & JOHN BRADLEY, Surviving Partners of )
VANCE, KING & BRADLEY                              )
              Vs                                   )  T.V.A.
SAMUEL THORNTON                                    )
```

For reasons appearing to the Court ordered that the non suit had on the
third day of this term be set aside in this suit.

```
HUGH F. BELL, Adminir )
     Vs               )  Debt
SAMUEL CRAFT          )
```

The Defendant in this case by his attorney filed the following reasons
for an Appeal (to wit) that he is not ready to pay the money　　　　W.Z.

(p-808) JOHN McCLAIN)
Vs) Debt
JAMES PIERCE)

The Defendant in this case being solemnly called came not but made default. Therefore it is considered by the Court that the Plaintiff recover against the Defendant agreeable to Specialty with interest as also his costs about his suit in this behalf expended & the Defendant in Mercy &

Execution stayed by the Plaintiff to 1st Decr. 1809.
Same Justices

ASAHEL BRUNSON, Junr.)
Vs) Debt
VINSON COOPER)

The Defendant in this case being solemnly called came not but made default. Therefore it is considered by the Court that the Plaintiff recover against the Defendant agreeable to to Specialty with interest as also his costs about his suit in this behalf expended & the Defendant in Mercy &

JAMES JACKSON, WASHINGTON JACKSON & SAMUEL BAXTER)
Vs) Debt
LEWIS PICKETT)

The Defendant being solemnly called came not but made default. Therefore it is considered by the Court that the Plaintiff recover against the Defendant the debt in Plaintiffs declaration mentioned as also the interest thereon also his costs about his suit in this behalf expended & the Defendant in Mercy &

Mary Waggoner's & others petition. It is ordered by the Court that it be continued untill next term.

(p-809) THOMAS SMITH)
Vs)
REUBEN LOGGINS &) Debt
WILLIAM LOGGINS)

The Defendants Reuben Loggins & William Loggins being solemnly called came not but made default. Therefore it is considered by the Court that the Plaintiff recover against the Defendants agreeable to Specialty & interest thereon as also his costs about his suit in this behalf expended & the Defendant in Mercy &

JAMES BAXTER & CO.)
Vs) In Debt
THOMAS TRAVISE)

On motion of the Plaintiffs Counsel it is ordered that the order of the case be reversed & that an alias execution issue immediately on the rise of the court.
Court adjourned untill tomorrow at 10 O'clock.
Court met according to adjournment Tuesday September the 26th, 1809.

Present   Hugh McClure   ⎫ Esquires
                           John H. Poston ⎬ Justices
                           James Baxter   ⎭

(p-310)   STATE OF TENNESSEE
          MONTGOMERY COUNTY

Pursuant to an order of the County Court of Montgomery issued at March term 1809, directed to Duncan Stewart, Samuel Allen & Samuel Gattis, George Bell came before us Duncan Stewart, Samuel Allen & Samuel Gattis this twenty seventh day of May 1809 (being a day adjourned to) at the house of John Moore on the blooming grove and being duly sworn on the holy evangelist of Almighty God deposeth & saith that in the year One thousand and seven hundred eighty five (as well as he recollected) John Nichols employed him the same deponent to locate two tracts of land of two hundred & twenty eight acres each & that to the best of his recollection he the said deponant located & superentended the surveying said two tracts of land some time in the year 1805 aforesaid & that the land the said John Moore now occupies & claims on the blooming grove creek, is the same land located & as aforesaid & that a poplar tree on the west side of said creek at which there is a fallin poplar he rarely believes to be the beginning of said two tracts of land, & that a poplar tree at which there is a fallen black oak on the east side of said creek, he does believe to be the southeast corner of the lower tract of said two tracts on said creek.

And further this deponant sayeth not.

                                                              GEORGE BELL

Sworn to this Twenty Seventh day of May 1809
   Duncan Stewart
   Samuel Allen
   Samuel Gattis

(p-311)   Court adjourned untill court in course.

                                                         Hugh McClure, J.P.
                                                         John H. Poston, J.P.
                                                         James Baxter, J.P.

163

The Worshipful Court of Montgomery County have met according to adjournment Monday Decr. 18th, 1809.
Present

     John Blair   )
     Sterling Neblett)
     James Hambleton) Esquires
     William Bearden) Justices

The Court adjourned unto the House of James Carreway & met according to adjournment.
Panel for the Grand Jury

1 John Stewart   9 Abraham Whitehead
2 Thomas Moore   10 Benjamin Cowen
3 David Davis   11 Edward Clifton
4 William M. Marr   12 John Hillis
5 William Cerlew   13 Samuel Wooldridge
6 James Boyd   14 Benjamin Adams
7 William Grayson   15 Samuel Fillingim
8 Brittain Bayless

Who being duly elected tried & sworn, retired to enquire for the body of the County, the Grand Jury served 3 days & was dismissed.

Harbert Wheeling Constable sworn to attend the Grand Jury during their setting, proves 3 days attendance.

(p-312) Ordered that Montgomery Bell have a license to keep a public Ferry across Cumberland River, opposite his lott formerly occupied by Peters & Minott in the town of Clarksville. He gave bond with John Stewart, James Huling, Joseph Penrice, James Hambleton his securities bond agreeable to Act of Assembly in the sum of Two Thousand Dollars & was received by the Court.

 1 Deed of Conveyance to Hugh McClure to William Farrior one lott in Clarksville known by No. 67 proven by the Oaths of James Bunting & Davis Bunting witnesses thereto & ordered to registeration.

 Bill of Sale Thomas Clinton to James Baxter & Company for one negro proven in Court by the Oaths of J. B. Reynolds & Jas. H. Russell witnesses thereto and ordered to registeration.

 2 Deed of Conveyance Thomas H. Oneal to Thomas Brantley for 80 acres of land proven in Court by the Oaths of James A. Bunting & David Bunting witnesses thereto & ordered to be registered.

 3 Deed of Conveyance John Cocke Shff. to Henry Pugh was acknowledged in Open Court & ordered to registeration for 80 acres.

 Ordered that John Bailey be appointed overseer of that part of the road in place of John Nevill & that Joseph Woolfolk Esq. appoint the hands to work.

(p-313) Ordered that Stephen Owens be appointed overseer of the road in place of Haydon Wells.

   Ordered that James Perry be appointed overseer of the road in place of Allen Anderson.

 4 Deed of Conveyance Daniel Welbourn to Gabrial Greathouse for 105 acres of land proven by the Oaths of Marvell McFarlin & Archellis McFarlen witnesses thereto & ordered to be registered.

 On motion, ordered that John Johnson have letters of Administration upon the Estate of Nancy Fowler, he gave bond with Archellas McFarlen, Marvell McFarland, David McFaden & John Mackey his securities bound in the sum of One Thousand Dollars.

Ordered that Joseph Woolfolk & Samuel Norrington Esquires let to the lowest bidder an insane person Benjamin Smith for the term of twelve months.

5 Deed of Conveyance John Cocke Sheriff to Absolam Tribble for 220 acres of land acknowledged in Open Court & ordered to registeration.

Ordered that William Lyons & Ebenezer Frost be exonerated from attending as Jurors this term.

(p-314) Robert Prince, Sterling Niblett, Samuel Vance, John Blair, Abner Harris, Nathan McGraw, William Bearden.

On motion ordered by the Court that no Justice be quallifyed into office for this county only agreeable to the constitution of the State of Tennessee.

Ordered that Sterling Neblett Esquire give the list of hands to work under William Niblett overseer of the road.

6 Deed of Conveyance Peter Onnal to Thomas Travis Senr. for 100 acres of land proven by the Oath of John H. Poston & Daniel Anderson witnesses thereto & ordered to registeration.

The Court proceeded to appoint a Venire to _____ Term _____ (Viz) James C. Brown, John Copeland, David Peoples, Asahal Brunson, Richard Whitehead, David Lench, William Allen, Josiah C. Duke, Thomas Brantley, Amos Hatcher, James Bailey, John Henderson, James McCarrell, Thomas Bunch, Archebauld McCorkle, Samuel Mitchell, Alexander McCrabb, Alexander Trousdale, Joshua Beggars, Fendall Whitworth, Philmore Whitsworth, Henry J. Williams, Benjamin Wilson, Samuel Thornton (p-315) James Wilson, James Morrow, William Morrow, Elisha Ramey, John Rudolph, John Haygood, David R. Slaughter, William Reasons, Nicholas Darnold, John Bristo, David Bunting, George Fransisco, Samuel McNichols, Jesse Craft, George Ury.

The Court adjourns untill tomorrow 9 O'clock.

Tuesday 19th December. The Court met according to adjournment. Present

Robert Prince)
Thomas Smith) Esquires
James Baxter) on the Bench

7 Deed of Conveyance Bennett Searcy to James Huling 50 acres of land proven by James H. Russell & Henry Fort subscribing witnesses & ordered to registeration.

Robert Prince, Thomas Smith, James Baxter Esqrs.

PHILLIP PARCHMENT)
Vs) O. Attach't.
EDWARD PLATON)

Thomas Blakeney summoned as Garnishee appeared was sworn & saith he ows nothing nor knows of any person that does.

8 Deed of Conveyance John Cocke Shrff. to James Huling was acknowledged in Open Court & ordered to registeration for 4 Town Lotts.

Same Justices.
(p-315)
JAMES & WASHINGTON JACKSON Asgee.)
Vs) Debt
ADAM HARMON Senr.)

165

This day came the parties by their Attornies & thereupon came a Jury of good and lawfull men, to wit,

1 Colmore Duvall
2 James Williams
3 William Farrior
4 James Trice
5 Absolam Tribble
6 Henry Funk
7 Daniel Mitchell
8 Thomas Collier
9 John Malone
10 Robert W. Temple
11 Thomas Blakeney
12 Robert Ray

Who being duly elected tried & sworn the truth to speak upon the Issue joined upon their Oath do say that they find the Issue for the Plaintiff and assess their damage by reason of the detention of the debt in the declaration mentioned to Twenty Four Dollars & Twenty Five Cents & that there is a ballance due of sd. debt of Two Hundred & Two Dollars & Eighteen Cents said ballance of Debt & Interest amounting in all to Two Hundred and Twenty Six Dollars & Forty Three Cents. Therefore it is considered by the Court that the Plaintiffs recover against the Defendant the said debt & damages amounting to said sum & their costs about their suit in this behalf expended.

9 Deed of Conveyance Allen Hunter to Nicholas Choat was acknowledged in Open Court for 100 acres of land & ordered to registeration.

(p-316) William Weaks, John Trousdale, Samuel Thornton, Samuel Allen, James Loggans, Edwin Gibson, Benjamin Organ, ~~Benjamin Weeks~~.
Who being summoned to attend this term & serve as Jurors were solemnly called & came not, therefore it is considered by the Court that they be fined ~~in the sum~~ agreeable to the Act of Assembly.

On petition of Ann Sugg widow of Samuel Sugg Deceased. It is ordered by the Court the Sheriff summon Jury of good & lawfull men to appear on the premises and lay of the Dower of the said Ann Sugg out of the lands which the said Samuel Sugg died possessed of.

On motion ordered that Francis Penrice be appointed Guardian to Jency Channell, James Channell & Henry Channell infant heirs of Elisha Channell decd. under the age of 21 years on given bond agreeable to law.

Deed of Conveyance Duncan Stewart to Aaron Laws was acknowledged in Open Court & ordered to be certifyed for 500 acres of land.

10 Deed of Conveyance Haydon Wells to the heirs of Lemuel Sugg proven in Court by the Oaths of Samuel Vance & Thomas Porter witnesses thereto & ordered to be registeration.

(p-317) Samuel Gattis, Nathan McGraw, Robert Prince Esquires.

TIMOTHY MURRICK)
        Vs   ) Case
JOHN STEWART   )

This day came the parties by their attornies and thereupon came a Jury of good and lawfull men, to wit,

1 Joseph Penrice
2 Peter Holt
3 James Williams
4 William Whitehead
5 William Hust
6 Benjamin Wilson
7 William Ford
8 William Good
9 John Teasley
10 David Bunting
11 William Goodwin
12 James Wilson

Who being duly elected tried & sworn the truth to speak upon the Issue joined upon their Oaths do say that they find for the Plaintiff & assessed his damages to Two Hundred & Twenty Three Dollars Seventy Four Cents. Therefore it is considered by the Court that the Plaintiff recover against the Defendant Two Hundred & Twenty Three Dollars Seventy Four Cents the Verdict of the Jury in form aforesaid as also his costs about his suit in this behalf expended & the Defendant in Mercy &

The Defendant not being satisfied with the Verdict of the Jury prayed and obtained an Appeal.

11 Deed of Conveyance David Slocumb to Morgan Brown for 160 acres proven in Open Court by the Oaths of Samuel Vance & George W. Jinkins witnesses thereto and ordered to registration.

(p-318) Deed of Conveyance Haydon Wells to John Barns for 150 acres of land acknowledged in Open Court and ordered to registration.

Robert Prince, Samuel Gattis, David McGraw, Esquires, Justices
James Lockert Esq.

William Bogard, Joseph Bogard & Charles Bogard)
Vs) Detenue
JOHN SHELBY)

This day came the parties by their Attornies and thereupon a Jury of good and lawfull men, to wit,

1 Henry Funk
2 Buckner Killebrew
3 Stephen Hendlen
4 William Mitchell
5 Barney Duff,
6 Samuel Mitchell
7 John Stewart
8 Thomas Collier
9 Mordica Johnson
10 Francis Penrice
11 William Farrier
12 Isaac Kittrell

Who being duly elected tried & sworn the truth to speak upon the Issue joined do upon their Oaths say that the Plaintiffs the Bogard be entitled to that Bond when they come into Court & acknowledge the executing of the Deed of Conveyance to the Defendant.

This suit is dismissed by the Plaintiffs Attorney ~~by mutual consent and~~ the Plaintiff assumes all costs with stay of Execution untill April Term next.

William E. Williams & James Bowers Esquires produced a commission from his Excellincy the Govenor of this State as Justices of the Peace took the necessary Oaths of office accordingly.

(p-319) Esther Cooper Adminx. of John Cooper Deceased returned on Oath an account of Sales of the said Deceased.

13 Deed of Conveyance James Dickson by his Attorney in fact William Dickson to Haydon Wells for 276 acres of land proven by Edward Neblett & Benjamin Wells witnesses thereto & ordered to registration.

14 Deed of Conveyance Haydon Wells to William Barns for 157 acres of land acknowledged in Court & ordered to registration.

15 Deed of Conveyance Timothy Anderson Senr. to Timothy Anderson, Jr. for 100 acres acknowledged in Open Court and ordered to registration.

On sufficient reasons shewn to the Court they exonirated James Wilson & Benjamin Wilson as Jurors to this term & that they may Depart.

16 Deed of Conveyance from Haydon Wells to Benjamin Wells 252½ acres acknowledged & ordered to registration.
Justices Present.

1 Robert Prince
2 Samuel Vance
3 Hugh McClure
4 James Baxter
5 John H. Poston
6 Thomas Smith
7 James Lockert
8 Nathan McGraw
9 Samuel Gattis

(p-320) On motion ordered that George W. L. Marr Esquire be allowed the sum of Fifty Dollars as County Solicitor for the County of Montgomery up to this term & that the County Trustee pay the same.
Bill of Sale Abraham Whitehead to John Bayless acknowledged in Open Court for one negro woman & ordered to registration.
Bill of Sale Abraham Whitehead to John Bayless for a negro boy acknowledged in Court & ordered to registration.

STATE OF TENNESSEE)
MONTGOMERY COUNTY) December Term 1809

To the Worshipfull the Justices of the Court of Pleas & Quarter Sessions for the County of Montgomery.
Your Petitioner Timothy Acoff resident of this State & the owner of a slave which he is desierous of seting free humbly represent to your Worships that Richard Acoff a negro man slave the property of your petitioner is a man true faithfull & honest humble & modest in his deportment warm & sincear in his affections industrious attentive & careful paying a strict regard to his own concerns & medling not with those of others for these & other reasons equally operative your petitioner prays your Worships the premises considered that you would emancipate said negro & in Virtue of an Act of the General Assembly in such case made & provided secure to him the enistimable blessings of freedom blessings which by the laws of God & nature belong to man & to which this negro man hath a further claim in his own high deserts.

Timothy Acoff

The matters & things contained in the foregoing petition being considered & fully understood by the Court now here they are fully understood by the Court they are of opinion that their according to the same is consistant with the interest & policy of this State in Testimony whereof Robert Prince Chairman of said Court have indorsed this report on the back of said Petition & have hereunto subscribed my name.
Done in Open Court
this 18th of Decr. 1809.

Robert Prince

(p-321) Court adjourned untill tomorrow at 9 O'clock.

The Worshipfull Court of Montgomery County have met according to adjournment Wednesday December 20th 1809.
Present

Robert Prince   ) Esquires
William E. Williams) Justices
Hugh McClure   )

168

17 Deed of Conveyance Joseph Oneal to John Hignight for 58 acres of land proven by the Oaths of Peter Oneal & Peter Lighaker witnesses thereto & ordered to registration

Stephen Cooke, Barney Duff & Stephen Thomas Esquires produced a commission as Justices of the Peace for Montgomery County from his Excellency the Governor & took the necessary Oaths of qualifications

1 Covenant Bond Robert Nelson to William M. Marr for 60 acres of land proven by George W. L. Marr a subscribing witness thereto & by Anthony Crutcher who proves said Nelson's signature and ordered to registration.

Ebenezer Frost gives in his resignation as overseer of the road.

(p-322) Robert Prince, William E. Williams, Stephen Thomas, Stephen Cooke, Barney Duff Esquires Justices. Benjamin Hawkins Esq.

CURDWELL BREATHELL)
Vs) Case
WILLIAM FARRIER)

This day came the parties by their Attornies & thereupon came a Jury of good and lawfull men, to wit,

1 Joseph Penrise
2 Henry Funk
3 Daniel Mitchell
4 William Mitchell
5 James Mitchell
6 Peter Holt
7 Robert Edmonston
8 Thomas Collier
9 Vinson Cooper
10 George West
11 William Good
12 John Bayley

Who being elected tried & sworn ~~diligently to enquire of damages to well~~ ~~their oaths say~~ the truth to speak upon the Issue joined do say that they find that the Defendant is not guilty as in pleading he hath alledged. Therefore it is considered by the Court that the Defendant go without day & that the Plaintiff pay to the Defendant his costs about his suit in this behalf expended from which judgment the plaintiff prayed an Appeal. Appeal granted.

(p-323) Stephen Cooke, Stephen Thomas, William E. Williams Esquires on the Bench.

Ordered that no Civil Cause shall be taken up tomorrow.

Isham Trotter Guardian for Robert Trotter renders into Court a list of the property in his hands belonging to the said Robert Trotter as Guardian & ordered to registration.

The last Will & Testament of John Ferman was proven by the Oaths of Robert Duke & Joseph Prise witnesses thereto & ordered by the Court to be registered.

The Court adjourned untill tomorrow 9 O'clock.
Thursday 21st Decr. 1809 the Court met according to adjournment.
Present

Sterling Niblett)
Stephen Cooke) Esquires
Stephen Thomas) Justices

18 Deed of Conveyance Hugh F. Bell administrator of Robert Nelson to Isam Trotter was proven in Open Court by the Oath of Robert W. Temple & Absolum Tribble subscribing witnesses thereto for 55 acres of land.

2 Covenant Bond Robert Nelson to William Barton for 100 acres of land the signature of said Robert Nelson was proven by Charles Stewart (mill) & Anthony Crutcher and was ordered to registeration.

(p-324) C. BREATHELL)
                 Vs   ) Case
         WM. FARRIER) Reasons for Appeal

The Plaintiff in this case prays an Appeal to the Circuit Court for Montgomery County for the following reasons to wit, that the Verdict of the Jury is contrary to law and the evidences of the case which I am of an opinion are sufficient reasons to authorise an Appeal.

J. B. Reynolds, Atty. for Plaintiff

And entered into Bond with James Baxter & Samuel Lynes his securities bound in the sum of Five Hundred Dollars.

Bill Sale Charles Stewart to William Chisholm was acknowledged in Open Court & ordered to registeration for one negro.

Bill of Sale William Chisholm to Charles Stewart was proven in Open Court by the Oath of Robert W. Temple & John Stewart subscribing witnesses thereto for one negro & ordered to be registered.

Ordered that Burrell M. Williamson have a license to keep a Ferry across Cumberland River on the South side at his landing at the Town of Palmyra and entered into Bond with Joseph Penrice, Vinson Cooper & George West his security bound in the sum of Two Thousand Dollars.

(p-325) John Sterling, Sterling Neblett, Henry H. Bryan Esquires.

        STATE   )
         Vs   ) Indictment
        JOHN H. HYDE)

The Defendant in this case comes in proper person & submits himself to the Court. Therefore it is considered by the Court that he be fined Five Dollars & that he pay all costs of suit in this behalf expended.

Henry H. Bryan, Sterling Neblett & Stephen Cocke Esquires, Barney Duff Esquire also on the Bench.

        STATE   )
         Vs   ) Indictment
        WILLIAM WHITE)

The Defendant in this case submitts to the Court & prays Mercy, therefore it is the oppinion of the Court that the Defendant be fined Eleven Dollars & Twenty five cents and that he pay all costs.

        THE STATE   )
           Vs   ) Indictment
        CHARLES STEWART)

The Defendant in this case submitts himself and prays Mercy. Therefore it is considered by the Court that he be fined Eleven Dollars & Twenty five Cents & that he pay all costs in this suit expended.

(p-326) MARY TRIBBLE
Vs } Imorality
JAMES MEDLOCK

On motion & argument it is ordered by the Court that James Medlock & his securities be discharged from their recognizance bond in this case.

Edwin Gibson who was summoned to appear at this term as a Juror offers to this Cort his excuse on affidavit and is cleared.

THE STATE
Vs }
PETER HEROD

The Defendant in this case comes here into Court and acknowledges himself bound in the sum of Five Hundred Dollars to be levied off his goods & chattles, Lands & tenements, but to be levied on condition that he make his personal appearance here from term to term untill after the child is born which Jimmey Funk is now big with, and will not depart hence without leave of the Court.

Peter Herod (Seal)

Charles Miles, James Morrow, James Boyd all acknowledge themselves bound in the sum of Five Hundred Dollars each to be levied off your goods & chattels lands & tenements but to be levied on condition that Peter Herod make his personally appearance (p-327) at our next County Court of pleas & quarter sessions and from term to term untill after the child is born which Jimmy Funk is now big with & not to depart the Court without leave.

Charles Miles (Seal)
James Morrow (Seal)
Jas. Boyd (Seal)

STATE
Vs } Indictment
JAMES TRIBBLE

James Medlock acknowledges himself bound in the sum of Two Hundred & Fifty Dollars to be levied of his goods & chattels lands & tenements but to be void on condition that he appear at our next County Court of pleas and quarter sessions and from term to term & prosecute the suit the State against James Tribble & not depart the Court without leave.

James Matlock (Seal)

STATE
Vs } Indictment
JOHN M. TRIBBLE

James Melock binds himself in the sum of Two Hundred & Fifty Dollars that he personally appear at our next Court of pleas and quarter sessions for Montgomery and prosecute the suit the State against John M. Tribble & not depart the Court without leave.

James Matlock (Seal)

(p-328) Elizabeth Kittrell qualified as Executrix to the Estate of John Ferman & quallified accordingly.

THE STATE)
Vs)
JAMES TRIBBLE)

John Tribble, Absolam Tribble and Joseph Whitehead securities bound to deliver up the bodies of John Trible and James Tribble to the Court of Pleas and Quarter sessions at our December term 1809, being solemnly called to bring into Court the bodies of the said Defendant failed to do so and therefore they forfited their recognizance. Therefore it is ordered by the Court that Seire facias Issue against the securities, the forfitness sett aside by consent.

James Blackwell & Joshua P. Vaughn produced a commission from his Excellency the Governor as Justices of the Peace and qualified accordingly.

TIMOTHY MURRIEH)
Vs) Case
JOHN STEWART)

Reasons for Appeal (to wit) that the Verdict is contrary to law and evidence, which reasons he considers are sufficient to authorize this Appeal.

J. B. Reynolds, Atty.

And entered into Bond)
with James Carreway,)
Charles Stewart his)
securities bound in the)
sum of Four Hundred & Forty Seven)
Dollars & Forty Eight Cents.)

(p-329) Court adjourned untill tomorrow at 9 O'clock.

The Worshipful Court of Montgomery County has met according to Adjournment Friday December 22nd 1809.
Present

Robert Prince)
Stephen Cocks) Esquires
James Hambleton) Justices

WILLIAM & DAVID COCHRAM)
Vs) Debt
JOHN SUMMERVILL)

The Plaintiffs in this case dismissed their suit. Therefore it is considered by the Court that the Plaintiff recover against the Defendant their costs about their suit in this behalf expended.
Same Justices

JAMES WALL Executor of)
ALEXANDER M. ROBERTS)
Vs) Sci fa
SHADRICK TRIBLE)
SPILSBY TRIBBLE)
JESSE TRIBBLE)
ABSOLAM TRIBBLE)
ANDREW TRIBBLE)
JAMES TRIBBLE)

JOHN TRIBBLE
GOODMAN TRAYWICK & His Wife, NANCY
RICHARD COCKE & ELIZABETH COCKE his Wife
POLLY TRIBBLE heirs of SPILSBY TRIBBLE, Decd.

Being solemnly called came not, it is therefore (p-330) considered by the Court that the said James Watt Executor as aforesaid have execution against the said Defendant for the aforesaid sum of Seven Hundred & Ninety Two Dollars & Sixty three cents & costs according to Sci facias & also his costs for suing forth & prosecuting this Siere facias.

Same Justices

JOSEPH WOOLFOLK & DRURY FORD, Admrs.
JAMES FORD Decd.
Vs
JAMES BOYD & CHARLES MILES, his Security

This day came the parties Plaintiffs by their Attorneys and it appearing to the satisfaction of the Court that the said Plaintiff heretofore, to wit, on the Twenty Second Day of March Eighteen Hundred & Nine obtained Judgment against the said James Boyd for the sum of Sixty Dollars & costs the satidfaction of which Judgement the said James Boyd gave Bond with Charles Miles his security dated the Fifth day of September 1809 said Bond being for the satisfaction of said Judgment & the interest and costs due thereon according to the provisions of the Act of the General Agsembly in such case made & provided entitled an Act concerning executions & for other purposes and it also appearing to the satisfaction of the Court that the said Judgment interests & costs have not been satisfyed according to the condition of said bond. On motion of said Plaintiffs by their Attorney, it is therefore considered by the Court that the Plaintiffs recover against the said James Boyd (p=331) & Charles Miles his security in said Bond the sum of Sixty Dollars the amount of the Judgment aforesaid & all interest due thereon & also Seven Dollars Seventeen & one half cents and also thereon his costs by them about their motion herein this behalf expended and the Defendant in Mercy &

Motion for an Appeal which is granted & gave Bond with Daniel Anderson & George West their securities bound in the sum of One Hundred & Thirty four Dollars & Thirty five cents & filed the following reasons.

The Defendant says the following are his reasons for praying an Appeal Viz that the Judgment is enegutious & irregular which are in my opinion a sufficient for appealing takeing also into consideration the hard times

WM. SMITH
Atty.

MCCLURE & ELDER
Vs   Debt
HAYDON WELLS

The Plaintiffs in this case agree to relinquish & release the present bail James Perry & James Morrow in this obligation and the said Defendant giving Benjamin Wells as special bail on security.

J. B. Reynolds, Atty.

DAVID WILLIAMS
Vs
JOHN GRIFFEN

Motion entered by Plaintiffs Attorney to strike out Defendants Demurrer. Motion withdrawn.

(p-332) Justices present, James Hambleton, Henry H. Bryan, Stephen Cooke, Esquires.

JOHN H. POSTON, Surviving Partner of
KING & POSTON
Vs
ROEZBERT PRINCE

Debt

The Defendant in this case being solemnly called came not but made default. Therefore it is considered by the Court that the Plaintiff reciver against the Defendant the debt in the declaration mentioned with interest from the 14th January 1809 untill Judgment, amounting in all to Two Hundred & Sixty Three Dollars Ninety Cents and also his costs of suit in behalf expended.

James Hambleton, Henry H. Bryan, Hugh McClure, Justices on the Bench.

GOODMAN TRAYWICK & WIFE
Vs
SHAIRICK TRIBBLE Admr. of
SPILSBY TRIBBLE? Decd.

Case

This day came the parties by their Attornies and thereupon came a Jury of good & lawfull men, to wit,
Joseph Penrice, Daniel Mitchell, Peter Hott, Henry Funk, William Benjamin Wells, James Williams, Thomas Collier, John French, Philip Duke, William Goodwin, Moses Parker, John Hogan, Robert W. Temple,
Who being duly elected tried & sworn the truth (p-333) to speak upon the Issue joined do upon their Oath say that the Intestate Spilsby Tribble in this life time did assume in manner & form as charged in the Plaintiffs said Plaintiffs declaration and assess the Plaintiffs damages to the sum of One Hundred & Sixty Six Dollars & Forty Cents and they do further find that the said Defendant has fully administered all and singular the goods and chattels rights and credits, that were of the Intestate at the time of his death and which have come to his hands to be administered, and the Jury do further find that there are outstanding judgments to the amount of Eleven Hundred Dollars unsatisfied and to be paid out of the goods & chattels & of the deceased when they shall come by the hands of the said Defendant to be administered. It is therefore considered by the Court that the said Plaintiff do recover the said sum of One Hundred & Sixty Six Dollars & Forty Cents to be levied on the goods & chattels & of the deceased when they shall come to the Defendants hands to be administered beyond the amount of value of the said sum of Eleven Hundred Dollars and the Defendant in Mercy &

On petition of Judith Ford widow & relict of James Ford deceased, it is ordered that the Sheriff summon a Jury of lawful men to lay off her Dower of all the land that the said James Ford died seased of & make return to next term.

On petition that, Henry H. Bryan, Richard Carney & Samuel Norrington, John Baker, Senr. & John Edmonston be appointed Commissioner to lay of to ~~pays of division between~~ Drury Ford, Ephraim Drake & Capandra his wife, William L. Boyd & Salley B. Boyd his wife ~~Legatees~~ Distributees of James ~~Boyd his wife~~ Ford Deed. ~~and pays return thereof~~ their respective distributive shares of the Estate of the said James Ford and make return thereof to next Court.

(p-334) Deed James Fentress to Elijah Parker was acknowledged in Open Court & ordered to registration for 100 acres of land.

JOHN COUTS
Vs
LEMUEL PETERS
&
JOHN STEELE, his Security

This day came the Plaintiff by his Attorney, and it appearing to the satisfaction of the Court that the said Plaintiff heretofore, to wit, on the Twenty Fourth day of June Eighteen Hundred and Nine obtained Judgment in this Court against the said Lemuel Peters and John Minott whereupon the said Lemuel Peters gave bond with John Steele his security dated the 16th day of September Eighteen Hundred and Nine said bond being for the satisfaction of said Judgment and the interest and cost due thereon according to the provisions of the Act of the General Assembly in such case made and provided entitled an Act concerning executions and for other purposes and it appearing to the satisfaction of the Court that the said Judgment interest and costs have not been satisfied according to the condition of said bond on motion of said Plaintiff by his Attorney. It is therefore considered by the Court that the Plaintiff recover against the said Lemuel Peters and John Steele his security the sum of One Hundred and Thirteen Dollars Sixty five cents the (p-335) amount of the Judgment aforesaid and all interest due and also Eight Dollars thirty three and three fourth cents the costs due thereon and also his costs by him about his motion herein this behalf expended.

JOHN COUTS
Vs
LEMUEL PETERS &
JOHN STEELE his Security

This day came the Plaintiff by his Attorney and it appearing to the satisfaction of the Court that the said Plaintiff heretofore to wit, on the Twenty Fourth day of June Eighteen Hundred and Nine obtained Judgment in this Court against the said Lemuel Peters and John Minott. Whereupon the said Lemuel Peters gave bond with John Steele his security dated the 16th day of September Eighteen Hundred and Nine, said bond being for the satisfaction of said Judgment and the interest and cost due thereon according to the provisions of the Act of the General Assembly in such case made and provided Entitled an Act concerning execution and for other purposes and it also appearing to the satisfaction of the Court that the said Judgment interest and cost have not been satisfied according to the condition of said bond. On motion of said Plaintiff by his Attorney, it is therefore considered (p-336) by the Court that the Plaintiff recover against the said Lemuel Peters and John Steele his security in said bond the sum of One Hundred and Twenty Eight Dollars sixty six cents and all interest due and also the sum of Eight Dollars thirty three & three fourth cents the costs due thereon and also his costs by him about his motion here in this behalf expended.

JOHN COUTS
Vs
LEMUEL PETERS
&
JOHN STEEL, his Security

This day came the Plaintiff by his Attorney and it appearing to the satisfaction of the Court that heretofore to wit, on the Twenty Fourth day of June Eighteen Hundred and Nine the said Plaintiff obtained Judgment against Lemuel Peters and John Minott whereupon the said Lemuel Peters gave bond with John Steele his security dated the 16th day of September Eighteen Hundred and Nine said bond being for the satisfaction of said Judgment and the Interest and costs due thereon according to the provision of the Act of the General Assembly entitled an Act concerning Executions and for other purposes and it also appearing to the satisfaction of the Court (p-337) that the said Judgment interest and costs have not been satisfied according to the condition of said Bond. On motion of the Plaintiff by his Attorney it is therefore considered by the Court that the Plaintiff recover against the said Lemuel Peters and John Steele his security in said Bond the sum of Seventy Five Dollars Sixty Cents the amount of the Judgment aforesaid with all interest due and also Eight Dollars Thirty three & three fourth Cents the costs due thereon and also his costs by him about his motion herein this behalf expended.

NICHOLAS CONRAD
Vs
WILLIAM MCDANIEL &
THOMAS WILLIAMS, his Security

This day came the Plaintiff by his Attorney and it appearing to the satisfaction of the Court the said Plaintiff heretofore to wit, on the Twenty Fourth day of September Eighteen Hundred and Eight obtained Judgment in this Court against the said William McDaniel whereupon the said William McDaniel gave bond with Thomas Williams his security dated the Sixth day of August Eighteen and Nine said Bond being for (p-338) the satisfaction of the said Judgment and the interest and costs due thereon according to the provisions of the Act of the General Assembly in such case made and provided Entitled an Act concerning Executions and for other purposes and it also appearing to the satisfaction of the Court that the said Judgment Interest and costs have not been satisfied according to the condition of said Bond. On motion of the Plaintiff by his Attorney it is therefore considered by the Court that the Plaintiff recover against the said William McDaniel and Thomas Williams his security in said bond the sum of One Hundred and Fifty Six Dollars Fifty Six and one half cents the amount of the Judgment aforesaid with all interest due and also the sum of Seven Dollars Seventy three & three fourth cents the costs due thereon and also his costs by him about his motion here in this behalf expended.

JAMES BOWERS
  Vs
VINSON COOPER &
JONATHAN CHANDLER &
BURRELL BAYLESS, his Security

This day came the Plaintiff by his Attorney and it appearing to the satisfaction of the Court, that the said Plaintiff (p-339) heretofore to wit, On the Twenty Eighth day of June Eighteen Hundred and Nine obtained a Judgment in this Court against the said Vinson Cooper whereupon the said Vinson Cooper gave bond with Jonathan Chandler and Burrell Bayless, his Securities said Bond being for the satisfaction of the said Judgement with the interest and costs due thereon according to the provisions of the Act of the General Assembly in such case made and provided Entitled an Act concerning Executions and for other purposes. And it also appearing to the satisfaction of the Court that the said Judgment interest and costs have not been satisfied according to the condition of the said Bond. On motion of the Plaintiff by his Attorney it is therefore considered by the Court that the Plaintiff recover against the said Vinson Cooper and Jonathan Chandler and Burrell Bayless his Securities in said Bond the sum of Sixty Dollars Ninety Cents the Amt. of the Judgment aforesaid and all interest due thereon & also the sum of _____ the costs due thereon & also the costs about their motion herein this behalf expended.

(p-340) HUGH MCCLURE &
         JAMES ELDER
           Vs
         ANDREW BEATY and
         RICHARD PERDUE, his Security

This day came the Plaintiff by their Attorney and it appearing to the satisfaction of the Court that the said Plaintiff heretofore, to wit, On the Twenty Seventh day of June Eighteen Hundred and Nine obtained Judgment in this Court against Andrew Beatie, whereupon the said Andrew Beatie gave bond with Richard Perdue his Security dated the Fourteenth day of September Eighteen Hundred and Nine said Bond being for the satisfaction of the said Judgment with the interest and cost due thereon according to the provisions of the Act of the General Assembly in such case made and provided Entitled an Act concerning Executions & for other purposes. And it also appearing to the satisfaction of the Court that that the said Judgment interest and costs have not been satisfied according to the condition of said Bond. On the motion of the Plaintiffs by their Attorney, it is therefore considered by the Court that the Plaintiffs recover against the said Andrew Beatie and Richard Perdue his security the sum of Fifty Four Dollars Forty Eight Cents the amount (p-341) of the Judgment aforesaid and all interest due and also Six Dollars Twenty One & a half cents the costs due thereon and also his costs about his motion herein this behalf expended.

HUGH MCCOLLUM
  Vs
WILLIAM FARRIER &
JAMES HULING, his Secy.

This day came the Plaintiff by his Attorney and it appearing to the satisfaction of the Court that the said Plaintiff heretofore to wit, On the Twenty Fifth day of September Eighteen Hundred and Nine obtained Judgment in this Court against the said William Farrier whereupon the said William Farrier gave bond with James Huling his security dated the 30th day of November Eighteen Hundred & Nine said Bond being for the satisfaction of the said Judgment with the interest and costs due thereon according to the provisions of the Act of Assembly Entitled an Act concerning Executors and for other purposes in such case made and provided and it also appearing to the satisfaction of the Court that the said Judgement interest and costs have not been satisfied according to the condition of said Bond. On the motion of the Plaintiff by his Attorney, it is therefore considered by the Court that (p-342) the said Plaintiff recover against the said William Farrier and James Huling his Security in said Bond the sum of One Hundred and Sixty five Dollars Seventy Three cents the amount of the Judgement aforesaid and all interest due thereon and also Seven Dollars Sixty One & a half cents - the costs due thereon and also his costs about his motion herein this behalf expended.

WILLIAM TAIT)
Vs)
JOSHUA P. VAUGHN)
&)
BARNY DUFF, his Secy.)

This day came the Plaintiff by his Attorney and it appearing to the satisfaction of the Court that the said Plaintiff heretofore, to wit, On the Twenty Seventh day of June Eighteen Hundred and Nine obtained Judgement in this Court against the said Joshua P. Vaughn whereupon the said Joshua P. Vaughn gave bond with Barny Duff his Security dated the Sixth day of September Eighteen Hundred and Nine, said Bond being for the satisfaction of said Judgment with the interest and costs due thereon according to the provisions of the Act of the General Assembly in such case made and provided Entitled an Act concerning Executions and for other purposes. And it appearing (p-343) to the satisfaction of the Court that the said Judgment interest and costs have not been satisfied according to the condition of said Bond.

On the motion of said Plaintiff by his attorney, it is therefore considered by the Court that the Plaintiff recover against the said Joshua P. Vaughn and Barny Duff his security the sum of One Hundred and Fifty One Dollars Seventy Cents the amount of the Judgment aforesaid and interest due thereon and also _____ the costs due thereon and also his costs about his motion herein this behalf expended.

HUGH MCCLURE &)
JAMES ELDER)
Vs)
DANIEL WILLIAMS &)
NEEDHAM WHITFIELD, his Security)

This day came the Plaintiffs by their Attorney and it appearing to the satisfaction of the Court that the said Plaintiff heretofore to wit,
On the Twenty Ninth day of March Eighteen Hundred and Nine, obtained Judgment in this Court against the said Daniel Williams, gave bond with Needham Whitfield his security dated the Twenty Ninth day of (p-344)

May Eighteen Hundred and Nine said Bond being for the satisfaction of said Judgement with the interest and costs thereon according to the provisions of the Act of the General Assembly in such case made and provided Entitled an Act concerning executions and for other purposes and it also appearing to the satisfaction of the Court that the said Judgment interest and costs have not been satisfied according to the condition of said Bond.

On the motion of the Plaintiff by their Attorney it is therefore considered by the Court that the said Plaintiffs recover against the said Daniel Williams and Needham Whitfield his security the sum of Sixty Dollars Seventeen cents the amount of the Judgement aforesaid and all interest due thereon and also Eight Dollars One and a Half cents the costs due thereon and also his costs by him about his motion herein this behalf expended.

EBENEZER FROST
Vs
JAMES D. DAVIS and
SAM'L. LYNES, his Security

This day came the Plaintiff by his Attorney and it appearing to the satisfaction of the Court (P-345) that heretofore to wit,

On the 19th day of September Eighteen Hundred and Nine the said Plaintiff obtained a Judgment in this Court against the said James D. Davis whereupon the said James D. Davis gave bond with Samuel Lynes his security dated the Eighth day of November Eighteen Hundred and Nine said Bond being for the satisfaction of the said Judgment with the interest and costs due thereon according to the provisions of the Act of Assembly in such case made and provided Entitled an Act concerning Executions and for other purposes, and it also appearing to the satisfaction of the Court that the said Judgement Interest and Costs have not been paid according to the condition of said Bond.

On the motion of the Plaintiff by his attorney it is therefore considered by the Court that the the Plaintiff recover against the said James D. Davis and Samuel Lynes his security in said Bond the sum of Eighty Four Dollars with all interest due thereon and also _____ the costs due thereon and also his costs by him about his motion (p-346) herein this behalf expended.

EBENEZER FROST
Vs
DAVID DAVIS &
SAMUEL LYNS, his Security

This day came the Plaintiff by his Attorney and it appearing to the satisfaction of the Court that the said Plaintiff heretofore to wit, on the 19th day of September Eighteen Hundred and Nine obtained Judgment in this Court against the said David Davis. Whereupon the said David Davis gave bond with Samuel Lynes his security dated the 28th day of November Eighteen Hundred and Nine said Bond being for the satisfaction of the said Judgement with the interest & costs due thereon according to the provisions of an Act of the General Assembly in such case made and provided Entitled an Act concerning executions and for other purposes and it also appearing to the satisfaction of the Court that the said Judgement interest and costs have not been paid according to the condition in said Bond on the motion of the Plaintiff by his Attorney. It is therefore considered by the Court that the Plaintiff (p-347) recover against the said David Davis and

Samuel Lynes his security in said Bond the sum of Eighty Four Dollars Sixty Cents the amount of the Judgement aforesaid with all interest due thereon and also _____ the costs due thereon and also his costs by him about his motion here in this behalf expended.

    ADRAIN DAVENPORT &)
    EMANUEL ENSINGER   )
              Vs   )
    JAMES D. DAVIS &   )
    SAM'L. LYNES, his Secy.)

This day came the Plaintiffs by their Attorney and it appearing to the satisfaction of the Court the the said Plaintiffs heretofore to wit,

On the 19th day of September Eighteen Hundred and Nine obtained Judgement in this Court against the said James D. Davis, whereupon the said James D. Davis gave bond with Samuel Lynes his security dated the Eighth day of November Eighteen Hundred and Nine said Bond being for the satisfaction of the said Judgement with the interest and costs due thereon according to (p-348) the provisions of the Act of the General Assembly in such case made & provided Entitled an Act concerning Executions and for other purposes, and it also appearing to the satisfaction of the Court that the said Judgement interests and cost have not been paid according to the condition of said Bond. On motion of the Plaintiffs by their Attorney, it is therefore considered by the Court that the Plaintiffs recover against the said James D. Davis and Samuel Lynes his security in said Bond the sum of Eighty Five Dollars Fifty Six and Three Fourth cents, the amount of the Judgement aforesaid with all interest due thereon and also _____ the costs due thereon and also their costs by them about their motion here in this behalf expended

    JOHN H. POSTON, Surviving Partner of)
    KING & POSTON   )
              Vs   )
    WILLIAM GORDON and   )
    JAMES HAMILTON, his Security   )

This day came the Plaintiff by his Attorney and it appearing to the satisfaction of the Court the the said Plaintiff heretofore to wit, (p-349)

On the Twenty Seventh day of March Eighteen Hundred and Nine obtained Judgement in this Court against the said William Gordon whereupon the said William Gordon gave bond with James Hambleton his security dated the Twenty-fifth day of May One Thousand Eight Hundred and Nine said bond being for the satisfaction of the said Judgement with the interest and cost thereon according to the provisions of the Act of the General Assembly in such case made and provided Entiled an Act concerning executions and for other purposes and it also appearing to the satisfaction of the Court that the said Judgement interest and cost have not been paid according to the condition of said Bond.

On the motion of the Plaintiff by his Attorney, it is therefore considered by the Court that the Plaintiff recover against the said William Gordon and James Hambleton his security in said Bond the sum of One Hundred and Forty Nine Dollars Ninety Eight and One forth cents the Amt. of the Judgement aforesaid and all interest due thereon and also Seven Dollars Sixty One & a half cents the costs due thereon and (p-350) also his costs by him about his motion herein this behalf expended.

ABEL OLIVER
VS
ISAAC SHELBY and
SAMUEL LYNES, his Security

This day came the Plaintiff by his Attorney and it appearing to the satisfaction of the Court that the said Plaintiff heretofore to wit, On the Twenty Second day of September Eighteen Hundred and Nine obtained Judgment against the said Isaac Shelby whereupon the said Isaac Shelby gave bond with Samuel Lynes his security dated the Twenty Ninth day of November Eighteen Hundred and Nine said Bond being for the satisfaction of the Judgement aforesaid with the interest and costs thereon according to the provisions of the Act of the General Assembly in that case made and provided Entitled an Act concerning executions and for other purposes and it also appearing to the satisfaction of the Court that that the said Judgement interest and costs have not been paid agreeable to the condition of said Bond. On motion of the Plaintiff by his Attorney it is considered by the (p-351) Court that the said Plaintiff recover against the said Isaac Shelby and Samuel Lynes his security in said Bond the sum of One Hundred and Four Dollars Twenty Five cents the Amt. of the Judgement aforesaid with all interest due thereon and also _____ the costs due thereon and also his costs by him about his motion here in this behalf expended.

ROBERT SEARCY
Vs
SAMUEL LYNES &
ISAAC SHELBY his Secy.

This day came the Plaintiff by his Attorney and it appearing to the satisfaction of the Court that the said Plaintiff heretofore to wit, On the Twenty Fifth day of September Eighteen Hundred and Nine obtained Judgement in this Court against the said Samuel Lynes, gave bond with Isaac Shelby his security in the sum of dated the Twenty Ninth day of November Eighteen Hundred and Nine said bond being for the satisfaction of said Judgement with the interest and Costs due thereon according to the provisions of the Act of the General Assembly in such case made and provided Entitled an Act concerning executions and for other purposes, and it also appearing to the satisfaction (p-352) of the Court that the Judgment, Interest and Costs have not been satisfyed according to the condition of said Bond. On motion of the Plaintiff by his Attorney it is therefore considered by the Court that the Plaintiff recover against the said Samuel Lynes and Isaac Shelby his Security in said Bond the sum of One Hundred and Eighty Seven Dollars and Ninety Cents the amount of said Judgment with all interest due thereon and also the sum of Seven Dollars Ninety Cents the costs due thereon and also his costs by him about his motion here in this behalf expended.

Motion for an Appeal Appeal granted to the Circuit Court of Montgomery County.

JAMES BAXTER & CO.
Vs
LEWIS PICKET &
JOHN COCKE his Secy.

This day came the Plaintiffs by their attorney and it appearing to the satisfaction of the Court that the said Plaintiff heretofore to wit,

On the 25th day of September Eighteen Hundred and Nine obtained Judgement in this Court against Lewis Picket whereupon the said Lewis Picket gave bond with John Cocke his security dated the Twenty First day of October Eighteen Hundred and Nine, said Bond being (p-353) for the satisfaction of said Judgment with the interest and costs due thereon according to the provisions of the Act of the General Assembly in such case made and provided Entitled an Act concerning executions and for other purposes, and it also appearing to the satisfaction of the Court that said Judgement, Interest and Costs have not been satisfied according to the condition of said Bond.

On the Motion of the Plaintiffs by their Attorney, it is therefore considered by the Court that the Plaintiffs recover against the said Lewis Picket and John Cocke his security in said Bond the sum of Ninety Three Dollars Twenty Six & one half cents, the amount of the Judgement aforesaid with all interest due thereon and also _____ the costs due thereon and also his costs by him about his motion here in this behalf expended.

    WILLIAM CLEMENTS
    SAMUEL THORNTON &
    HOWEL TATUM
        Vs
    BENJAMIN HAWKINS
    &
    ADAM HARMAN for his Security

This day came the Plaintiffs by their Attorney and it appearing (p-354) to the Court that the said Plaintiffs heretofore to wit,

On the Thirtieth day of March Eighteen Hundred and Nine obtained Judgement in this Court against the said Benjamin Hawkins whereupon the said Benjamin Hawkins gave bond with Adam Harman, Senior his security, said bond being dated the Ninth day of June Eighteen Hundred and Nine and for the satisfaction of the said Judgement with the interest and costs due thereon, according to the Act of Assembly in such case made and provided Entitled an Act concerning executions and for other purposes, and it also appearing to the satisfaction of the Court that the said Judgment, Interest and Cost have not been satisfied according to the condition of said Bond. On the motion of the Plaintiffs by their attorney it is therefore considered by the Court that the Plaintiffs recover against the said Benjamin Hawkins and Adam Harman, Senr. his security in said Bond (p-355) the sum of Twenty Five Dollars Twenty Five Cents the amount of the Judgement aforesaid with all interest due thereon and also Six Dollars Eighty Seven & Three Fourth Cents the costs due thereon and also their costs by them about their motion here in this behalf expended.

    SAMUEL VANCE & JOHN BRADLEY
    Surviving Partners of
    VANCE, KING & BRADLEY
        Vs
    EDMUND SUTER & JOSEPH PEIRCE,
    his Security

This day came the Plaintiffs by their Attorney and it appearing to the satisfaction of the Court that the said Plaintiffs heretofore to wit,

On the thirteenth of March Eighteen hundred and nine obtained Judgement in this court against the said Edmund Suter, Whereupon the said Edmund Suter gave bond with Joseph Penrice his security dated the ninth day of June Eighteen hundred and nine, said bond being for the satisfaction of the said judgement with the interest and costs due thereon, according to the provision of the Act of the General Assembly (p 358) Entitled and Act concerning executions and for other purposes, and it also appearing to the satisfaction of the court that the said judgement, interest and costs have not been satisfied according to the condition of said bond.

On motion of the plaintiff by their attorney it is therefore considered by the court that the plaintiffs recover against the said Edmund Suter and Joseph Penrice his security in said bond the sum of thirty eight dollars, ninety eight and one fourth cents the amount of judgement aforesaid with all interest due thereon and also ---- the costs due thereon and also their costs by them about their motion in this behalf expended.

SAMUEL C. HAWKINS AND
SAMUEL THORNTON
VS
GUTHRIDGE LYONS AND
WILLIAM LYONS, HIS SECURITY

This day came the plaintiffs by their attorney and it appearing to the satisfaction of the court that the said plaintiffs heretofore, towit, on the twenty eighth (p 357) day of March eighteen hundred and nine obtained judgement in this court against the said Guthridge Lyons, thereupon the said Guthridge Lyons gave bond with Elisha Willis and William Lyons, his securities dated the seventh day of August eighteen hundred and nine said bond being for the satisfaction of the said judgement with the interest and costs due thereon according to the provision of the Act of General Assembly in such case made and provided entitled an Act concerning executions and for other purposes and it also appearing to the satisfaction of the court that the said judgement interest thereon and costs have not been satisfied according to the condition of said bond, on the motion of the plaintiffs by their attorney, It is therefore considered by the court that the plaintiffs recover against the said Guthridge Lyons and Elisha Wells and William Lyons his securities in said bond the sum of thirteen dollars, ninety seven cents the amount of the judgement aforesaid and all interests due thereon and also (p 358) the costs due thereon and also their costs by them about their motion in this behalf expended.

SAMUEL C. HAWKINS &
SAMUEL THORNTON
VS
GUTHRIDGE LYONS &
ELISHA WELLES AND
WILLIAM LYONS HIS SECYS.

This day came the plaintiffs by their attorney and it appearing to the satisfaction of the court that the said plaintiffs heretofore to wit on the twenty eighth day of March eighteen hundred and nine obtained judgement against the said Guthridge Lyons whereupon the said Guthridge Lyons gave bond with Elisha Willis and William Lyons, his securities dated the seventh day of August eighteen hundred and nine said bond being for the satisfaction of the said judgement with the interest and costs due thereon according to the provisions of the Act of the General Assembly in such case made and provided entitled an Act concerning executions and for other purposes and it appearing also to the satisfaction of the court that the said Judgement (p 359) Interest and costs have not been paid according to the condition of said bond.

On the motion of the plaintiff by his attorney, It is therefore considered by the court that the plaintiff recover against the said Guthridge Lyons and Elisha Wells and William Lyons his securities in said bond the sum of eleven dollars sixty cents the amount of the judgement aforesaid and all interest thereon and also the costs due thereon and also their costs by them about their motion in this behalf expended.

JOHN H. POSTON, Surviving Partner of)
KING & POSTON
VS
DAVID SLOCUM AND
JOHN KETHLEY his security

This day came the plaintiff by his attorney and it appearing to the satisfaction of the court that the said plaintiff heretofore to wit,
On the thirteenth day of March eighteen hundred and nine obtained judgement in this court against the said David Slocum, whereupon the said David Slocum gave bond with John Kethley his security dated the (p 360) twenty ninth day of May eighteen hundred and nine, said bond being for the satisfaction of said judgement with the interest and costs due thereon according to the provisions of the Act of the General Assembly in such

(cont. on page 183)

case made and provided and it also appearing to the satisfaction of the Court that the said Judgement, Interest and Costs have not been paid according to the condition of said Bond, on the motion of the Plaintiff by his Attorney. It is therefore considered by the Court that the Plaintiff recover against the said David Slocum and John Kethly his security in said Bond the sum of Eighteen Dollars Eighty Three Cents with all interest due thereon, and also _____ the costs due thereon and also his costs by him about his motion here in this behalf expended.

```
GEORGE WILSON & JOHN EASTIN  )
            Vs               )   Certiorari
         HUGH McCOLLAME       )
```

The Plaintiff in this case was solemnly called & made default therefore was non suited. Therefore it is considered by the Court that the Defendant recover against the Plaintiff his costs about his suit in this behalf expended.

(p-361) The same Justices on the Bench.

```
JAMES & WASHINGTON JACKSON   )
            Vs               )
         PETER MOSLEY        )   Appeal
              &              )
       MONTGOMERY BELL       )
```

This day came the Plaintiffs by their Attorney and it appearing to the satisfaction of the Court that the said Plaintiff heretofore, to wit,

On the Nineteenth day of September 1809 obtained Judgement in this Court against the said Peter Mosley whereupon the said Peter Mosley gave bond with Montgomery Bell his security dated the 28th day of November 1809, said bond being for the satisfaction of said Judgement & the Interest and Costs due thereon ~~and it also appearing to the~~ according to the provisions of the Acts of the General Assembly in such case made and provided Entitled an Act concerning executions and for other purposes and it also appearing to the satisfaction of the Court that the said Judgement, Interest and costs have not been satisfied according to the condition of said bond.

On motion of said Plaintiffs by their Attorney, it is therefore considered by the Court that the Plaintiffs recover against the said Peter Mosley and the said Montgomery Bell, his security in said Bond the sum of One Hundred & Four Dollars & Fifty Cents the amount of the Judgement aforesaid & all Interest due thereon also Seven Dollars Seventy Three & Three Forths Cents Costs due thereon & their costs about their suit in this behalf expended, motion for appeal which is granted & gave bond with William Smith ~~& Montgomery Bell~~ their security bond in the sum of Two Hundred & Nine Dollars and filed the following reasons. The Defendants in (p-362) this case files the following reasons for an Appeal, that is the Judgement is unconstitutional and Iniquitions which are in my oppinion sufficient reasons for an Appeal.

Wm. Smith, Atty.

```
Same Justices        )
ANTHONY FOSTER       )
      Vs             )
  JAMES MOORE        )
```

This day same the Plaintiff by his Attorney, and it appearing to the satisfaction of the Court that the said Plaintiff heretofore, to wit,

On the Seventeenth day of April Eighteen Hundred & Seven obtained Judgement in this Court against the said James Moore, whereupon the said James Moore gave bond with John Moore his security dated the Seventeenth day of June 1809, said Bond being for the satisfaction of said Judgement & the Interest and Costs due thereon according to the provisions of the Acts of the General Assembly in such case made & provided Entitled an Act concerning executions and for other purposes and it also appearing to the satisfaction of the Court that said Judgement & costs have not been satisfied according to the condition of said Bond.

On motion of said Plaintiff by his Attorney, it is therefore considered by the Court that the Plaintiff recover against said James Moore & the said John Moore his security in said Bond the sum of Four Thousand Sixty five Dollars & Thirty Cents _____ and all interest due thereon also _____ costs due thereon his costs about his suit in this behalf expended & the Defendants in Mercy &

(p-363) Court adjourned untill tomorrow at 9 O'clock.

The Worshipful Court of Montgomery County have met according to adjournment Saturday December 23rd 1809.
Present

JAMES HAMBLETON)
HUGH MCCLURE) Esquire
BARNY DUFF) Justices

STATE
Vs
JOHN M. TRIBBLE and
JAMES TRIBBLE
} Indictment for Assault & Battery

Be it remembered that the said John M. Tribble and James Tribble and Joseph Whitehead and Andrew Tribble their securities this day personally appeared in Court and acknowledged themselves to be indebted to the State of Tennessee, the said John M. Tribble and in the sum of Five Hundred Dollars each and the said Joseph Whitehead and Andrew Tribble in Two Hundred and Fifty Dollars each, to be levied of their and each of their goods and chattels lands and tenements. This obligation to be void of the said John M. Tribble and James Tribble shall make their personal appearance at the next August Term of the Circuit Court of Montgomery County to answer the State on an indictment for an assault and battery on the body of James Matlock and (p-364) shall then and there abide by and perform the Judgment of the Court and shall not depart the same without leave.

Acknowledged in Open Court Decr. 23rd,
1809. Teste
W. C. Jamison, Clk.

John M. Tribble (Seal)
James Tribble (Seal)
Joseph Whitehead (Seal)
Andrew Tribble (Seal)

Same Justices

WILLIAM BOGARD
Vs
WILLIAM R. BELL &
JOHN SHELBY
} Covenant

On motion of Plaintiffs Attorney to amend the declaration & argued on both sides it is the oppinion of the Court that they have leave to amend and the Defendants plead at next term.

Same Justices

ISAAC KITTRELL)
    Vs   ) Trespass Vict Annis
ROBERT WELLS)

The Defendant by his Attorney withdraws his motion in Arrest of Judgement, therefore it is considered by the Court that the Plaintiff recover against the Defendant the sum of Twenty Nine Dollars Seventy Five Cents, damages as assessed by the Jury (p-365) and his costs about his suit in this behalf expended. The attorney for the Plaintiff stays the execution untill April term next.

Same Justices

SAMUEL VANCE & JOHN BRADLEY,) Surviving
Partners of)
    VANCE, KING & BRADLEY)
        Vs) Debt
WILLIAM DAVIDSON)

The Defendant in this case being solemnly called came not but made default. Therefore it is considered by the Court that the Plaintiffs recover against the Defendant debt in the declaration mentioned amounting to Ninety Three Dollars Thirty Seven & a half cents together with the further sum of Eleven Dollars Twenty Cents damages by the Court herewith the assent of the Plaintiff adjudged to him for the detention of the said Debt together with his costs in this behalf expended & the Defendant in Mercy &

Same Justices

ROBERT WEAKLEY)
    Vs   ) Debt
NATHAN MCGRAW)

By consent of the parties the plea in abatement withdrawn & Demurrer the Defendant pleads payment. Issue joined & the cause is continued.

Same Justices

    Weakly)
ISAAC KITTRELL)
    Vs   ) Debt
ISAAC KITTREL)

This day came the Plaintiff by his (p-366) Attorney & the Defendant being solemnly called came not but made default. Therefore it is considered by the Court the Plaintiff recover against the Defendant the debt in the declaration mentioned amounting to One Hundred ~~Forty~~ & Twenty ~~Twenty~~ Dollars together with the ~~six Dollars~~ the further sum of Six Dollars and Seventy Five Cents damages by the Court herewith the assent of the assent of the Plaintiff adjudged to him for the detention of the said debt together with his costs in this behalf expended & the Defendant in Mercy &

Same Justices

DAVID WILLIAMS Assee)
    Vs   ) Covenant
JOHN GRIFFIN   )

This day came the parties by their Attornies & the Defendants Demurrer to the Plaintiffs declaration being argued, it is the oppinion of the Court that the said declaration is sufficient in law for the Plaintiff to maintain his action aforesaid against the Defendant. Therefore it is considered by the Court that the Plaintiff recover against the Defendant his damages by occasion of his non performance of the Covenants in the declaration mentioned to be inquired of by a Jury at next Court.

JOHN DEN Lessee of John Moore)
        Vs   )
BRITAIN BAYLESS   ) Ejectments
        &   )
JOSIAH HORN   )

De Po to the Plaintiffs on affidavit to take the Deposition of George Bell, Senr. Debeneessee. Notice to Defendant Ten Days.

STEPHEN STEWART)
    Vs   ) Debt
LUKE DILLARD   )

This day came the parties by their Attornies and and the matters of law arriving upon the defendants Demurrer (p-367) and the Plaintiffs declaration being argued, it is considered by the Court that the said Demurrer be overruled. And that the Plaintiff recover against the Defendant the debt in the declaration mentioned and interest thereon from the Seventeenth day of December 1808 amounting in all to the sum of Three Hundred & Sixty Four Dollars & Three Cents together with his costs about his suit in this behalf expended &

ROBERT BOWEN, Senr.)
    Vs   ) Debt
WILLIAM LOVE & JOHN)
JAMES LOVE   )

This day came the parties by their Attornies and the matters of Law arrising upon the Defendants Defendants Demurrer to Plaintiffs declaration being argued, it is considered by the Court that the said Demurrer be overruled & that the Plaintiff recover against the Defendant the Debt in the declaration mentioned and interest thereon from the first day of Sept. 1808 amounting in all to the sum of Fifty Four Dollars Two & a half cents together with his costs about his suit in this behalf expended &

Bill of Sale John Garth to James B. Reynolds proven in Open Court by the Oath of James McClure & Hugh McClure for one negro & ordered to registeration.

Bill of Sale for one negro woman Samuel Peters to James Miller proven by William S. Bailey & Anthony Crutcher & ordered to be registered.

Frances Penrice comes into Court & entered into Bond with Stephen Cocke & Joseph Penrice his securities bound in the sum of Three Thousand Dollars for his true performance as Guardian to Jency Channell, James Channell & Henry Channell heirs of Elisha Channell deceased & which securities was received by the Court & the said Bond is ordered to be recorded.

(p-368) Court adjourned agreeable to the Acts of the General Assembly untill Court in Course.

James Hambleton
Bryan Whitfield
Barny Duff

MONTGOMERY COUNTY

COUNTY COURT MINUTE BOOK, VOL. 2
1808-1810

NEW INDEX

Note: Page numbers in this index refer to those of the original volume from which this copy was made. These numbers are inserted within parentheses throughout the text, as (p 124).

Acoff, Richard, 207
Adams, Benjamin, 26,37,99,100, 105,108,269,311
Adams, James, 1,133,149
Adkinson, Jane 72,109,234
Adkinson, James, 166,230
Adkinson, Richard, 72
Akins, Robert, 184,185,273,278, 281
Allen, Captain, 65,157,161
Allen, William, 2,43,50,51,53,98, 136,139,141,143,145,314
Allen, Samuel, 152,157,170,183, 185,186,188,193,223,269,310, 316,175
Allison, John, 185
Anderson, Allen, 49,50,54,312
Anderson, Charles, 21,30,43,46, 49,78,102,230,245,250,254
Anderson, Daniel, 17,126,136, 202,213
Anderson, Johnson, 154
Anderson, Timothy, 319
Arnold, Price, 256

Bailey, James, 234,314
Bailey, John, 255,312,322,145,194
Bailey, William, 110,158,251,367
Bailess, Burrell, 109,135,177, 270,279,289,290,293,299,303, 339
Bailess, John, 26
Barnes, John, 242,318
Baker, John, 12,20,39,45,49,51, 68, 261
Baker, Joseph, 205
Baker, William, 154,205
Barton, William, 156,160,314
Barnes, Matthew, 92
Bartee, James, 324
Barton, John, 113,160,225,277

Barton, William, 113,125,197,225, 214,227,323
Bosley, John, 139
Bates, Andrew, 45
Bayliss John, 37,144,320
Baylis, Brittain, 37,155,266,269, 311,366
Bayliss, William, 61
Batson, Thomas, 6,141
Baxter, John, 60,100
Baxter, James, 18,32,36,37,39,43, 62,76,78,82,110,114,116,117, 153,174,178,192,200,203,215, 217,238,251,252,260,277,297, 300,301,303,308,309,311,312, 315,352
Baxter, Joseph, 299
Bean, John, 215
Bearden, William, 160,225,311
Beatie, Andrew, 272,270
Beates, Captain, 272
Beatie, Frances, 272
Blair, John, 1,3,7,10,36,37,39,41, 43,47,70,76,78,91,92,98,133, 139,146,161,162,163,164,165,169, 170,171,184,189,193,222,227,235, 239,257,264,269,270,279,282,285, 311,314
Blount, John G. 268,287
Bowen, Joseph, 89,152
Bowen, Robert, 367
Blount, Willie, 8,32,36,37,39,62,107, 152,268,275,287
Boatwright, Joshua, 133,150,163
Bogard, Charles, 266,289,318
Bogard, Joseph, 266,289,318
Bogard, William, 239,243,253,256,318, 364
Bonds, Wright, 14,40,57,169,273
Bonds, Hugh, 169
Boyd, James, 33,37,91,166,235, 311,326,330

Boyd, Sallie, B. 333
Bradley, Thomas, 314
Brantley, Thomas, 13,37,93,266, 267,273,312
Brawner, Hyde, 214
Brawner, Hyde, 214
Brawner, Peter, 43
Brunson, Asbel, 303
Bryan, Henry H. 220,223,285,288, 290,291,325,332,333
Bristow, John, 315
Brigham, David, 37,126,155
Brigham, Henry, 35
Berel, Henry, 207
Benham, John, 202
Bennett, Mason, 243
Berry, Jonathan, 133
Berry, William, 133
Bell, Daniel, 27
Bell, John, 41,63,95,157,227
Bell, George, 186
Bell, Hugh F. 18,44,89,132,154, 165,168,169,184,225,255,272, 294,295,296,298,303,307,323
Bell, Montgomery, 312
Bell, William M. 195
Bell, Morgan, 9
Bell, William R. 138,140,178,296
Bird, Amos, 67,79,144,154,221
Bird, Blodgett, 37,83
Black, Ezekial, 205
Blackney, Thomas, 315
Bone, Abner, 222
Bowers, James, 1,89,93,126,133, 261,302,318,333
Bradshaw, Jonathan, 2,6,21
Brantley, James, 20,21,266,267
Brathell, C. 324
Bray, James, 53,58,61,105,133
Breathell, Cardwell, 168
Briggs, Asa, 207
Brigham, John, 135,288
Biggers, Joshua, 314
Bigger, Robert, 28,37,83,148
Brown, Alexander, 25,32,103
Brown, John, 178,196
Brown, James C. 23,98,174,314
Brown, James, 93,134,160,239,242, 247,250,255
Bryant, Capt. 161
Bryant, Jacob, 14
Bryant, Henry H. 94,282,286
Bull, Daniel, 56
Bull, Balim, 36
Bull, Jerry, 56

Bull, Molly, 56
Bull, Dempsey, 56
Bullard, Reuben, 37,99,101,105,108, 110,118,221
Brown, Abel, 183
Brown, Darden, 5,30,250,254
Brown, Morgan, 1,11,68,82,95,151, 163,181,184,293,317
Broom, William, 52,164,165,167
Bumpas, John, 178
Bumpas, Samuel, 270,282,290,293, 299,303
Bunting, David, 266,312,315,316
Bunting, James A. 22,57,98,99,102, 109,115,120,147,173,179,181, 187,190,312
Bunch, Thomas, 72,152,239,242,247, 250,254,255,314
Burney, David 87,98,132,243

Calhoon, William, 90,108,160,173, 218
Campbell, John D.F. 206
Carns, Alexander, 223,270,282,290, 293,299,303
Carney, Richard, 278,333
Carney, Thomas L. 275
Caraway, James, 127,162,292,328
Carr, William, 21
Carrell, James, 262
Carrell, Zelpha, 262
Cashen, Pleasant, 205
Chambless, Mark, 266
Chandler, Jonathan, 270,338
Channell, Elisha, 367
Channell, James, 267
Channell, Henry, 367
Channell, Jency, 367
Cheatham, Edward, 33
Cherry, Charles, 155
Cheslan, John, 27,89
Chisham, John, 266, 268
Chisenhall, Ruben, 206
Chisham, Taylor, 266
Chisham, William, 266,301
Clements, Hyde, 215,249,258
Clements, Wm. 1,11,90,128,159,201, 211
Clifton, Edward, 311
Clifton, William, 212
Clinton, Thomas, 18,101,312
Cobb, Jesse, 145,157,188
Cobb, Hannah, 153
Cooke, John, 19,20,27,36,55,80,98, 121,136,143,157,158,159,162,163, 202,204,205,224,241,242,249,275 287,285,288,300,312,313,315,332

Cocks, Abraham, 40,43,46,50,54,178,
Cocks, Peter, 200
Cocks, Stephen, 9,15,36,37,40,42,
   46,56,58,64,75,91,103,200,
   223,321,322,323,329,367
Cocks, Sterling, 264
Coffee, John, 54,149,267,272
Cane, or Cone, 278
Collier, Daniel, 93,126
Collier, Thomas, 269,290,316,318,322,
   331
Collins, David, 275
Conrad, Nicholas, 115
Cooksey, Jesse, 196,232,246
Cooper, Easter, 229,245,319
Cooper, John, 87,118,122,229,245,
   319
Cooper, Vincent, 29,134,224,261,
   308,322,324,338,339
Copeland, John, 314
Corbin, Camell, 222
Corbin, William, 40,42,46,51,57,
   61,68,87
Corlew, Wm. 2,3,5,10,12,15,20,22,
   35,56,64,218,311
Couts, John, 245,335,336
Cowan, Benjamin, 79,86,269,311
Crabb, Alexander M. 30
Craft, Jessie, 315
Craft, Samuel, 279,296,307
Creswell, Samuel 2,3,4,9,12,15,19,
   21,37,40,101,118
Cross, Drury H. 233
Crutcher, Anthony, 221,259,271
Crutcher, M. 96
Crutcher, William, 62
Cunningham, William, 284

Davenport, Adrin, 274,276,347
Davidson, John, 292,293
Davidson, William, 292,365
Davis, David, 269,276,311,346,347
Davis, James, D. 274,284,285,344,345,
   347
Davis, John, 202
Davis, Rebecca, 267
Davis, Thomas, 23
Davis, William, 287
Dean, Thomas, 206
Dennis, Zebedee, 67,72,162,164,165,
   167,172,175,182,183,188,195
Denn, John, 95,143,170,271,304,
   366
Denson, Jesse, 231
Dickson, James, 34,178,219
Dickson, Joseph, 25,160,233,264

Dickson, Michael, 219
Dickson, Ruben, 232
Dickerson, Samuel, 44,95,143
Dixon, James, 94,179
Dikas, John, 218,354
Dixon, Loggins, 202
Dikas, John, 50,56,61
Dillard, Luke, 168
Dodd, Thomas, 37,44,83
Donald, Nicholas, 315
Douglass, Henry, 285
Downs, Benjamin, 30,42
Drake, Captain, 75,333
Drake, Robert, 78,164
Duff, Philip, 206
Drake, Timothy, 12,13,142,182,192,
   212,216,301
Duff, Barney, 1,3,4,20,21,22,67,
   70,100,126,162,313,321,322,
   342,343,365,368
Duke, Admun, 71
Dunbar, James, 61
Duke, John, 71,74
Duke, Joseph R. 38,43,53,58,98
Duke, Josiah, A. 49,51,59,71,171,
   314
Duke, Patsy, 71,74
Duke, Philip, 71,74,331
Duke, Timothy, 9,10,19
Dunbar, Thomas, 124,140,176,234,
   259
Duncan, Adam, 64
Duncan, Daniel A. 24
Dunn, John W. 96
Duvall, Colmire, 20,21,22,49,91,
   140
Duvall, Louisa Ann, 221
Dupree, David, 37,83,264,290
Duncan, Ashel, 206

Edmondson, John, 14,103,167,172,
   175,179,182,195,286,299
Edmondson, Robert, 93,141,147,322
Edmonston, Archbard, 163
Edwards, James, 134,140,147,189,
   283
Edwards, Joseph, 239,247,253,269
Elder, James, 23,67,72,79,80,155,
   184,201,203,212,250,340,343
Elliott, George, 262
Elliott, John, 245
Elliott, Lewis, 115
Ennis, Vinson, 205
Enlow, Capt. 161
Enshinger, Emanul, 274
Epps, Daniel, 22

Faith, Alex, 2,48,54,57,87,177,
    200,230,254,281
Falk, William, 218
Farland, John R. 91
Farmer, John, 323,328
Farrar, William, 86,94,151,153,
    173,188,255,303,305,312,322,
    324,341
Farrell, Barnabus, O. 185
Fenn, Richard, 74,109
Fentress, James, 28,29,32,39,42,
    44,89,90,334
Ferrell, Barnabus, 229
Flack, Thomas, 205
Ferrell, William, 200,289
Fletcher, Aaron, 51,77,228
Fletcher, John G. 37,205
Ford, Drewry, 35,166,333
Ford, Henry, 34,225,315
Ford, James, 18,35,197,330
Ford, Judith, 333
Ford, Moses, 176
Ford, William, 34,105,218,342,
    317
Fort, Josiah, 55
Foster, Anthony, 120,137,362
Fort, Elias, 168,255,261,
Fowler, Nancy, 313
French, John B. 225,264,331
Frost, Ebeneza, 160,269,276,284,
    302,321,344,346
French, Joseph, 37,290
Frost, Edward, 313
Funk, Henry, 40,42,56,57,64,75,
    83,160,225,318,331
Furguson, John, 106

Gardner, James, 53
Garner, John, 52
Garner, Joshua, 13
Garner, Shaderick, 205
Garrett, John B. 2
Garth, John, 367
Gattis, George, 310
Gattis, Samuel, 1,3,7,25,33,36,
    47,67,71,107,113,116,151,161,
    185,218,229,235,273,290,317,
    318,319
Gattis, Isaac, 1,206
Gaskell, Evans, 305
George, John, 268
Gibson, Edward, 269,316,325,148,
    132,93
Gibson, George, 49,139,262
Gibson, John, 181

Gibson, William R. 181,218,220,223,
    268,279,288,290,291,292,293
Gihson, Wilson, 53,93,152,228
Gillibe, James, 66,67,70
Glover, Richard, 247,250,254,255
Gonter, Jacob, 113
Good, William, 93,126,243,316,322
Gordon, George, 127,196,271
Gordon, William, 52,177,187,195,196,
    271,288,348,349
Goodwin, William, 264,290,317,331
Gore, Edwin, 205
Goss, Martin, 78,97,144,152,164,202,
    210,212
Goss, Frederick, 13,25,41,97
Grant, Dickson, 163
Grant, James, 53,70,97,145,175,196
Grant, Zachariah, 52,156
Graves, James, 206
Gray, James, 206
Gray, James, 153
Gray, John, 152,258
Gray, Joseph, 28
Grayson, Robert, 170
Grayson, William, 25,93,311
Grayson, Reuben, 5,11,41,53,58,95,137,
    227
Green, Thomas, 113,197,198
Grewin, Andrew, 208
Griffin, John, 93,132,143,164,262,306,
    331,366
Griffin, Spencer, 202
Grimes, John, 231

Hagler, John, 239,242,250
Hall, Abraham, 25
Hall, Joseph, 206
Hamilton, Benjamin, 201
Hamilton, James, 1,3,13,25,36,51,53,
    61,73,82,91,93,95,99,107,110,113,
    126,139,143,172,174,175,177,78,
    183,184,189,194,203,216,223,231,
    241,243,244,246,249,251,252,254,
    260,264,272,279,288,290,303,304,
    311,312,329,332,349,363,368
Hamilton, George, 129
Hamilton, Henn, 13
Hanley, Joseph, 60,97,124
Handley, Samuel, 214
Handley, Stephen, 1,3,4,5
Hamblin, Stephen, 264,292
Hardkin, Joseph, 160
Harmon, Adam, 70,77,90,91,96,105,135,
    142,159,222,230,240,243,255,260,
    263,269,293,316,353,354

Harmon, Amos, 305
Harmon, Capt. 161
Harmon, John, 293
Harris, Abner, 29,32,36,39,45,49,
   53,69,83,161,165,171,223,224,227,
   229,230,235,237,264,291,314
Harris, Hugh, 157
Harris, John, 37,150
Harris, William H. 233,256
Harris, Thompson, 200
Harris, Victor, 221,264
Hart, Charles, 151
Harwell, Mark, 247,260
Hawkins, Benjamin, 1,2,4,5,10,12,15,
   19,20,22,211,221,229,230,235,
   296,322,353,354
Hawkins, Philip, 166,217,283
Hawkins, Samuel C. 26,196,198,240,
   241,242,356,358
Hawkins, Stephen, 2
Hawkins, Thornton, 154
Hawkins, Thomas, 14
Hays, Leonard, 40
Henderson, John, 49,50,161,205,
   218,314
Henderson, Philip, 206
Hendlen, Stephen, 227,318
Hensley, Charles, 77
Herod, Peter, 325
Herring, Bright, 161,223,234,265,
   270,282,290,293,303
Herring, Simeon, B. 177
Herring, William, 303
Hicks, Hamlin, 20,128
Hickman, Thomas, 282,298
Highnight, John, 34,71,160,228
Hightower, William, 37,41,98,103,
   105,108,110,210,
Hill, Green, 31,150,249
Hill, John, 150
Hillard, Richard, 16,69
Hitler, John, 93,126
Hogan, John, 351
Hogan, William, 205
Holland, Willis, 205
Holmes, Simon, 244,247,258
Holt, James, 93,139,141,147
Holt, Peter, 54,132,141,269,317,322
Horn, Josiah, 304,366
Hoskins, John, 272,278
Houston, William, 144
Hubbard, Frances, 111,179,194
Hubbard, John, 88
Hubbard, Peter, 14,28,93,141,146,
   147,271,290,293,299,303

Hubbard, Thomas, 193
Hubbard, William, 4,156
Hughes, James, 77
Huling, James, 35,122,132,157,181,
   196,263,286,287,312,315
Hully, Isaac, 228
Humphrey, George, 153,157,165,247,
   260
Humphrey, John, 36,40,54,131,141,
   146
Humphrey, Perry W. 79,231,275
Hunt, John, 153
Hunter, Allen, 127,316
Hunter, Dempsey, 26
Hunter, Thomas, 143
Hust, John, 273
Hust, William, 57,91,317,153,273
Hutton, Leonard, 133
Hutton, Mary, 133
Hyde, John H. 26,149,154,201,228,
   325
   /177,188,238,288
Ingram, Sterling, 15,51,77,145,157,
Instone, John, 98
Irwin, Andrew, 37,83
Isaacs, Jesse, 198
Izzle, Thomas, 132

Jackson, Alexander, 64
Jackson, Brice, 153,157
Jackson, James, 20,120,142,192,203,
   260,263,275,284,308,316,361
Jackson, Washington, 20,44,192,203,
   260,263,275,284,308,316
Jackson, Robert, 243
Jackson, Willis, 239,254,257
Jamison, William C. 66,108,157,222,
   224,235
Jenkins, George W. 282
Jenkins, James, G. 282
Jenkins, Thomas W. 282
Jeffree, James, 85,132,271
Johnson, John, 46,315
Johnston, Jones, 60
Jones, Charles, 28
Johnson, Jonathan, 223,264
Johnson, Mordica, 157
Jones, John, 10,14,17,23,199
Jones, William, 127,206
Jordan, William, 25,170,171
Joyce, Alexander, 28
Joyce, Thomas, 199
Justice, William, 206

Karr, William, 20,22,46,52,105

Keathley, John, 98,132,136,148,
 181,206,271,279,282,290,299,
 359
Kenkrick, Alexander, 14
Kendrick, Olsemus, 118,179,180
Kendrick, William, 14,179,180
King & Bradley, 153,166,191,194,
 207,208,215,217,285,365
King & Foster, 331
King, James, 27
King, John, 114,139,141,164,165,
 170,172,175,179,181,183,186,
 195
King, Nathan, 6
King & Poston, 129,187,207,213,
 254,328   /307,365
King & Vance, 124,128,236,283,
King, William, 301
Killebrew, Bucknersl, 143,318
Killebrew, Glidwell, 37,63
Kitrell, Isaac, 56,93,147,179,
 182,196,213,242,271,278,354,
 356
Killebrew, William, 45
Knighton, Moses, 9
Knight, William, 206
Kittrell, Elizabeth, 327
Kyle, Daniel, 157

Lagrand, Melikia, 64,68,75
Laurence, Elias, 52
Laws, Aaron, 318
Leach, David, 303
Lee, John, 160
Leech, Jacob, 37,83,93,154,221,
 223,246,270,282,290,293,299,
 303
Lee, Richard, 273
Leech, Edward, 14,27,38,239,241,
 242,247,250,54,255
Leggett, Absolam, 58,59,70,72
Lester, James, 53,161,234
Lewis, Jeremiah, 140,142
Linch, David, 93,223,282,290,
 293,314
Lewis, William, 285
Little, John, 149
Lockert, James, 11,33,36,39,99,
 161,222,224,271,273,274,279,
 286,319
Lockner, John, 206
Loggins, Dixon, 15,21,54,73,215
Loggins, Guthridge, 9,87
Loggins, James, 10,51,54,72,191,
 215,269,316

Loggins, Reuben, 9,10,15,47,112,308,
 309
Loggins, Robert, 74
Loggins, Martin, 48,51,57,88
Loggins, William, 9,12,15,47,49,58,
 60,112,306,309
Long, Frances, 49,178,196
Lowther, John W. 40,83,98,271
Lyons, Guthridge, 26,37,60,116,134,
 159,284,356,358,359
Lyons, Samuel, 37,103,124,145,186,
 215,255,256,305,324,345,349,350
Lyons, William, 54,55,107,147,223,
 269,313,357
Lynes, James, 344
Lynes, Willard, 357
Lytaker, Peter, 125,178
Lytle, Andrew, 293
Lytle, William, 96,276

Madden, Sterling, 1
Magbee, Obediah, 222
Malone, John, 216
Malone, Lewis, 84
Malone, Robert, 315
Mallory, James, 29,43,49,289
Mallory, Stephen, 27
Mann, Abel, 226
Mann, Robert, 243
Marr, John, 68,83
Marr, George W.L. 67,76,110,112,
 182,320
Marr, William, M. 311, 321
Marshall, John, 1,3,4,9,12,15,19,21,
 132,164,167,170,172,175,179,182,
 188,195,183
Martin, Ambrose, 89
Martin, Isaac, 14,16,75
Martin, Jesse, 12,15,38,65,160
Martin, Thomas, 119,200,267
Mason, Benjamin, 117
Mattlock, James, 247,268,327,363
Matthews, Isham, 40,42,45,52,57,
 64,75,139,146,123,
Matthew, William, 196
Maxwell, George, 133
Maxwell, James, 23
Medlock, James, 325,327
Medlock, Samuel, 327
Meares, John, 202
Mitchell, Samuel, 25
Miles, Charles, 327
Miller, James, 186,306,367
Mills, Gideon, 212
Mimm, John, 206

Minor, Henry, 49,72,117,121,230, 231
Minor, Thomas C. 225,270,271,282
Minott, John, 5,60,97,174,186, 213,243,248
Mitchell, Daniel, 269,332
Mitchell, James, 322
Mitchel, John, 206
Mitchell, Samuel, 164,165,167,170, 172,179,182,183,186,195,318
Mitchell, William, 37,93,126,15, 318,322
Montgomery, Joseph, 206
Montgomery, William, 37,98
Morris Hollow, 41
Morris, Samuel, 41
Moody, Frederick, 170,178
Moon, James, 24,26,37,41,51,52, 82,116,152
Moore, Charles, 201
Moore, Frederick, 167
Moore, Gully, 131
Moore, James, 42,48,85,94,107, 123,150,153,157,161,193,221, 231,237,242,243,255,362
Moore, John, 171,185,229,305,362, 366
Moore, Robert, 127
Moore, Saunders, 206,249
Moore, William, 202,206,250
Moore, Thomas, 152,158,269
Morgan, Allen, 205
Morgan, Isaac, 1,3,4,9,12,15,19, 22,30,40,46,49,50,158,201
Morgan, Mathews, 131
Morrel, John, 299
Morrison, Adam, 70
Morris, David, 206
Morris, James, 142
Morris, Nathan, 133
Morris, Thomas, 183
Morrow, James, 223,270,282,290, 291,293,303,315,325,327,331
Morrow, William, 160,218,315
Moseley, James, 42,90
Moseley, John, 42,265
Moseley, Peter, 202,275,361
Moseley, & Watson, 122,176
Moss, Joseph, 205
Murfree, Hardy, 39
Murphy, Andrew, 206
Murphy, George, 206
Murry, Charles, 19,36,103,178,179

McCallester, John, 257
McBride, Henry, 19

McCarrell, John, 270,282,293
McCarrell, James, 11,25,89,245
McCarrell, Zilpha, 245
McCauley, Daniel, 214
McCauley, John, 35,37,39,42,45,49, 52,53,54,115,147,218,225,227,230, 231,235,239,241,243,244,246,286, 288,290
McClure & Elder, 62,121,158,191,192, 211,331
McClure, Hugh, 3,7,11,19,23,36,39,54, 59,82,104,126,155,163,165,167,169, 172,176,177,184,193,200,201,263, 269,294,297,301,303
McClure, James, 367
McClure, John, 205,308
McClure, William, 205
McCorkle, Archibald, 314
McCrabb, Captain, 44,93
McCrabb, Alexander, 25,314
McCraw, Nathan, 32,36,39,317,319,365
* McColloch,Alexander, 8
McCulloch, Benjamin, 8,62
McCullum, Hugh, 15,84,314
McCullouch, Samuel, 8
McDonand, John, 125
McDaniel, William, 28,29,32,161,237, 266,337
McDowell, Nelson, 79,125
McElrath, Thomas R. 27,30,108
McFadden, David, 37,83,152,165,167, 172,179,183,186,195,313
McFarland, James, 106,114,169
McFarland, Kellis, 106,172
McFarland, John R. 1,9,12,21,22,66, 110,182,258,294
McGowan, Edward, 219
McGowen, James, 37,103,108,110
McGowan, John, 219
McGowen, William, 219
McGowan, William, 37
McKee, John, 206
McKey, John, 26,206
McLain, John, 290
McGlaughen, Robert, 223,270,290,293, 303
McGraw, Cornelius, 158
McLaughlin, Robert, 25
McNichols, Samuel, 314
McNatt, Mitchell, 85,115
McPerson, John, 204
McRoberts, Alexander, 329
McRoberts, James, 202
* McCray, William, 94
Neblett, Edward, 36,37, 87,88,89, 228
Neblett, John, 228

Neblett, Sterling, 1,3,25,27,29,32, 35,54,60,83,86,128,169,172,180, 183,184,189,193,218,227,229,235, 237,241,249,254,264,291,292,294, 311,314,325,39
Neblett, William, 76,219,314
Nelson, Alexander, 204
Nelson, John H. 155,204,289
Nelson, Robert, 76,84,123,130,132, 136,137,154,155,156,159,163,169, 173,183,221,224,228,231,256,270, 292,272,279,289,294,296,303,321,323
Nelson, William, 61,156,183
Nicholas, James, 206
Nevell, George W. 247,253,273
Nevell, John, 103,117,132,148,159, 247,253
Nevell, Joseph B. 103,104
Norrington, Samuel, 225
Norman, Robert, 205
Northington, Michal, 142

O'Gwin, Stephen, 45,46,50,56,57,58, 61,64,75,86,148,
Ohira, John, 4
Oldham, Joe R. 75,84,120,147,178, 268
Oldham, Jesse, 273
Oldham, Moses, 37,53,75,99,101, 105,110,142,146,161,162,234
Oliver, Abel, 297,350
O'Neal, John, 202
O'Neal, Joseph, 71,229,270,321
O'Neal, Marmaduke, 60,84
O'Neal, Peter, 9,12,19,37,42, 45,49,52,83,142,170,175,220, 224,271
O'Neal, Stephen, 15
O'Neal, Thos. H. 271,312
Organ, Benjamin, 38,87,92,269,270, 316
Outlaw, Alahon, 31
Outlaw, David, 26,40,42,46,50,56, 57,64,75,159
Outlaw, Nancy, 159
Outlaw, Wright, 20,26,40,42,44,49, 53,54,264
Overton, John, 86
Overton, Thomas, 181
Owen, Stephen, 313

Pardus, Richard, 1,3,5,20,22,46,50, 340
Pardue, William, 113
Pare, Joel, 29
Park, Joseph, 175
Parchman, Philip, 315
Parker, Moses, 19,53,61,64,75,178, 186,188,331
Pasmore, David, 37
Patlock, Robert, 186
Payzer, George, 44
Pearce, James, 46,50,292
Peoples, David, 314
Pennington, William, 90,173
Penrice, Frances, 138,297,316,318, 367
Penrice, James, 72
Penrice, John, 355
Penrice, Joseph, 2,44,66,136,139, 141,143,146,215,237,312,316,322
Penrice, William, 297
Penny, David C. 173
Penny, William D. 90
Perdue, Owen, 43,142
Perry, James, 154,313,331
Perry, Samuel, 154
Peters & Minnott, 299
Pertes, Samuel, 153,172,213,243,278, 281,286,306,334,336,337,
Peterson, Andrew, 61,156,169,223
Peterson, Isaac, 18,126,161,223,234, 271
Peterson, Poland, 39,169,268
Peterson, Samuel, 32,61,133
Paterson, Susannah, 157
Pettis, Lunsford, 151
Phillips, Joseph, 10,50
Phillips, Mann, 138
Picket, Charles, 102
Picket, Lewis, 102,308,352,353
Pierce, James, 40,45,53,58,70,292, 308
Pollock, George, 138
Pollock, Robert, 188,195
Pollard, Ruben, 18,133,149
Porter, Captain, 91,161
Porter, William, 56,244,253,258
Poston, John H. 3,23,24,36,39,60,82, 110,113,119,120,148,155,158,161, 157,176,177,178,187,195,220,203, 207,216,249,257,259,263,288,292, 294,297,299,304,309,311,319,331
Powell, Cuthbert, 281
Powell, Stephen, 202
Prewitt, Jacob, 120
Price, Joseph, 37,87,323
Price, William, 206
Prince, John, 230
Prince, Robert, 36,39,46,66,92,98, 101,109,114,117,129,139,142,144, 165,170,176,178,180,183,224,230, 146,151

8

231,235,245,246,248,269,273,
282,285,292,293,314,315,316,
317,319,320,321,329,331,322
Pritchard, David, 37,172
Pritchard, John, 174
Pucket, Lewis, 9,49,103
Puckett & Long, 9,50,136
Puckett, Selah, 9,49,122,196
Rushing, Robert, 232

Ramsey, Elisha, 315
Ray, Robert, 17,315
Reasons, William, 315
Ray, Joseph, 27,235,239
Reynolds, James M. 1,21,22,86,110,
111,130,132,233,257,253,263,
324,328,367,287,294
Reynolds & McFarland, 79,87,121,
124,137,176,178,197,214,259,
279,302
Richardson, Alexander, 301
Ryburn, Matthew, 265,270,282,290,
291,299
Ryburn, William, 79
Roach, Pleasant, 282,298
Roberts, George, 72,230
Roberts, Samuel, 87,172,228
Robertson, Elijah, 204
Robertson, George, 207
Robertson, Willie, 39
Rochell, Amos, 16
Rogers, Isaac, 150
Robinson, Israel, 79,97,135,145,
43,70,186,195,196
Robinson, Joel, 162
Robinson, John, 137,271
Robinson, Joseph, 32,35,36,38,44,
124,142,143,156,163,167,182,
223,224,261,264
Robinson, Zachariah, 199
Roland, Bunch, 239,242
Ross, James, 271
Ross, John, 206
Ross, William, 10,35,37,40,90,99,
105,108,110,153,155,231,272,
288,315
Rudder, David, 9,95,126,255
Rudolph, Jacob, 25,303
Rudolph, John, 15,25,225,230,239,
242,247,250,254,278,315
Rushing, Robert, 208,232
Russell, James H. 10,17,23,86,312
Rutledge, John, 38,255

Satterfield, Isaac,43,46,50
Sawyer, Robert, 57
Saunders, John, 18
Saunderson, Nathaniel, 96
Scott, John D. 240
Scott, Nancy, 283
Scott, Samuel, 270
Scott, Solomon, 283
Senny, Eli, 206
Searcy, Bennett, 19,20,110,202,315
Searcy, Bennett, 19,20,110,202,315
Searcy, Robert, 35,42,44,179,225,305
Sellen, Matthew, 84   /351
Shelby, John, 33,93,97,126,135,150,
221,256, 318,364,
Shelby, Isaac, 191,250,295,297,299,
350,351
Shelby, Thomas, 234
Selters, Thomas, 34
Simmons, Broxton, 234
Sims, Payton, 76
Slocumb, David, 206,317,359
Sinsel, John, 47
Simmons, Thomas, 95,181
Slater, DIR.731
Small, Henry, 24,79,80,90,122,144,
162,168,183,251,279
Smith, Benjamin, 144
Smith, Charles, 205
Smith, Eli, 206
Smith, Job, 47,93
Smith, Samuel, 36,43,66,92,161,210,
225,229,250,273,274
Smith, Thomas, 1,3,19,23,27,36,43,
45,46,51,61,70,86,78,126,150,
184,189,218,239,274,309,315,319,290
Smith, William, 44,155,231,248,361
Sneeling, Barnard, 118
Sneeling, Barnett, 271
Sugg, Melton B. 227
Sugg, Samuel, 155,159,316
Sullivant, William, 56,112,156
Staley, Jacob, 150
Staley, William, 1,11
Starr, Isaac, 243,254
Steel, James, 268
Steele, John, 31,81,85,139,182,239,
240,334,335,336
Steel, Moses, 12,65,99,158
Stephen, Jonathan, 120,205
Stewart, John, 44,52,56,61,65,72,86,
118,179,180,187,268,311,317,325,
328

Stewart, Andrew, 28
Stewart, Charles, 44,84,86,89,156,
    178,323,324,325,328
Stewart, Duncan, 8,29,62,79,132,
    290,310,316
Stewart, James, 14,18,69,77,156,
    218,295
Stewart, Sarah, 28,97,105
Stewart, Stephen, 70,107,140,258,
    259,366
Stewart, White, 84
Sterling, George, 220
Sterling, John, 36,45,46,120,126,
    127,131,132,151,188,224,250,
    254,259,260,264,282
Stroud, William, 40,42,45,50,56,
    57,68,75
Stump, Frederick, 73,307
Sullivant, Jesse, 91
Suter, Edmund, 165,167,170,172,
    175,179,182,183,186,188,218,355
Sugg, Anne, 154,226,227,316
Sugg, Elizabeth, 227
Sugg, Howell, 227
Summerville, John, 329
Sugg, Leonard, 160,227
Sugg, Lucinda, 227

Taggart, Robert, 64,68,75
Tate, Adam, 202
Tate, Alexander, 28,202
Tate, William, 23,282
Tatum, Howell, 128,211
Taylor, Daniel, 161,234
Taylor, Henry, 95,120
Taylor, John, 256
Taylor Minoah, 18,95,96,69,120
Taylor, Thomas, 205
Teasley, John, 27,83,132,164,165,
    167,170,172,175,179,183,195,282,
    290,293,299,317
Temples, Robert M. 19,20,22,53,66,70,
    72,103,170,182,183,195,224,316,322,
    331
Tennen, Thomas, 84
Tennen, Hugh, 218
Thomas, Christopher, 141
Thomas, Benjamin, 253
Thomas, John, 2,3,4,5,6,210,225
Thomas, Lewis, 206
Thomas, Stephen, 1,2,4,5,6,142,
    153,223,264,321,322,323
Thompkins, Frances, 27,90,294
Thompkins, John, 43
Thompson, Lewis, 25,129

Thornton, Samuel, 16,87,89,93,102,
    128,134,197,198,211,269,285,
    305,307,316,353,356,358
Tygurts, Thomas, 18
Trawick, Goodman, 55
Travis, Thomas, 132,143,251,275,
    309
Tribble, Absolam, 64,167,196,225,
    243,313,323,329
Tribble, Andrew, 66,70,72,74,80,
    82,103,141,329,328
Tribble, Jesse, 329
Tribble, James, 41,55,95,137,
    227,328,329
Tribble, John, 289,329
Tribble, Mary, 325
Tribble, Spilsby, 74,80,98
Trice, Edward, 128
Trice, James, 12,13,37,70,98,99,
    108,113,272,287,316
Trice, John, 101
Trigg, Gray S, 301
Trigg, William, 220
Trotter, Absolom, 253
Trotter, George, 23,253
Trotter, James, 41,93,141,143,147,
    210
Trotter, Isham, 37,68,103,108,110,
    257,300,30
Trotter, John, 1,21,4,5,10,12,15,
    19, 21,22,246,333
Trotter, Robert, 291,325
Trousdale, Alexander, 314
Trousdale, John, 218,269,316
Tucker, Daniel, 206
Tygert, Robert, 85
Tyre, Elizabeth, 173
Tyre, Thomas, 173

U

Vance, Captain, 40
Vance & Bradley, 209,210,217
Vance, Samuel, 1,5,7,13,15,37,55,
    93,94,98,105,108,113,115,117,
    193,194,203,221,288,292,306,
    324,335,365
Vaughn, Joseph, P. 323
Vaughan, Joshua, 113,134,140,143,
    164,

Vick, Roland, 17,26,206

Waggoner, John, 14,41

Waggoner, Mary, 251
Walker, Andrew, 170,206
Walker, Jeremiah, 245
Walker, Zeke, 245
Wall, James, 329
Wallace, Jobe, 245
Waller, James, 287
Washington, Joseph, 125
Waters, Thomas, 202
Watkins, Benjamin, H. 54
Watkins, John, 143,146,230,232
Watkins, Thomas, 206
Watkins & Nelson, 161
Watson, Thomas, 33
Watt, James, 248,330
Weakley, Benjamin, 19,24,28,31,85
Weakley, Capt. 161
Weakley, Isaac, 37,85,86,127
Weakley, John, 202
Weakley, Joseph, 1,2,5,14,16,75,
 117
Weakley, Robert, 24,113,365
Weekley, Thomas, 259
Weeks, William, 269,316
Weathers, John, 268
Wells, Archilles, 126
Wells, Benjamin, 45,49,93,319
Wells, Heydon, 28,156,221,222,316,
 318,331
Wells, Robert, 1,42,56,74,200,
 226,237,242,243,364
West, George, 126,132,179,225,322
Wendson, Thomas, 202
Westmer, George, 213
Wheelan, James, 90
Wheeler, James, 158
Wheeler, John, 241
Whillis, Herbert, 156
Whipple, Pray, 52,173
White, William, 50,161,254,325
Whitfield, Bryan, 138,136,180,
 213,222,265,270,299,301,303,
 363
Whitfield, Capt. 161
Whitfield, Needham, 45,61,102,143,
 149,264,343
Whitledge, Robert, 159
Whiteheed, Abraham, 26,41,43,50,
 269,311,320
Whitehead, Benjamin, 153
Whitehead, Joseph, 37,99,102,
 108,328,364
Whitehead, Richard, 37,218,230,
 239,242,247,250,254

Whitehead, Thomas, 40,43,52,58,66,67,
 70,140
Whitehead, William, 37,48,99,100,102,
 108,110,171,317
Whitledge, John, 100,155,205,206
Whitworth, Philmore, 265,314
Wilcox, Samuel, 173
Willis, Elijah, 79,93,134,142,147,149
Williams, Arthur, 196
Williams, Burrell M. 26,37,83,124,134,
 249,278,324
Williams, David, 201,203,204,202,230,
 306,313,345,366
Williams, George, 12,38,64,99
Williams, Henry, 127,218,234,265,314
Williams, James, 49,56,57,61,64,72,93,
 103,109,120,132,140,150156,166,
 166,234,236,237,243,253,316
Williams, Love, 242
Williams, Proxy, 93
Williams, Ralph, 37,215,230,239,242
Wilson, Samuel J. 315
Williams, Thomas, 26,195
Williams, William, 28,33,37,135,201,
 318,321,322,323
Willis, Elijah, 286,357
Wilson, Benjamin, 179,269,314,316
Wilson, George, 360
Wilson, James, 269,318,319
Wilson, William B. 53,67,262
Wimberley, Joseph, 105,107,110,119,140
Woods, Samuel, 86,155
Woods, William, 206
Woolfolk, Joseph, 19,23,24,32,35,56,70,
 83,85,92,97,144,161,133,164,312,
 313,330
Wooldridge, Samuel, 153,165,167,170,
 175,182,188,195,269,311
Wright, John, 122,176
Wyatt, Walter, 266

Yarbrough, James, 133
Yarbrough, Thomas, 278
Yoes, John, 43
Young, Robert, 204

www.ingramcontent.com/pod-product-compliance
Lightning Source LLC
Chambersburg PA
CBHW020650300426
44112CB00007B/315